Praise for **PALM SUNDAY**

"He is either the funniest serious writer around or the most serious funny writer." —*Los Angeles Times Book Review*

"In *Palm Sunday* it's Vonnegut instead of his characters who is saying surprising and revealing things. . . . There is no more wry and witty, nor more whimsical, touching writer around than Kurt Vonnegut."
—*Chicago Tribune Book World*

"A modern Mark Twain . . . *Palm Sunday* is Vonnegut at the top of his form, and it is wonderful. So it goes. Ting-a-ling, too." —*Newsday*

"Kurt Vonnegut is the Danny Kaye of American letters, a world-famous jester whose sweet and zany style has never been sealed by the academy as the high art of a Chaplin or a Keaton . . . a modest, polite, sentimental family man, a planetary patriot and a writer to whose stubborn simplicity the modern American novel owes a great thanks."
—*The Nation*

"A rollicking overview of the life and times of one of America's most popular writers straight from the horse's mouth. . . . Humor is his message; wisdom is his glue."
—*The Kansas City Star*

". . . what a great conversationalist and raconteur."
—*Los Angeles Herald Examiner*

"It's all been described before—the clarity and simplicity of phrase, the perfect sense of timing, the funny incongruity, and the shrewd sense of idiom. He is, at his best, fit company for his idol, Mark Twain. —*The New York Times*

BY THE SAME AUTHOR

KURT VONNEGUT

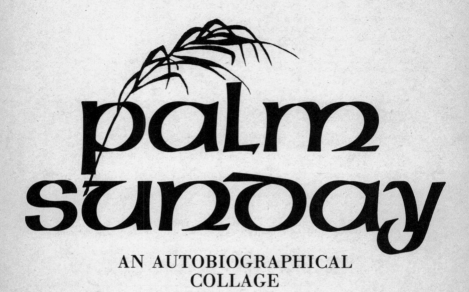

palm sunday

AN AUTOBIOGRAPHICAL COLLAGE

A DELL TRADE PAPERBACK

A DELL TRADE PAPERBACK BOOK
Published by
Dell Publishing Co., Inc.
1 Dag Hammarskjold Plaza
New York, New York 10017

ACKNOWLEDGMENTS

Grateful acknowledgment is made for permission to use the following material:

"An account of the Ancestry of Kurt Vonnegut, Jr., by an Ancient Friend of his Family" by John G. Rauch: Used by permission of William Rauch.

Excerpts from *Indianapolis* magazine used by permission.

"How to Write with Style" by Kurt Vonnegut: Reprinted by permission from International Paper Company's "Power of the Printed Word" Program.

"Self-Interview" appeared originally in *The Paris Review*, Issue #69. Copyright 1977 by The Paris Review. Reprinted by permission of The Viking Press.

"Who in America Is Truly Happy?": Reprinted from *Politics Today*, January 1979. Used by permission.

Review of SOMETHING HAPPENED by Joseph Heller: © 1974 by The New York Times Company. Reprinted by permission.

"Introduction" to WRITE IF YOU GET WORK: THE BEST OF BOB AND RAY by Bob Elliott and Ray Goulding: Used by permission of Random House, Inc.

"Class of '57" by Harold Reid and Don Reid: © Copyright 1972 by House of Cash, Inc., Hendersonville, Tennessee 37075. Used by permission.

Viking Penguin, Inc. for "Louis-Ferdinand Céline" as the Introduction to the Penguin edition of CASTLE TO CASTLE, RIGADOON and NORTH by Louis-Ferdinand Céline.

"Dresden Revisited" was originally an introduction for the limited edition of SLAUGHTERHOUSE-FIVE published by The Franklin Library and signed by the writer. The work is reprinted with the permission of The Franklin Library.

"Flowers on the Wall" by Lewis DeWitt: Copyright © 1965, 1966 by Southwind Music, Inc. Rights controlled by Unichappell Music, Inc. (Rightsong Music, Inc., Publisher). International Copyright Secured. All Rights Reserved.

Lines from "Howl" by Allen Ginsberg: Copyright © 1956, 1959 by Allen Ginsberg. Reprinted by permission of City Lights Books.

Acknowledgment is made to the following publications in whose pages these essays first appeared:

The New York Times for "Un-American Nonsense": *Again, Dangerous Visions* edited by Harlan Ellison for "The Big Space Fuck"; and *The Nation* for "Mark Twain" and "Palm Sunday" as "Hypocrites You Always Have With You."

Dell ® TM 681510, Dell Publishing Co., Inc.

ISBN: 0-440-57163-4

Reprinted by arrangement with Delacorte Press
Printed in the United States of America

First Dell Trade Paperback printing—March 1982

For my cousins the de St. Andrés everywhere.

Who has the castle now?

TABLE OF CONTENTS
(BITS OF THE COLLAGE)

ix

INTRODUCTION

*t*HIS is a very great book by an American genius. I have worked so hard on this masterpiece for the past six years. I have groaned and banged my head on radiators. I have walked through every hotel lobby in New York, thinking about this book and weeping, and driving my fist into the guts of grandfather clocks.

It is a marvelous new literary form. This book combines the tidal power of a major novel with the bone-rattling immediacy of front-line journalism—which is old stuff now, God knows, God knows. But I have also intertwined the flashy enthusiasms of musical theater, the lethal left jab of the short story, the sachet of personal letters, the oompah of American history, and oratory in the bow-wow style.

This book is so broad and deep that it reminds me of my brother Bernard's early experiments with radio. He built a transmitter of his own invention, and he hooked it up to a telegraph key, and he turned it on. He called up our cousin Richard, about two miles away, and he told Richard to listen to his radio, to tune it back and forth across the band, to see if he could pick up my brother's signals anywhere. They were both about fifteen.

My brother tapped out an easily recognizable message, sending it again and again and again. It was "SOS." This was in Indianapolis, the world's largest city not on a navigable waterway.

Cousin Richard telephoned back. He was thrilled. He said that Bernard's signals were loud and clear simply everywhere on the radio band, drowning out music or news or drama, or whatever the commercial stations were putting out at the time.

❦

THIS is certainly that kind of masterpiece, and a new name should be created for such an all-frequencies assault on the sensibilities. I propose the name *blivit*. This is a word which during my adolescence was defined by peers as "two pounds of shit in a one-pound bag."

I would not mind if books simpler than this one, but combining fiction and fact, were also called blivits. This would encourage *The New York Times Book Review* to establish a third category for best sellers, one long needed, in my opinion. If there were a separate list for blivits, then authors of blivits could stop stepping in the faces of mere novelists and historians and so on.

Until that happy day, however, I insist, as only a great author can, that this book be ranked in both the fiction and nonfiction competitions. As for the Pulitzer prizes: this book should be eligible for a mega–grand slam, sweeping fiction, drama, history, biography, and journalism. We will wait and see.

❧

THIS book is not only a blivit but a collage. It began with my wish to collect in one volume most of the reviews and speeches and essays I had written since the publication of a similar collection, *Wampeters, Foma & Granfalloons,* in 1974. But as I arranged those fragments in this order and then that one, I saw that they formed a sort of autobiography, especially if I felt free to include some pieces not written by me. To give life to such a golem, however, I would have to write much new connective tissue. This I have done.

The reader should expect me to chat about this and that, and then to include a speech or a letter or a song or whatever, and then to chat some more.

I do not really consider this to be a masterpiece. I find it clumsy. I find it raw. It has some value, I think, as a confrontation between an American novelist and his own stubborn simplicity. I was dumb in school. Whatever the nature of that dumbness, it is with me still.

I have dedicated this book to the de St. Andrés. I am a de St. André, since that was the maiden name of a maternal great-grandmother of mine. My mother believed that this meant that she was descended from nobles of some kind.

This was an innocent belief, and so should not be mocked or scorned. Or so I say. My books so far have argued that most human behavior, no matter how ghastly or ludicrous or glorious or whatever, is innocent. And here seems as good a place as any to include a statement made to me by Marsha Mason, the superb actress who once did me the honor of starring in a play of mine. She, too, is from the Middle West, from St. Louis.

"You know what the trouble is with New York?" she asked me.

"No," I said.

"Nobody here," she said, "believes that there is such a thing as innocence."

*Whoever entertains liberal views
and chooses a consort that is captured
by superstition risks his liberty
and his happiness.*

—CLEMENS VONNEGUT (1824–1906)
Instruction in Morals
(The Hollenbeck Press,
Indianapolis, 1900)

PALM
SUNDAY

I

THE FIRST
AMENDMENT

I am a member of what I believe to be the last recognizable generation of full-time, life-time American novelists. We appear to be standing more or less in a row. It was the Great Depression which made us similarly edgy and watchful. It was World War II which lined us up so nicely, whether we were men or women, whether we were ever in uniform or not. It was an era of romantic anarchy in publishing which gave us money and mentors, willy-nilly, when we were young —while we learned our craft. Words printed on pages were still the principal form of long-distance communication and stored information in America when we were young.

No more.

Nor are there many publishers and editors and agents left who are eager to find some way to get money and other forms of encouragement to young writers who write as clumsily as members of my literary generation did when we started out. The wild and wonderful and expensive guess was made back then that we might acquire some wisdom and learn how to write halfway decently by and by. Writers were needed that much back then.

It was an amusing and instructive time for writers—for hundreds of them.

Television wrecked the short-story branch of the industry, and now accountants and business school graduates dominate book publishing. They feel that money spent on someone's first novel is good money down a rat hole. They are right. It almost always is.

So, as I say, I think I belong to America's last generation of novelists. Novelists will come one by one from now on, not in seeming families, and will perhaps write only one or two novels, and let it go at that. Many will have inherited or married money.

The most influential of my bunch, in my opinion, is still J. D. Salinger, although he has been silent for years. The most promising was perhaps Edward Lewis Wallant, who died so young. And it is my thinking about the death of James Jones two years ago, who was not all that young, who was almost exactly my age, which accounts for the autumnal mood of this book. There have been other reminders of my own mortality, to be sure, but the death of Jones is central —perhaps because I see his widow Gloria so often and because he, too, was a self-educated midwesterner, and because he, too, in a major adventure for all of us, which was the Second World War, had been an enlisted man. And let it here

be noted that the best-known members of my literary generation, if they wrote about war, almost unanimously despised
officers and made heroes of sketchily educated, aggressively
unaristocratic enlisted men.

❧

JAMES JONES told me one time that his publisher and Ernest
Hemingway's, Charles Scribner's Sons, had once hoped to
get Jones and Hemingway together—so that they could
enjoy each other's company as old warriors.

Jones declined, by his own account, because he did not
regard Hemingway as a fellow soldier. He said Hemingway
in wartime was free to come and go from the fighting as he
pleased, and to take time off for a fine meal or woman or
whatever. Real soldiers, according to Jones, damn well had
to stay where they were told, or go where they were told, and
eat swill, and take the worst the enemy had to throw at them
day after day, week after week.

❧

IT may be that the most striking thing about members of my
literary generation in retrospect will be that we were allowed
to say absolutely anything without fear of punishment. Our
American heirs may find it incredible, as most foreigners do
right now, that a nation would want to enforce as a law
something which sounds more like a dream, which reads as
follows:

"Congress shall make no law respecting an establishment
of religion, or prohibiting the free exercise thereof, or abridg-
ing the freedom of the press, or the right of the people

3

peaceably to assemble, and to petition the Government for a redress of grievances."

How could a nation with such a law raise its children in an atmosphere of decency? It couldn't—it can't. So the law will surely be repealed soon for the sake of children.

And even now my books, along with books by Bernard Malamud and James Dickey and Joseph Heller and many other first-rate patriots, are regularly thrown out of public-school libraries by school board members, who commonly say that they have not actually read the books, but that they have it on good authority that the books are bad for children.

❦

My novel *Slaughterhouse-Five* was actually burned in a furnace by a school janitor in Drake, North Dakota, on instructions from the school committee there, and the school board made public statements about the unwholesomeness of the book. Even by the standards of Queen Victoria, the only offensive line in the entire novel is this: "Get out of the road, you dumb motherfucker." This is spoken by an American antitank gunner to an unarmed American chaplain's assistant during the Battle of the Bulge in Europe in December 1944, the largest single defeat of American arms (the Confederacy excluded) in history. The chaplain's assistant had attracted enemy fire.

So on November 16, 1973, I wrote as follows to Charles McCarthy of Drake, North Dakota:

Dear Mr. McCarthy:

I am writing to you in your capacity as chairman of the Drake School Board. I am among those American writers whose books have been destroyed in the now famous furnace of your school.

Certain members of your community have suggested that my work is evil. This is extraordinarily insulting to me. The news from Drake indicates to me that books and writers are very unreal to you people. I am writing this letter to let you know how real I am.

I want you to know, too, that my publisher and I have done absolutely nothing to exploit the disgusting news from Drake. We are not clapping each other on the back, crowing about all the books we will sell because of the news. We have declined to go on television, have written no fiery letters to editorial pages, have granted no lengthy interviews. We are angered and sickened and saddened. And no copies of this letter have been sent to anybody else. You now hold the only copy in your hands. It is a strictly private letter from me to the people of Drake, who have done so much to damage my reputation in the eyes of their children and then in the eyes of the world. Do you have the courage and ordinary decency to show this letter to the people, or will it, too, be consigned to the fires of your furnace?

I gather from what I read in the papers and hear on television that you imagine me, and some other writers, too, as being sort of ratlike people who enjoy making money from poisoning the minds of young people. I am in fact a large, strong person, fifty-one years old, who did a lot of farm work as a boy, who is good with tools. I have raised six children, three my own and three adopted. They have all turned out well. Two of them are farmers. I am a combat infantry veteran from World War II, and hold a Purple Heart. I have earned whatever I own by hard work. I have never been arrested or sued for anything. I am so much trusted with young people and by young people that I have served on the faculties of the University of Iowa, Harvard, and the City College of New York. Every year I receive at least a dozen invitations to be commencement speaker at colleges and high schools. My books are probably more widely used in schools than those of any other living American fiction writer.

If you were to bother to read my books, to behave as educated persons would, you would learn that they are not sexy, and do not argue in favor of wildness of any kind. They beg that people be kinder and more responsible than they often are. It is true that some of the characters speak coarsely. That is because people speak coarsely in real life. Especially soldiers and hardworking men speak coarsely, and even our most sheltered children know that. And we all know, too, that those words really don't damage children much. They didn't damage us when we were young. It was evil deeds and lying that hurt us.

After I have said all this, I am sure you are still ready to respond, in effect, "Yes, yes—but it still remains our right and our responsibility to decide what books our children are going to be made to read in our community." This is surely so. But it is also true that if you exercise that right and fulfill that responsibility in an ignorant, harsh, un-American manner, then people are entitled to call you bad citizens and fools. Even your own children are entitled to call you that.

I read in the newspaper that your community is mystified by the outcry from all over the country about what you have done. Well, you have discovered that Drake is a part of American civilization, and your fellow Americans can't stand it that you have behaved in such an uncivilized way. Perhaps you will learn from this that books are sacred to free men for very good reasons, and that wars have been fought against nations which hate books and burn them. If you are an American, you must allow all ideas to circulate freely in your community, not merely your own.

If you and your board are now determined to show that you in fact have wisdom and maturity when you exercise your powers over the education of your young, then you should acknowledge that it was a rotten lesson you taught young people in a free society when you denounced and then burned books—books you hadn't even read. You should also resolve to expose your children to all sorts of opinions and information, in order that they will be better equipped to make decisions and to survive.

Again: you have insulted me, and I am a good citizen, and I am very real.

❧

THAT was seven years ago. There has so far been no reply. At this very moment, as I write in New York City, *Slaughterhouse-Five* has been banned from school libraries not fifty miles from here. A legal battle begun several years ago rages on. The school board in question has found lawyers eager to attack the First Amendment tooth and nail. There is never a shortage anywhere of lawyers eager to attack the First Amendment, as though it were nothing more than a clause in a lease from a crooked slumlord.

At the start of that particular litigation, on March 24th of 1976, I wrote a comment for the Op-Ed page of the Long Island edition of *The New York Times*. It went like this:

A school board has denounced some books again—out in Levittown this time. One of the books was mine. I hear about

7

un-American nonsense like this twice a year or so. One time out in North Dakota, the books were actually burned in a furnace. I had a laugh. It was such an ignorant, dumb, superstitious thing to do.

It was so cowardly, too—to make a great show of attacking artifacts. It was like St. George attacking bedspreads and cuckoo clocks.

Yes, and St. Georges like that seem to get elected or appointed to school committees all the time. They are actually proud of their illiteracy. They imagine that they are somehow celebrating the bicentennial when they boast, as some did in Levittown, that they hadn't actually read the books they banned.

Such lunks are often the backbone of volunteer fire departments and the United States Infantry and cake sales and so on, and they have been thanked often enough for that. But they have no business supervising the educations of children in a free society. They are just too bloody stupid.

Here is how I propose to end book-banning in this country once and for all: Every candidate for school committee should be hooked up to a lie-detector and asked this question: "Have you read a book from start to finish since high school? Or did you even read a book from start to finish in high school?"

If the truthful answer is "no," then the candidate should be told politely that he cannot get on the school committee and blow off his big bazoo about how books make children crazy.

Whenever ideas are squashed in this country, literate lovers of the American experiment write careful and intricate explanations of why all ideas must be allowed to live. It is time for them to realize that they are attempting to explain

America at its bravest and most optimistic to orangutans.

From now on, I intend to limit my discourse with dim-witted Savonarolas to this advice: "Have somebody read the First Amendment to the United States Constitution out loud to you, you God damned fool!"

Well—the American Civil Liberties Union or somebody like that will come to the scene of trouble, as they always do. They will explain what is in the Constitution, and to whom it applies.

They will win.

And there will be millions who are bewildered and heart-broken by the legal victory, who think some things should never be said—especially about religion.

They are in the wrong place at the wrong time.

Hi ho.

❦

WHY is it so ordinary for American citizens to show such scorn for the First Amendment? I discussed that some at a fund raiser for the American Civil Liberties Union at Sands Point, New York, out on Long Island, on September 16, 1979. The house where I spoke, incidentally, was said to be the model for Gatsby's house in F. Scott Fitzgerald's *The Great Gatsby*. I saw no reason to doubt the claim.

I said this in such a setting:

"I will not speak directly to the ejection of my book *Slaughterhouse-Five* from the school libraries of Island Trees. I have a vested interest. I wrote the book, after all, so why wouldn't I argue that it is less repulsive than the school board says?

"I will speak of Thomas Aquinas instead. I will tell you my dim memories of what he said about the hierarchy of laws on this planet, which was flat at the time. The highest law, he said, was divine law, God's law. Beneath that was natural law, which I suppose would include thunderstorms, and our right to shield our children from poisonous ideas, and so on.

"And the lowest law was human law.

"Let me clarify this scheme by comparing its parts to playing cards. Enemies of the Bill of Rights do the same sort of thing all the time, so why shouldn't we? Divine law, then, is an ace. Natural law is a king. The Bill of Rights is a lousy queen.

"The Thomist hierarchy of laws is so far from being ridiculous that I have never met anybody who did not believe in it right down to the marrow of his or her bones. Everybody knows that there are laws with more grandeur than those which are printed in our statute books. The big trouble is that there is so little agreement as to how those grander laws are worded. Theologians can give us hints of the wording, but it takes a dictator to set them down just right—to dot the *i*'s and cross the *t*'s. A man who had been a mere corporal in the army did that for Germany and then for all of Europe, you may remember, not long ago. There was nothing he did not know about divine and natural law. He had fistfuls of aces and kings to play.

"Meanwhile, over on this side of the Atlantic, we were not playing with a full deck, as they say. Because of our Constitution, the highest card anybody had to play was a lousy queen, contemptible human law. That remains true today. I myself celebrate that incompleteness, since it has obviously been so good for us. I support the American Civil Liberties Union because it goes to court to insist that our government officials be guided by nothing grander than human law. Every time the circulation of this idea or that one is discouraged by an official in this country, that official is scorning the Constitution, and urging all of us to participate in far grander systems, again: divine or natural law.

"Cannot we, as libertarians, hunger for at least a little natural law? Can't we learn from nature at least, without being burdened by another person's idea of God?

"Certainly. Granola never harmed anybody, nor the birds and bees—not to mention milk. God is unknowable, but nature is explaining herself all the time. What has she told us so far? That blacks are obviously inferior to whites, for one thing, and intended for menial work on white man's terms. This clear lesson from nature, we should remind ourselves from time to time, allowed Thomas Jefferson to own slaves. Imagine that.

"What troubles me most about my lovely country is that its children are seldom taught that American freedom will vanish, if, when they grow up, and in the exercise of their duties as citizens, they insist that our courts and policemen and prisons be guided by divine or natural law.

"Most teachers and parents and guardians do not teach this vital lesson because they themselves never learned it, or because they dare not. Why dare they not? People can get into a lot of trouble in this country, and often have to be defended by the American Civil Liberties Union, for laying the groundwork for the lesson, which is this: That no one really understands nature or God. It is my willingness to lay this groundwork, and not sex or violence, which has got my poor book in such trouble in Island Trees—and in Drake, North Dakota, where the book was burned, and in many other communities too numerous to mention.

"I have not said that our government is anti-nature and anti-God. I have said that it is non-nature and non-God, for very good reasons that could curl your hair.

"Well—all good things must come to an end, they say. So American freedom will come to an end, too, sooner or later. How will it end? As all freedoms end: by the surrender of our destinies to the highest laws.

"To return to my foolish analogy of playing cards: kings and aces will be played. Nobody else will have anything higher than a queen.

"There will be a struggle between those holding kings and aces. The struggle will not end, not that the rest of us will care much by then, until somebody plays the ace of spades. Nothing beats the ace of spades.

"I thank you for your attention."

❦

I spoke at Gatsby's house in the afternoon. When I got back to my own house in New York City, I wrote a letter to a friend in the Soviet Union, Felix Kuznetzov, a distinguished critic and teacher, and an officer in the Union of Writers of the USSR in Moscow. The date on the letter is the same as the date of the Sands Point oration.

There was a time when I might have been half-bombed on booze when writing such a letter so late at night, a time when I might have reeked of mustard gas and roses as I punched the keys. But I don't drink anymore. Never in my life have I written anything for publication while sozzled. But I certainly used to write a lot of letters that way.

No more.

Be that as it may, I was sober then and am sober now, and Felix Kuznetzov and I had become friends during the previous summer—at an ecumenical meeting in New York City, sponsored by the Charles F. Kettering Foundation, of American and Soviet literary persons, about ten to a side. The American delegation was headed by Norman Cousins, and included myself and Edward Albee and Arthur Miller and William Styron and John Updike. All of us had been published in the Soviet Union. I am almost entirely in print over there—with the exception of *Mother Night* and *Jailbird.* Few, if any, of the Soviet delegates had had anything published here, and so their work was unknown to us.

We Americans were told by the Soviets that we should be embarrassed that their country published so much of our work, and that we published so little of theirs. Our reply was that we would work to get more of them published over here, but that we felt, too, that the USSR could easily have put together a delegation whose works were admired and published here—and that we could easily have put together a delegation so unfamiliar to them that its members could have been sewer commissioners from Fresno, as far as anybody in the Soviet Union knew.

Felix Kuznetzov and I got along very well, at any rate. I had him over to my house, and we sat in my garden out back and talked away the better part of an afternoon.

But then, after everybody went home, there was some trouble in the Soviet Union about the publication of an outlaw magazine called *Metropole.* Most of *Metropole*'s writers and editors were young, impatient with the strictures placed on their writings by old poops. Nothing in *Metropole,* incidentally, was nearly as offensive as calling a chaplain's assistant a "dumb motherfucker." But the *Metropole* people were denounced, and the magazine was suppressed, and ways were discussed for making life harder for anyone associated with it.

So Albee and Styron and Updike and I sent a cable to the Writers' Union, saying that we thought it was wrong to penalize writers for what they wrote, no matter what they wrote. Felix Kuznetzov made an official reply on behalf of the union, giving the sense of a large meeting in which distinguished writer after distinguished writer testified that those who wrote for *Metropole* weren't really writers, that they were pornographers and other sorts of disturbers of the peace, and so on. He asked that his reply be published in *The New York Times,* and it was published there. Why not?

And I privately wrote to Kuznetzov as follows:

Dear Professor Kuznetzov—dear Felix—
I thank you for your prompt and frank and thoughtful letter of August 20, and for the supplementary materials which accompanied it. I apologize for not replying in your own beautiful language, and I wish that we both might have employed from the first a more conversational tone in our discussion of the *Metropole* affair. I will try to recapture the amiable, brotherly mood of our long talk in my garden here about a year ago.

You speak of us in your letter as "American authors." We do not feel especially American in this instance, since we spoke only for ourselves—without consulting with any American institution whatsoever. We are simply "authors" in this case, expressing loyalty to the great and vulnerable family of writers throughout the world. You and all other members of the Union of Writers surely have the same family feelings. Those of us who sent the cable are so far from being organized that I have no idea what sorts of replies the others may be making to you.

As you must know, your response to our cable was printed recently in *The New York Times*, and perhaps elsewhere. The controversy has attracted little attention. It is a matter of interest, seemingly, only to other writers. Nobody cares much about writers but writers. And, if it weren't for a few of us like the signers of the cable, I wonder if there would be anybody to care about writers—no matter how much trouble they were in. Should we, too, stop caring?

Well—I understand that our cultures are so different that we can never agree about freedom of expression. It is natural that we should disagree, and perhaps even commendable. What you may not know about our own culture is that writers such as those who signed the cable are routinely attacked by fellow citizens as being pornographers or corrupters of children and celebrators of violence and persons of no talent and so on. In my own case, such charges are brought against my works in court several times a year, usually by parents who, for religious or political reasons, do not want their children to read what I have to say. The parents, incidentally, often find their charges supported by the lowest courts. The charges so far have been invariably overthrown in higher courts, those closer to the soul of the Constitution of the United States.

Please convey the contents of this letter to my brothers and sisters in the Writers' Union, as we conveyed your letter to *The New York Times*. This letter is specifically for you, to do with as you please. I am not sending carbon copies to anyone. It has not even been read by my wife.

That homely detail, if brought to the attention of the

Writers' Union, might help its members to understand what I do not think is at all well understood now: That we are not nationalists, taking part in some cold-war enterprise. We simply care deeply about how things are going for writers here, there, and everywhere. Even when they are declared nonwriters, as we have been, we continue to care.

※

KUZNETZOV gave me a prompt and likewise private answer. It was gracious and humane. I could assume that we were still friends. He said nothing against his union or his government. Neither did he say anything to discourage me from feeling that writers everywhere, good and bad, were all first cousins—first cousins, at least.

And all the argle-bargling that goes on between educated persons in the United States and the Soviet Union is so touching and comical, really, as long as it does not lead to war. It draws its energy, in my opinion, from a desperate wish on both sides that each other's utopias should work much better than they do. We want to tinker with theirs, to make it work much better than it does—so that people there, for example, can say whatever they please without fear of punishment. They want to tinker with ours, so that everybody here who wants a job can have one, and so that we don't have to tolerate the sales of fist-fucking films and snuff films and so on.

Neither utopia now works much better than the Page typesetting machine, in which Mark Twain invested and lost a fortune. That beautiful contraption actually set type just once, when only Twain and the inventor were watching.

Twain called all the other investors to see this miracle, but, by the time they got there, the inventor had taken the machine all apart again. It never ran again.

Peace.

II

ROOTS

I am descended from Europeans who have been literate for
a long time, as I will presently demonstrate, and who
have not been slaves since the early days of the Roman
games, most likely. A more meticulous historian might suggest that my European ancestors no doubt enslaved themselves to their own military commanders from time to time.
When I examine my genealogy over the past century and a
little more, however, I find no war lovers of any kind.

My father and grandfathers were in no wars. Only one of
my four great-grandfathers was in a war, the Civil War. This
was Peter Lieber, born in Düsseldorf, Germany, in 1832. My
mother's maiden name was Lieber. This Peter Lieber, who

is no more real to me than to you, came to America with one million other Germans in 1848. His father was a brush manufacturer. He was living in New Ulm, Minnesota, running a general store and trading for furs with the Indians, when the Civil War broke out. When Abraham Lincoln called for 75,000 volunteers, Peter Lieber joined the 22nd Minnesota Battery of Light Artillery, and served for two years until wounded and honorably discharged.

"The knee-joint of his right leg was permanently damaged, and he walked with a limp to the end of his days," according to my Uncle John Rauch (1890–1976). Uncle John was not in fact my uncle, but the husband of a first cousin of my father, Gertrude Schnull Rauch. He was a Harvard graduate and a distinguished Indianapolis lawyer. Toward the end of his life, he made himself an historian, a *griot,* of his wife's family—in part my family, too, although he was not related to it by blood, but only by marriage.

I am a highly diluted relative of his wife, and did not expect to appear as more than a footnote in the history—and so I was properly astonished when he one day made me a gift of a manuscript entitled "An Account of the Ancestry of Kurt Vonnegut, Jr., by an Ancient Friend of His Family." It was painstakingly researched and better written, by Uncle John himself, than much of my own stuff, sad to say. That manuscript is the most extravagant gift I ever expect to receive—and it came from a man who had never spoken favorably of my work in my presence, other than to say that he was "surprised by my convincing tone of authority," and that he was sure I would make a great deal of money.

When I published my first short story, which was "Report on the Barnhouse Effect," in *Collier's,* its hero was a man who could control dice by thinking hard about them, and who could eventually loosen bricks in chimneys a mile away, and so on—and Uncle John said, "Now you will hear from every nut in the country. They can all do that."

When I published the novel *Cat's Cradle,* Uncle John sent me a postcard saying, "You're saying that life is a load of crap, right? Read Thackeray!" He wasn't joking.

I was no literary gentleman in his eyes, surely, and one satisfaction he may have found in writing about my ancestry was demonstrating how a gentleman wrote. I stand instructed.

❦

WHEN Uncle John speaks of "Kurt" in his account, he means my father, Kurt Vonnegut, Sr. He commonly calls me "K," which was my nickname when a child. People who knew me before I was twelve years old still call me that. So do my descendents.

I have never identified with the "K" in Kafka's works, by the way. Having grown up in a democracy, I have dared to imagine that I know at all times who is really in charge, what is really going on. This could be a mistake.

The opening pages of Uncle John's manuscript give an impersonal account, such as might be found in an encyclopedia, of the settling of this country by European immigrants, and the consequent growth of commerce, industry, agriculture, and so on. The largest of the waves was German—the second was Italian, the third was Irish.

Uncle John's conclusion to this prologue is worth setting down here: "The two world wars in which the United States was arrayed against Germany were painful experiences for German-Americans. They hated to be obliged to fight their racial cousins, but they did so, and it is significant that of the millions of German descendants in the United States during those dreadful wars there was not one case of treason.

"The Germans, while loving the country of their origin, did not approve of Kaiser Wilhelm II and his warlords, nor Hitler and his wretched Nazis. Their sympathies were with England, and their adoption of the culture of England determined their attitude. When England was in trouble in 1917 and again in 1941, the German-Americans rallied to her support against the Fatherland. This is a phenomenon little remarked upon."

So be it.

❧

As I have said in other books, the anti-Germanism in this country during the First World War so shamed and dismayed my parents that they resolved to raise me without acquainting me with the language or the literature or the music or the oral family histories which my ancestors had loved. They volunteered to make me ignorant and rootless as proof of their patriotism.

This was done with surprising meekness by many, many German-American families in Indianapolis, it seems to me. Uncle John almost seems to boast of this dismantling and quiet burial of a culture, a culture which surely would have been of use to me today.

But I still get a *frisson* when I encounter a German-American who was raised, amazingly, to loath Woodrow Wilson for calling into question the loyalty of what he called "hyphenated Americans," for egging on those who loved democracy so much that they defaced the walls of German social and gymnastic and educational associations across the country, and refused to listen to German music or, even, to eat sauerkraut. As nearly as I can remember, none of my relatives ever said anything much, one way or another, about Woodrow Wilson to me.

❧

ONE German-American friend of mine, an architectural historian my own age, can be counted on to excoriate Woodrow Wilson after he has had several strong drinks. He goes on to say that it was Wilson who persuaded this country that it was patriotic to be stupid, to be proud of knowing only one language, of believing that all other cultures were inferior and ridiculous, offensive to God and common sense alike, that artists and teachers and studious persons in general were ninnies when it came to dealing with problems in life that really mattered, and on and on.

This friend says that it was a particular misfortune for this country that the German-Americans had achieved such eminence in the arts and education when it was their turn to be scorned from on high. To hate all they did and stood for at that time, which included gymnastics, by the way, was to lobotomize not only the German-Americans but our culture.

"That left American football," says my German-American friend, and someone is elected to drive him home.

❧

To return to Uncle John:

"All of Kurt Vonnegut, Jr.'s eight great-grandparents were part of the vast migration of Germans to the Midwest

22

in the half century from 1820 to 1870. They were: Clemens Vonnegut, Sr., and his wife, Katarina Blank; Henry Schnull and his wife, Matilde Schramm; Peter Lieber and his wife, Sophia St. André; Karl Barus and his wife, Alice Möllman. They were preceded only by four of his sixteen great-great-grandparents, who were Jacob Schramm and his wife, Julia Junghans; and Johann Blank and his wife, Anna Maria Oger. The remaining twelve and their forebears are mostly unknown. They never left Germany. Their bones still repose there in anonymity.

"But all of the eight ancestors who did settle here were better educated and of higher social rank than the mine-run of immigrants. They were with the exception of Anna Oger's parents, burghers, city people, merchants and members of the upper middle class, in contrast to the bulk of German immigrants who were chiefly peasant farmers or skilled artisans.

"Thus, K's great-great-grandfather Jacob Schramm came from Saxony, where for generations his family had been grain merchants. He brought with him five thousand dollars in gold, six hundred books, and boxes of household goods, including a dinner set of Meissen porcelain. He bought at once a section of land near Cumberland, Indiana. He was a highly literate fellow, and wrote a series of letters back to Germany detailing his experiences and making valuable suggestions for the guidance of subsequent immigrants. These letters were printed and published in Germany. A copy of this publication is in the library of the Indiana Historical Society, which issued an English translation of it in 1928. Jacob Schramm traveled extensively—once around the world, quite by himself. He prospered. He bought a great deal of land, one parcel of over two thousand acres on the old Michigan Road just northwest of Indianapolis. He loaned money, secured by good mortgages, to later arrivals in the vicinity. When his only daughter, Matilda, married Henry Schnull in 1857, Jacob Schramm advanced the latter capital to help him start a wholesale grocery business and launch a successful mercantile career which made him a large fortune.

"K's paternal ancestors the Vonneguts, were likewise people of substance. They came from Münster, Westphalia, where the name derives from a distant forebear who had an estate—'ein Gut'—on the little River Funne; hence the surname FunneGut—the estate on the Funne. This name was subsequently changed from Funnegut to Vonnegut. Funnegut sounded too much like 'funny gut' in English.

"Clemens Vonnegut, Sr., was born in Münster in Westphalia in 1824; came to the United States in 1848 and finally settled in Indianapolis in 1850. His father had been an official tax-collector for the Duke of Westphalia.

"Clemens had a far better formal education than ninety-eight percent or more of the German or other immigrants. He had completed his *'Abitur'* at the *Hochschule* in Hannover; which meant that he had the equivalent at that time of an American college education and was qualified to attend one of the Universities as a candidate for a Ph.D. degree. He had an acquaintance with Latin and Greek, and spoke French fluently in addition to his native German. He had read widely in History and Philosophy; had acquired a fine vocabulary; and was able to write with clarity. Although raised and instructed in the Roman Catholic Church, he rejected formalized religion and disliked clergymen. He greatly admired Voltaire, and shared many of the latter's philosophical views. Instead of attending a University, Clemens became a salesman for a textile firm located in Amsterdam, Holland. At the age of twenty-four, in 1848, he decided to emigrate to the United States, where he first traveled about as agent for the textile mill. When he came to Indianapolis in 1850, he encountered a fellow countryman named Vollmer, who had been settled here a few years and was already established in business for himself in a small way as a retail merchant in hardware and sundry merchandise. The two became friends, and Vollmer invited Vonnegut to join him in this enterprise. The firm then became known as Vollmer & Vonnegut. After a short association Vollmer decided to make a journey out West to explore the new country and visit the gold fields recently discovered in California. He was never heard from again, and presumably lost his life in the 'Wild West.'

"Vonnegut thus became the sole proprietor of the small business which he in 1852, and later his sons and grandsons, made into a considerable enterprise as the Vonnegut Hardware Company.

"Across the street from his first modest shop on East Washington Street in the 1850s was a small German restaurant. One of the waitresses in this establishment was an attractive girl named Katarina Blank. She was one of seven children of a German immigrant family of peasants who came from Urloffen in Baden and settled on a farm in Wayne Township, Marion County, just west of Indianapolis. They were struggling to get their farm to be productive after felling the forest trees and draining the land. With so many children to feed and clothe, all had to work for their living after a few years of primary instruction in the common school. Katarina

Blank went to work as a waitress in this little cafe, and soon met Clemens Vonnegut, who fell in love with her. They were married in 1852. He was twenty-eight and she, twenty-four. They bought a modest home on West Market Street and raised their family in steadily improving material circumstances. Katarina was, like Clemens, small in stature and dark complected. Both spoke German in their home, but had considerable fluency in French as well. The training of their children was in the tradition and culture of nineteenth-century Germany. It is highly significant of Clemens's ascetic and puritanical ethics that his literary idol was Schiller and not Goethe, who was much the greater genius. He disapproved of Goethe's morals, and would not read him. Katarina, although of humble origin and little formal education, became a highly respected and extremely dignified matriarch, much beloved by her children and grandchildren.

"Clemens attained local distinction as an advocate of progressive public education. He served for twenty-seven years on the Board of School Commissioners of the City of Indianapolis; most of the time as Chairman and Chief Administrative Officer. He was an incorruptible and highly efficient officer. He was particularly interested in the High School, and saw to it that first-rate instruction was provided in the classics, history, and the social sciences. He was instrumental in the establishment of the second High School in 1894, known as Manual Training High School, where, under Professor Emmerich as Principal, instruction was provided with emphasis on Science, Mathematics, and Practical Engineering. Graduates of these two high schools were readily accepted at Harvard and Yale and other great Universities until about 1940; since then the prestige of these high schools has sadly declined as a result of lowered standards.

"Many tales were told of Clemens Vonnegut. When he was elected to the Board of School Commissioners, he found that the local banks did not pay interest on the somewhat large deposits which the Board carried to finance its operations. He demanded that the banks pay interest on the Board's deposits. This was then considered to be an offensive innovation in the customary and comfortable practice which until then had prevailed. The banker John P. Frenzel then called upon Clemens at his office and loudly upbraided him. Clemens pretended to be hard of hearing, and capped his ears. Frenzel shouted louder. Still Clemens pretended not to hear. Frenzel raised his voice and interjected profanity, but to no avail. Clemens would not 'hear' him. Finally Frenzel stormed out—still not heard. But thenceforth the banks paid interest and have continued to do so to this day.

"Upon another occasion a disgruntled contractor called upon him and protested the award of a contract for school construction to a bidder who did not have the 'right' political connections. Here again Clemens pretended to be hard of hearing; but, in addition, took out a pen-knife and pared his fingernails. The frustrated contractor then indulged in invectives. Clemens remained calm and silent. After he finished paring his fingernails, he took off his shoes and socks and proceeded to pare his toenails with intense but silent concentration. His visitor soon left in disgust, cursing this crazy German. Clemens remained imperturbable and undisturbed. Many similar tales were told of him, but at his death at age eighty-two in 1906 he was a greatly respected figure in the business and civic life of the community; next only to Henry Schnull as the first in prestige of the German immigrants to Indianapolis.

"Old Clemens, as he advanced into his seventies, turned

over management of his business to the competent hands of his three sons: Clemens, Jr., Franklin, and George. His son Bernard had a brief connection with the Company but disliked what he called 'the trade in nails' and confined his attention to his profession of architecture and to his avocations in the arts. He had never been as robust as his brothers, two of whom lived into their nineties. The old man set them all an example not only of the highest standards of moral integrity but of physical fitness through exercise of the body. To the end of his days old Clemens was a devotee of the teachings of Father Jahn: a sound mind in a sound body. He exercised daily in all weathers and ate and drank very sparingly. He never weighed much over one hundred and ten pounds. He could be seen striding vigorously about the streets swinging a large boulder in each hand. If he passed a tree with a stout branch within reach he would stop, lay down the boulders, and chin himself a number of times on the branch. On a cold December day in the year 1904, in his eighty-third year, he left his home for his usual walk. He apparently became confused and lost his way. When he did not return at his accustomed time, his family instituted a search with the assistance of the police. He was found several miles from his home lying by the side of a road—quite dead. It was the sort of death he would have welcomed—active to the very end."

❦

ALMOST all of my ancestors delivered themselves directly from Europe to Indianapolis, except for Peter Lieber and Sophia de St. André, who had the general store in New Ulm,

Minnesota. When Peter returned from the Civil War with a crippled leg, he was full of stories about how Indianapolis was booming. New Ulm was dead by comparison.

So Peter, according to Uncle John, wangled an appointment as one of the secretaries to Oliver P. Morton, the Governor of Indiana. The governor needed a German liaison secretary in his political activities. The pay was good and steady, and Peter remained in his office until the close of the war.

"In 1865 came an opportunity for Peter. The leading brewery of the city was known as Gack & Biser's. Owing to death of the proprietors, the business was offered for sale. Peter bought it and renamed it P. Lieber & Co. Peter knew absolutely nothing of the brewery business, but he engaged a skilled brewmaster named Geiger who did, and proceeded to brew and sell Lieber's Beer. It was a successful venture from the very start. Peter gave his principal attention to sales, at which he became adept. This involved political activity and manipulation of saloon outlets.

"Peter was always involved in politics. He had to be in order to get saloon licenses for his favored customers. Until 1880 he was a staunch Republican, as all the Civil War veterans were. But in that year the Republicans, at the insistence of the Methodist Church, adopted a plank in their platform recommending a restraint upon the beer and liquor trade. It was the first stirring of Prohibition. This outraged Peter and was a threat to his interests. He promptly changed his politics and was thereafter a Democrat—and an aggressive, active one.

"He contributed generously to Grover Cleveland's Campaign Funds, particularly in 1892, when Cleveland was elected President for the second time. He was rewarded by being appointed Consul General of the United States to Düsseldorf in 1893."

Peter Lieber sold his brewery to a British syndicate, which was eager to have Peter's oldest son, my grandfather Albert, run it for them.

Peter returned to Germany in 1893, where he bought a castle on the Rhine near Düsseldorf. He took with him President Cleveland's commission as Consul General of the United States to Düsseldorf. Uncle John says, "He hoisted the Stars and Stripes over his castle, delegated his negligible duties to subordinates, and finished his days in opulence and official grandeur."

His son Albert, who never went to college, stayed in Indianapolis and ran the brewery, and went to London once a year to report to its new owners.

❦

So there—Uncle John has now accounted for four of my great-grandparents, those who brought my mother's maiden name, Lieber, and my father's name, Vonnegut, into this country when there was still much wilderness. Four more great-grandparents and four grandparents and two parents must still be described.

Let me say now that the ancestor who most beguiles me is Clemens Vonnegut, who died by the side of the road.

"Clemens Vonnegut was a cultivated eccentric," says Uncle John. That is what I aspire to be.

"He was small in stature, but stout in his independence and convictions," says Uncle John. "While his forebears had been Roman Catholics, he professed to be an atheist or Free

Thinker." So do I profess. "He would more properly be called a skeptic, one who rejects faith in the unknowable." "Skeptic" is also the proper thing to call me.

"But he was a very model of Victorian asceticism, lived frugally, and eschewed excesses of any kind," says Uncle John. I try. I don't drink anymore, but I smoke like a house afire. I am monogamous, but I have married twice.

"He greatly admired Benjamin Franklin, whom he called an American saint, and named his third son after him instead of naming him for one of the saints on the Christian calendar." I myself have named my only son after Mark Twain, another American Saint.

"As a recognition of his service to public education," Uncle John goes on, "one of the City's schools was named after him. He was highly literate, well read, and the author of various pamphlets expounding his views on education, philosophy, and religion. He wrote his own funeral oration."

That oration, by the way, appears in Chapter XI. of this book, the chapter on religion. I read it out loud recently to my agnostic son, Mark, who is a physician now, but who set out during his undergraduate years to become a Unitarian minister.

Mark said this of the oration, grinding his teeth before and afterward: "The *guts* move." When you read the oration, and especially if you are a chess player like Mark, you are bound to admire the guts of Clemens Vonnegut.

Note: I do not have the guts to request that Clemens Vonnegut's oration be read at my funeral, too.

❦

To return to Uncle John:

"Another one of Kurt Vonnegut, Jr.'s great-grandfathers
who attained distinction locally was Henry Schnull, who,
with his brother, August, came to Indianapolis from the
town of Hausberge in Westphalia about ten years before the
Civil War. They had both been apprenticed as Kaufmann, or
merchant, in Germany and knew the methods of trade and
accounts. They first engaged in the business of buying and
selling farm produce in central Indiana. They traveled about
in a wagon to the farms in the area; bought grain, butter,
eggs, chickens, and salted and smoked pork, and resold these
farm products in the city at a profit.

"As they prospered by the hardest kind of work, they
enlarged their operation by trucking surpluses to Madison or
Jeffersonville, Indiana, on the Ohio River, where the merchandise was loaded on huge barges which were floated
down the Ohio and Mississippi rivers to New Orleans. One
or the other of the brothers would accompany the shipment
and attend to the trading in New Orleans. Here they would
sell the produce in a good market and buy coffee, rum and
sorghum, which was called 'New Orleans molasses.' These
products they then shipped north by barge and sold at a
profit in Cincinnati or Indianapolis. They are said to have
brought to Indianapolis one of the last shipments from the
South before the river was closed by the Confederates at
Memphis. The price of sorghum and coffee skyrocketed, and
the Schnull Brothers then had sufficient capital to establish
a wholesale grocery business and construct a warehouse
which still stands on the southeast corner of Washington and
Delaware Streets in Indianapolis. The firm was originally a
partnership known as A. & H. Schnull, later as Schnull &
Company. At the close of the Civil War, August announced
that he had enough money and wanted to return to Ger-

many. So he sold his interests to Henry and took two hundred thousand dollars back to Hausberge, where he bought a small Schloss and lived like a gentleman until his death in 1918.

"Henry Schnull elected to remain in the United States. He became one of the leading merchants of Indiana, and was a most highly regarded citizen. In addition to his wholesale grocery business he founded the Eagle Machine Works, which later became the great Atlas Engine Company, which manufactured stationary steam engines and farm implements. He also organized the American Woolen Company, the first textile mill in the State.

"Shortly after passage in 1865 of the law authorizing national banks, he established and was first President of the Merchants National Bank of Indianapolis, which has survived all of the intervening panics and is still operating.

"Henry Schnull was a man of immense industry, courage, and independence; intelligent, self-reliant, and resourceful; incorruptibly honest and reliable in his dealings; and completely dedicated to business and accumulation. He became very rich for his times, endowed his children with generous gifts, and left a fortune in 1905 which has assisted three generations of his progeny to live comfortably. He was so much engaged with his many activities that he was not much of a family man, and his children saw but little of him. His wife, Matilda Schramm, whom he met on one of his early buying visits to her father's farm in 1854, was as stern and tough as Henry, but she had a warm, lovable disposition and was the real matriarch of the family."

❦

ALL right now: Uncle John has now told us about my two sets of great-grandparents on my father's side, Clemens Vonnegut, whose wife was Katarina Blank, and Henry Schnull, whose wife was Matilda Schramm, and one set from my mother's side, the limping Civil War veteran Peter Lieber, whose wife was Sophia de St. André.

This brings me to my fourth set of great-grandparents—the only ones who had anything participatory to do with the arts. They were "Professor" Karl Barus, "the first real professional teacher of voice, violin, and piano in the city," according to Uncle John, and his wife, Alice Möllman.

"Professor Barus was highly respected, and in addition to his function as a private teacher he conducted orchestras, organized choral singing and other musical events. He was well educated and a definite intellectual. He never engaged in trade or business but made a good income by his teaching and lived well. Professor Barus originally settled in Cincinnati in the early fifties, where he was appointed Musical Director of the Cincinnati Sangverein.

"In 1858 Dr. Barus was invited to come to Indianapolis to conduct the mixed chorus of German singing societies from Indianapolis, Louisville, Cincinnati, and Columbus, Ohio, at a great Musical Festival. In 1882 he was invited by Das Deutsche Haus to come to Indianapolis to be musical director of the Maennerchor, in which position he remained until 1896.

"At his last concert in that year at Tomlinson Hall he was given a standing ovation and was presented with a silver laurel wreath as an expression of appreciation of his great contribution to the musical life of the whole community. For the remaining twelve years of his life he gave instruction in piano and voice to selected pupils and was always held in highest esteem. His influence on the musical taste and sophistication of the whole city was incalculable. No one ever seems subsequently to have quite taken his place."

❦

AND Professor Karl Barus the musician, and his wife Alice begat another Alice Barus, who, according to Uncle John, "is said to have been the most beautiful and accomplished young lady in Indianapolis. She played the piano and sang; also composed music, some of which was published."

She was my mother's mother.

Yes, and Peter Lieber, the limping war veteran, and his wife Sophia begat Albert Lieber, who became an Indianapolis brewer and *bon vivant.*

He was my mother's father.

Henry Schnull, the merchant and banker, and his wife Matilda begat Nanette Schnull, who, according to Uncle John, "was a very beautiful woman in her prime, and had a lovely speaking and singing voice. She often sang in public. She laughed readily, enjoyed people, and was greatly admired by a host of friends."

She was my father's mother.

And Clemens Vonnegut, the Free Thinker and founder of the Vonnegut Hardware Company, and his wife Katarina begat Bernard Vonnegut, who, Uncle John says, "was from earliest youth artistic. He could draw and paint with skill. Bernard was extremely modest and retiring. He had no intimates, and took but little part in social activities. He was never a happy, extroverted personality, but was inclined to be reticent, shy, and somewhat contemptuous of his environment."

He was my father's father.

❦

WE have come now to a rascal, Albert Lieber, whose emotional faithlessness to his children, in my humble opinion, contributed substantially to my mother's eventual suicide. As I have said, he was the son of the limping Civil War Veteran. When his father retired to Düsseldorf, Albert remained in Indianapolis to run the brewery that his father had sold to a British syndicate. He was born in 1863.

When I got to know him, there wasn't much to know. He was in bed all the time with a flabby heart. He might as well have been a Martian. What do I remember about him? His mouth was slackly open. It was very pink inside.

He was often in London on business when he was young. "He had his clothes tailored in Savile Row," says Uncle John, "and was the very model of Victorian sartorial elegance: broadcloth Prince Albert coats, silk hats, Scotch tweeds, starched shirts and collars, and handmade boots. He was handsome, friendly, and highly sociable. He loved parties, good eating, and fine wines. He was always much involved in a series of love affairs, passing feminine attachments, and ribald entertainment.

"The brewery was under the general supervision of a retired British army officer—Colonel Thompson—who visited Indianapolis every year or two to look things over and report back to London. He and Albert between them milked the local operation of most of the profits of the brewery through padded expense accounts, sales promotion schemes, public relations departments, political contributions and other devices to skim the cream off the profits. The syndicate demanded a five percent return upon its investment and got it. Albert and his cohorts lined their pockets.

"In contrast to his father, who was conservative, retiring, and extremely modest and unassuming, Albert was extroverted, flamboyant, sociable, and a big spender. He always lived on a very lavish scale in various large houses with lots of servants, horses, and carriages and then the earliest and finest motor cars. In his heyday he always had an English butler and a footman in livery. He entertained his friends without thought of cost: the choicest viands, rare wines, flowers, the whitest linens, and choicest porcelain chinaware.

"He soon acquired the reputation of a millionaire who counted the cost of nothing. He became a jolly companion of the town's 'fun boys' who consisted of other rich men's sons, among them Booth Tarkington. They gave fabulous parties. One of them owned the English Hotel on Monument Circle and English's Opera House where all the principal traveling shows played. He had a stage box reserved for his use on the right side of the house where he had a door which connected to the stage. This gave him and his cronies access to the stage and easy opportunity to meet actresses and particularly the chorus girls with musical comedies.

"At other times they would take over for the night the leading bagnio of the town—facetiously known as the University Club Annex—which was situated on the east side of

New Jersey Street about two blocks north of Washington Street. No cash changed hands to sully the dignified atmosphere of the Annex. Each month its devotees were billed discreetly for their share of maintenance. Here the local 'fun boys' would stage real bacchanalian orgies which provided choice and juicy gossip for the staid community. But they always committed their indiscretions, with due respect for the Victorian proprieties, in privacy behind doors—which is what doors are for.

"One of their charming folkways was to initiate congenial spirits into what they called their 'W-A Club.' Preceding an elaborate dinner at one of the clubs or hotels, the neophyte would be blindfolded and seated on a cool, fresh keg of Lieber's beer to which a spigot and faucet had been attached. At the turn of the faucet the beer would squirt out and drench the candidate. He was then said to have a wet ass and was qualified to be admitted to their fellowship. They even had a gold button made by a jeweler which could be worn on the coat lapel with the insignia 'W-A.' They were real devotees of sport and always chartered a private Pullman car to take them to championship prizefights, horse races, and other sporting events. They never used drugs or much profanity, and always respected respectable women. They were always suitably attired and were uniformly well-mannered and gentlemanly."

❧

THIS Edwardian sport married the beautiful and musical Alice Barus in 1885. They had three children. My mother was the oldest. And then Alice Barus died of pneumonia when Mother was six.

❦

"SHORTLY thereafter," says Uncle John, "Albert married a very attractive but extremely eccentric woman, who was never accepted by Albert's family or close friends. Her name was Ora D. Lane. She was an accomplished violinist and came from Zanesville, Ohio. She was familiarly known as 'O.D.' but most people referred to her as 'Odious.' She became a sort of storybook stepmother to Albert's children. She chastised and ill-treated them in subtle ways. She seemed to resent them and abused them so that they all suffered a distinctive psychic trauma from which they never fully recovered. Where formerly they had known nothing but loving and tender care, now they were subjected to every sort of indignity, humiliation, and neglect. She terrorized Albert as well, threatened his life, slept with a pistol under her pillow, and was a perfect demon and termagant. Kindly, gentle Albert stood it as long as he could and then divorced her; but he was obliged to settle a large alimony upon her which depleted his capital, which was not large. He had never been an accumulator and had spent freely, relying upon the brewery to carry him as usual with a large annual income.

"But nothing daunted, Albert soon was married a third time to a nondescript widow named Meda Langtry, a Canadian, who had a daughter whom Albert adopted and renamed Alberta.

"Meda was much younger than Albert. In fact she was about the same age as his daughter Edith."

"Shortly after Albert's third and last marriage came Prohibition in 1921," Uncle John goes on, "the brewery was closed. Albert lost his position, and from then on his affairs went from bad to worse until he died in what he would have regarded as relative poverty. The last years of his life were supported by the sale of several parcels of real estate including his former residence, a large house situated on an estate of a hundred acres on a hill overlooking White River and running north to Kessler Boulevard and West Fifty-sixth Street in the City of Indianapolis. This land would now be worth at least a million dollars or more.

"He, like all rich men, had a miscellaneous assortment of personal property which will be acquired not for investment but as adjuncts of abundant privileges such as miscellaneous securities, paintings, porcelains, furniture, and other art objects. Much had to be sold but he had a few securities left and his estate inventory came to $311,607.65. All that his children got out of the Peter Lieber fortune was a small remnant from Albert's estate and a few trust funds which Peter had established for them in Merchants Bank stock. And so the proverbial cycle of 'shirt sleeves to shirt sleeves' was completed in three generations due for them to Prohibition and Albert's extravagance and improvidence.

"But while Albert was still in his prime and riding high, his daughter, Edith—K's mother—was married on November 22, 1913, to Kurt Vonnegut. They were a charming and extremely attractive couple."

❧

As has already been said, my father's mother Nanette was cheerful and sociable, and uninterested in the fine arts save for music—and my father's father Bernard was a freak in the family for being able to draw and paint so well at an early age. He was also unsociable, and evidently unhappy in Indianapolis most of the time.

Uncle John said to me in conversation one time that my grandfather Bernard was probably relieved to die young—"to be well out of it." He died of intestinal cancer at fifty-three, five years younger than I am now. That was in 1908, so he did not see any of his grandchildren. He did not even see his children married.

"Like his brothers," says Uncle John, "he attended the public schools, the German-English school, and then the Indianapolis High School then situated at Pennsylvania and Michigan Streets. Recognizing his talents as an artist, Alexander Metzger, a friend of his father, suggested that Bernard be given a higher education. He was then sent to the Massachusetts Institute of Technology in Boston, where he studied architecture. He later studied in Hannover, Germany, and then worked as draftsman, for a couple of years, with a leading firm in New York.

"Returning to Indianapolis in 1883, he engaged in the practice of architecture, first in his own office and later with Arthur Bohn in what became the well-known firm of Vonnegut & Bohn, whose successors are in practice today. This firm designed and supervised construction of many fine residences and public buildings in Indianapolis, including the first Chamber of Commerce, the Athenaeum, the John Herron Art Museum, the L. S. Ayres store, the Fletcher Trust Building, and many others.

"He read the poems of Heine with delight. He was highly cultivated in the arts, but his sympathies and inclinations were definitely Germanic. He and his family frequently lived abroad, and he sent his two sons to school in Strasbourg abroad, and he sent his two sons to school in Strasbourg when they were quite young. He fathered three children: Kurt, born in 1884; Alex, in 1888; and then Irma, in 1890.

"Aside from his attachment to his profession, Bernard took little participation in the social or civic life of the community. He confined his activities to the arts. His favorite clubs were the Portfolio and the Lyra Casino. The former was composed of painters, sculptors, architects, and writers. It held monthly dinners and discussions, and considered itself to be the custodian of the aesthetic conscience of the community. The Lyra Casino was a society of musicians, and gave private concerts of classical music. Bernard was an active participant in both these organizations, and his son Kurt likewise joined them in his maturity. Bernard's wife, Nanette, had a thorough training in and acquaintance with musical literature, but she did not share her husband's other interests.

"When their children attained an age to enable them to make objective judgment, they agreed that their parents' marriage was not a particularly congenial one. Kurt and Irma definitely identified with their father, while Alex identified with his mother. Unlike his brothers, Bernard was never robust physically. He suffered much with indigestion and headaches."

❦

I, too, identify with this unhappy Bernard, although I am more or less robust and can say, knocking on wood, that I am seldom ill. I sleep well always. My digestion is good.

The family legend is that Bernard Vonnegut when a boy

was working with his brothers in the family hardware store, and he began to weep. He was asked what the trouble was, and he said that he didn't want to work in a store. He said he wanted to be an artist instead.

A child expressing such a wish in such a family in such a town was a troubling mystery.

The legend goes on that he became stagestruck, and wanted to be a theatrical designer, but learned that almost no one could make a living at that—so he became an architect instead.

The legend says that he was happy and productive and even sociable as a young architect here in New York City. But then he was told by his family that it was time for him to come home to Indianapolis, and to marry a woman from a nice German family. He was to surrender to the gravitational pull of the tremendous mass of respectability which his father and mother had amassed in the American wilderness in a little more than thirty years.

He should have disobeyed, if he did not want constant headaches and indigestion. He should have stayed in New York City.

He should have moved into the very house I live in now. This house was standing back then.

In a huge and rich and bustling and polyglot world city like this one, he surely found many friends as gifted as himself. So he must have made all sorts of jokes here about giftedness, made romantic speeches about the pain of bringing new works of art into the world, and on and on. There was a knowing audience here for talk like that.

When he got back to Indianapolis, where the practice of the arts was regarded as an evasion of real life by means of parlor tricks, the things that made him happy or sad were equally meaningless to his relatives and neighbors. So, yes, he became as silent as a clam. He died.

Wasn't it true that his wife was also gifted, that she sang beautifully? Yes, but she was not interested in creating any new music. She was a sort of frontier phonograph, reproducing melodies from the Old World, where creative artists belonged, where they were needed, where they were supposed to be.

❦

HE may even have been a genius, as mutations sometimes are.

❦

AND it is always the men, even if they were as reclusive and secretive and unfond of life as my grandfather Bernard, who are the stars in this account of my ancestors. There are reasons for this. "It is regrettable that so little is known of K's two grandmothers and four great-grandmothers," says Uncle John. "Practically everyone who knew any of them intimately is now dead. The Victorian age in which they lived was a man's world. Women's place was in the home, and no public notice was taken of them. They left no records of their own, and were expected to bask in obscurity in the reflected glory of their husbands' achievements—the most admired of which was the accumulation of money.

"But they bore the children, which was one thing the men could not do. They ran the households admirably, and provided their progeny with all their training in manners and morals which they received.

"The men were so much engaged in the struggle for material success that they gave but scant attention to their families. How they found time to father their children is conjectural. But in defense of the men it should be noted that they were emotionally and psychologically motivated to assert their own importance in a new environment: to achieve and to demonstrate their worth as individuals. Success was principally equated with money. To be rich was to be respected.

"The immigrants had been literally starved—materially and socially—in the nineteenth century of Western Europe. When they came here and found the rich table of the Midwest, they gorged themselves. And who can blame them? In the process they created an Empire by the hardest work and exercise of their inherent and varied talents. The men took the credit, but their womenfolk, if unnoticed, helped lay the foundation."

❧

LET Uncle John now run out his story of my family without further interruptions from me. There remain only a father and a mother to be described.

"K's father—Kurt, the eldest son of Bernard and Nannie —was very much like his father in outlook and pattern of behavior, but dissimilar in appearance. Bernard was dark complected, wore a beard, and was rather bald. Kurt was blue-eyed, and very fair complected, with finely modeled features, long thin fingers, and blond curly hair. He was a sort of Adonis and extremely handsome, without any trace of effeminacy. He was, like his father, artistic. He could draw and paint. He worked in ceramics, and created some beautiful objects in that technique. And, of course, he was a fine, sensitive architect.

"Kurt Vonnegut attended School No. 10, a grammar school, from 1890 to 1898. He then attended Shortridge High School in Indianapolis for somewhat over a year. He was subsequently sent to the American College in Strasbourg, Germany, for three years. This was a small private school under the direction of Professor Goss, who organized it as a school principally for American boys on the model of the German Gymnasia. It was a good school, with rigid standards and discipline. In this school Kurt was steeped in the German language and in German cultural patterns. Strasbourg had its own opera and symphony orchestra. Kurt was naturally devoted to music throughout his life, and in his formative years at this school became intimately acquainted with the whole classical repertoire.

"At the age of nineteen he was well prepared in a solid foundation of secondary education, and was admitted to the Massachusetts Institute of Technology, where he studied architecture and took his degree of Bachelor of Science in 1908—the year in which his father died. He then went with his widowed mother and his sister, Irma, to Berlin, and continued his architectural studies with the best masters. He returned to Indianapolis in 1910, and joined his father's surviving partner, Arthur Bohn, in the well-established firm of Vonnegut & Bohn. He was thus launched upon what promised to be a comfortable and successful career. His family had a prominent position in the community. They had plenty of money.

"Kurt was handsome in appearance, with charming manners, and although dignified and reserved, soon had many friends who remained devoted to him. He joined the University Club, then situated at Meridian and Michigan Streets, which was the most exclusive men's club in the City. He was received and accepted by the best families as a most eligible bachelor. He was generally approved by doting mamas looking for suitable mates for their daughters, and had the pick of the crop of debutantes. After a couple of years of a happy and carefree existence, Kurt began to court Edith Lieber, who was four years his junior and had likewise returned to an active social life after attending Miss Shipley's School at Bryn Mawr and traveling much abroad. Her father, Albert Lieber, was then in the full tide of success as one of the town's rich men. He resided on a beautiful estate of some hundred acres just to the northwest of the city, in a large residence which he had recently constructed."

❦

"EDITH was a very beautiful woman, tall and statuesque. Kurt always admired her beauty and was very proud of her. They fell in love, became engaged, and were married on November 22, 1913. They remained a devoted couple until the day of Edith's death thirty-one years later. The marriage was approved by both families; but the Schnull-Vonnegut clan was slightly condescending. In the pecking order in the social hierarchy of the community, and particularly in the German group it was generally understood that the Schnull-Vonnegut clan ranked ahead of the Lieber-Barus clan.

"Edith was a rather tall woman, about five feet eight inches, with a fine graceful figure. She was auburn-haired, not quite red, with a very fair, clear skin, finely modeled features, and blue-green eyes. She was stately and dignified in bearing. She had a lively sense of humor and laughed easily. Her adolescent years had been difficult with her odious stepmother, but she was strong enough in spirit and courage to endure her ordeal, although the scars were there.

"Prior to her engagement and marriage to Kurt, Edith had been engaged to other men but had each time broken her engagement. These suitors were all Europeans; for in the years from 1907 to 1913 Edith lived mostly abroad. As an extremely handsome woman and the daughter of an American millionaire she was much courted.

"She first became engaged to Kenneth Doulton, an Englishman, a grandson of Sir Henry Doulton, and a scion of the family which for generations had owned the world-famous Royal Doulton Porcelain Works in Lambeth. She met him while visiting the Thompsons for the London season of 1908 in the waning days of the Edwardian twilight of elegance and sophistication when the rich could still enjoy their privileges. Doulton was an attractive member of the upper-middle class with connections in the aristocracy. He was a charming idler and of course expected Albert to supply a suitable settlement as a dowry upon his lovely daughter. Albert enjoyed a large income at that time but was not enthusiastic to part with his modest capital. And Doulton was not about to go in the brewery business in Indianapolis. He wanted to marry Edith, have her father buy them a country place and a little house in Mayfair, and remain in old England. Edith demurred and the engagement was broken.

"In the First World War Doulton as a junior officer in a Guard's regiment lost his life while serving in the first British Expeditionary Force in the first months of the war.

"Edith then forsook merrie England and shifted her European base of operations from London to Düsseldorf. From 1909 to 1913 she spent most of each year staying with her grandfather, Peter, then past eighty, and her maiden aunt Laura, in the old man's Schloss on the Rhine. He was no longer Consul General of the United States but he kept the Stars and Stripes flying over his palace and retained his American citizenship to the end. But his three children, Laura, Emily, and Rudolph, became German citizens. Rudolph adopted a military career, went through the Cadet School and became Lieutenant Colonel of a regiment of cavalry—the Uhlans—garrisoned in the area of Düsseldorf. Emily married a German army officer. Edith was thus thrown into the company of subalterns in her uncle's famous regiment. At that time the Kaiser's army officers constituted a sort of elite social group with many privileges and much prestige. The Kaiser's pay and allowances to his officers were extremely meager. If an officer did not have substantial means to supplement his pay and maintain the position required of him, he was expected to marry a rich wife. In fact, he could not marry except with the consent of the colonel of his regiment; and the consent was withheld until the social position, reputability, and dowry of the bride were officially approved.

"Edith's first serious German suitor was Lieutenant Paul Genth of the Uhlans. She gave him the go-by after a brief courtship. Shortly afterward Captain Otto Voigt of the regiment proposed to her, and after a spirited courtship was accepted by her with the consent of her family and of his commanding officer. The Captain was a dashing figure in his colorful dress uniform with shako and 'Merry Widow' accoutrements.

"But here again the course of true love did not run true and smooth. There were difficulties about the dowry, and the prospect for Edith of a career as an army wife in the highly artificial and regulated life of the imperial army palled upon her. Captain Voigt was one of those heel-clicking Prussian-type officers who looked good in his uniform in command of his squadron of cavalry but was quite different from the easygoing, indulgent, and deferential American husbands of Edith's experience. She wavered. But Albert gave her carte blanche to buy a trousseau and she proceeded to do so. All of the linens were duly embroidered 'L-V.' The Liebers of the German branch thought it was a great match."

❧

"BUT Edith began to have misgivings. So did Albert, who never liked dowries anyway. And Edith did not want to make her permanent home in Germany. The captain was likewise not an enthusiastic candidate for a job in the brewery. At all events, the engagement was broken by mutual consent and Edith returned to Indianapolis where her father built for her a small cottage on his estate very attractively situated on a bluff overlooking White River. It was furnished to her taste; had a grand piano in the living room, a fireplace, comfortable lounge chairs and couches; and it was her own retreat when she wanted privacy—which was most of the time. But she got along well enough with her father and his third wife Meda and their two young children. She resumed contact with her old friends, went about in the social life of the city, and had plenty of suitors. Kurt Vonnegut, Sr., fell deeply in love with her and she reciprocated his affection. In every respect the match was universally approved.

"Edith and Kurt's wedding celebration was one long remembered in Indianapolis. It was probably the biggest and most costly party which the town had ever seen or is likely ever to witness again. The couple were married by the Reverend Frank S. C. Wicks, a Unitarian clergyman, in an evening ceremony in the First Unitarian Church attended by members of the two families—Lieber and Vonnegut—and a bevy of lovely bridesmaids and handsome ushers. But these families in three generations were then numerous and both clans had many friends. The Liebers and the Vonneguts with the Hollwegs, Mayers, Savereins, Schnulls, Rauchs, Frenzels, Pantzers, Haueisens, Kipps, Kuhns, Metzgers, and Kothes were the leading German families of the city. They were all convivial people, sentimental and emotional. And they loved to celebrate weddings, particularly between congenial clans of a common heritage and cultural background. The nuptials qualified to be celebrated in accordance with the best German traditions: food, drink, dancing, music, and song. Albert decided to give them a party to end all parties.

"In 1913 the Claypool Hotel, situated on the northwest corner of Washington Street and Illinois Street in the very heart of the city of Indianapolis, was one of the finest hostelries in the Midwest. It has just been completed about ten years before and was in prime condition. Eight stories high, it contained five hundred bedrooms. Its main lobby was 80 feet square and 60 feet high, elaborately decorated in the fashion of the time. The mezzanine story had a huge ballroom about 125 feet by 80 feet. This later was named the Riley Room after the Hoosier poet—James Whitcomb Riley. On the Illinois Street side of the mezzanine floor were a series of private dining rooms decorated in red and gold in Louis XV rococo. The proprietor of this garish caravansary was

Henry Lawrence. He and Albert Lieber were buddies. And so Albert decided to throw the wedding celebration party for Edith and Kurt in the Claypool. Henry Lawrence decided to give his all—and did so.

"In addition to the numerous relatives of the Lieber-Vonnegut clans Albert had a host of friends, a rigid selection of whom had to be invited. About six hundred of them came, including Colonel Thompson who journeyed from London to represent the English syndicate. The men guests were arrayed in white tie and tails, the women in long elaborate ball gowns. The chefs of the hotel were put to work days ahead and a large buffet of choice viands was served. Champagne of rarest vintages flowed like water. Then the floor was cleared and a large band of musicians played for dancing in the ballroom.

"A bar some sixty feet long had been specially erected. Here every variety of beverage was provided. The party lasted through the night and until six o'clock in the morning. Never before or since have so many otherwise respectable and thoroughly conservative citizens of the dull community passed out in so short a time. The consumption of spirits after the preliminary foundation of champagne was like pouring gasoline on a hot fire. It was estimated later that about seventy-five men and ten or fifteen women passed out cold. But Henry Lawrence was ready for the occasion. He had reserved plenty of bedrooms above and, as guests wavered and lost the coordination required for locomotion, they were gently assisted by the hotel waiters and bellmen to comfortable beds and the arms of Morpheus where a few of them were still reposing three days later.

"It was a grand occasion, but the Vonneguts and Schnulls thought it was all rather vulgar, and did not hesitate to express their disapproval. Some of the town wags, who were familiar with Albert's ways, in commenting on the huge cost of the bash said: 'What the Hell! Albert probably charged the tab to the brewery, and let the syndicate unwittingly give the party.' It was a strictly *fin de siècle* affair.

"The next year came the First World War and then Prohibition. The curtain fell on a glorious scene—never to be witnessed again."

❦

"KURT and Edith's marriage was a happy and congenial one —as marriages go. At first they were reasonably affluent— had servants, governesses for their children, and lived well. But they were both inclined to be extravagant. They traveled and entertained rather lavishly. If they needed money, they sold securities or borrowed. After Prohibition in 1921 Albert was no longer able to help them.

"But they had enough economic fat which, with Kurt's income from his profession, saw them through the twenties. Kurt's mother, Nannie Schnull Vonnegut, died in 1929 and left Kurt his share of her then modest fortune derived from her father, Henry Schnull. They soon used this up. Kurt had acquired a plot of land on the east side of North Illinois Street at about Forty-fifth Street. Here he designed and built a large and very beautiful brick residence. They sent their older children in the twenties and thirties to private schools; Bernard to Park School, and Alice to Tudor Hall School for girls. Bernard went on to the Massachusetts Institute of Technology where he took his degree of Bachelor of Science and remained to take his Ph.D. degree in Chemistry. He became and remains a distinguished scientist. Alice married

James Adams. But by the time K came along to his adolescence, the family was in financial trouble. He knew only the hard times of the 1930s. He was taken out of private school after the third grade, and sent to Public School No. 43 and then Shortridge High School. He was sent to Cornell University with specific instructions not to waste time or money on 'frivolous' courses, but to give full attention to practical studies, principally physics and chemistry and math.

"His parents were in straitened circumstances. There was practically no building in the Depression years and Kurt's professional income vanished. They began to live on their capital which, to a good bourgeois, is a heresy looked upon with horror and usually followed by disaster.

"It was obvious to them that they could not continue to support so large an establishment. This residence, by then heavily mortgaged, was sold. It still stands and is now the home of Evans Woollen III, a descendent of a well-known family and a distinguished architect in his own right. With the proceeds of their equity in this property and a few remaining assets, Kurt and Edith then purchased an attractive plot of land in William's Creek—a suburban development lying about nine miles due north of Monument Circle, to which many of the leading families migrated to escape the deteriorating conditions of the inner city. Here Kurt designed and built in 1941 a somewhat smaller and less pretentious dwelling, but it was well constructed of brick. It was surrounded by tall virginal forest trees—oaks, maples, and elms. It was a most attractive home, was well furnished, and displayed Kurt's artistic skills. In the basement Kurt had a small shop where he installed a kiln and dabbled in ceramics in which he produced some beautiful pieces. Here the family lived quietly and modestly with but little entertaining or traveling.

"They continued to invade their diminishing capital. But Kurt had two $1,000 corporate bonds which he had inherited from his mother. Edith, true to her delusions to grandeur, said: 'Let's take one more trip abroad.' So they sold the two bonds, went to Paris for three weeks and returned broke. But it was a rare example of *ésprit*—what the French call *panache*. It was going out with flair—all banners flying.

"Meanwhile came the Second World War in December 1941 and once again America was arrayed against Germany. Bernard at twenty-four escaped the draft, but Kurt, Jr., at nineteen was caught. He was enlisted in the army as a private and sent to training camp. This came as a great shock with acute distress to Edith. With her other financial problems the prospect of losing her son in the impending holocaust made her cup of troubles overflow. She became despondent and morose. Wanting money desperately, she attempted to write short stories which she could sell, but it was a futile, hopeless venture; a tragic disillusion. She simply could not see daylight. Kurt, Jr., got leave from his regiment to come home and spend Mother's Day in May 1944 with his family. During the night before, Edith died in her sleep in her fifty-sixth year on May 14, 1944. Her death was attributed to an overdose of sleeping tablets taken possibly by mistake. Her gross estate was inventoried in probate at $10,815.50. It was all that was left as her share of her grandfather's fortune and of her father's residue.

"She missed by a matter of two months the birth of her first grandchild, the son of her daughter Alice. She would miss seeing twelve grandchildren in all. She missed by seven months the capture of her son K by the Germans in the Battle of the Bulge, and his imprisonment in Dresden until the end of the war."

❦

"AFTER Edith's death Kurt lived almost as a recluse, for some ten years. But his sister, Irma Vonnegut Lindener, who was then a resident of Hamburg, Germany, paid him protracted visits—sometimes for months at a time. They were very congenial and deeply attached to each other. She understood his vagaries, respected his privacy and fierce independence, and gave him the only sort of companionship which he would tolerate. They resembled each other in many ways and were deeply empathetic. They were both blond and blue-eyed. They both spoke German fluently and shared their attachment to their German traditions of music and literature. Kurt acquired a sort of skeptical and fatalistic contempt for life—what the Germans call Weltschmerz.

"As Kurt aged and his fortunes waned, he could not continue to support this last abode of modest elegance. He sold it, and with the pittance left to him, some ten thousand dollars, Kurt then bought a small cottage in the country on a little hill on a winding road just north of Nashville, in Brown County, about twenty-five miles south of Indianapolis. Brown County is still a bucolic community but it has some of the highest hills and loveliest scenery in the Midwest. It is the abode of preference of artists. Here Kurt retired alone and lived in perfect seclusion. He had his books and the phonograph which his sister gave him and upon which he played his favorite recordings of classical music: principally Mozart, Beethoven, Wagner, Brahms, and particularly Richard Strauss. The four last songs of Strauss were his favorites. He played them over and over. They express his mood perfectly."

✾

"ALTHOUGH he suffered from emphysema, Kurt continued to smoke cigarettes heavily and drank whiskey in moderation. His health deteriorated slowly until it was found that he had a cancer in one of the lobes of his lungs. The surgeons wanted to operate but he wisely declined. As the cancer spread, he became extremely weak and short of breath with lack of oxygen. But he refused to go into a hospital or to remain in bed at home. He would get up in the morning, dress, eat very sparingly, and then lie about on a couch before a comfortable fire reading or listening to his records, quite alone. He had no nurses, was completely self-reliant, and never complained or feared death. Toward the end a faithful devoted old servant—Nelly—came down to look after him. Just before the end he had a trained nurse in attendance as he became bedfast. He died quietly in his sleep on October 1, 1957—quite alone. Two days later his remains were buried in the Vonnegut lot in Crown Hill Cemetery next to his wife Edith and his parents, Bernard and Nanette."

✾

THERE ends my Uncle John's essay, save for a grandiloquent coda not entirely in keeping with the facts. I have left a lot out, but nothing which has a direct bearing on what I myself have become. It is copyrighted.

The owner of the copyright is Uncle John's grandson, my

second cousin once-removed, William Rauch. He works here in New York now for Mayor Edward Koch. See how we disperse and disperse?

❦

Was I a sad child, knowing how rich my family had been? Not at all. We were at least as well off as most of the people I went to public school with, and I would have lost all my friends if we had started having servants again, and worn expensive clothes again, and ridden on ocean liners and visited German relatives in a real castle, and on and on. Mother, who was half-cracked, used to speak of the time when I would resume my proper place in society when the Great Depression ended, would swim with members of other leading families at the Indianapolis Athletic Club, would play tennis and golf with them at the Woodstock Golf and Country Club. She could not understand that to give up my friends at Public School No. 43, "the James Whitcomb Riley school," by the way, would be for me to give up *everything*.

I still feel uneasy about prosperity and associating with members of my parents' class on that account.

Henry David Thoreau said, "I have traveled extensively in Concord." That quotation was probably first brought to my attention by one of my magnificent teachers in high school. Thoreau, I now feel, wrote in the voice of a child, as do I. And what he said about Concord is what every child feels, what every child seemingly *must* feel, about the place where he or she was born. There is surely more than enough to marvel at for a lifetime, no matter where the child is born.

Castles? Indianapolis was full of them.

❧

ONE of my brother Bernard's favorite stories is about the farmer who decides to go to have a look at St. Louis, the nearest city. This would be in 1900, say. When he comes back to his farm after a week, he is gaga about all the human activities and machinery he has seen.

When he is questioned about this famous landmark or that one in St. Louis, it turns out that he knows nothing about them. He makes this confession: "Actually, I never got past the depot."

❧

MY father had few gifts for getting along famously with me. That's life. We did not spend much time together, and conversations were arch and distant. But Father's younger brother, Uncle Alex, a Harvard graduate and life insurance salesman, was responsive and amusing and generous with me, was my ideal grown-up friend.

He was also then a socialist, and among the books he gave me, when I was a high school sophomore, was Thorstein Veblen's *Theory of the Leisure Class.* I understood it perfectly and loved it, since it made low comedy of the empty graces and aggressively useless possessions which my parents, and especially my mother, meant to regain someday.

❧

IT will be noted that my mother attempted to be what I have in fact become—which is a professional writer.

It used to be a fairly reliable rule of American middle-class life that a son could be expected to try hard, with his own life, to make some of his disappointed mother's dreams come true.

This may no longer be the case. Things change.

❦

UNCLE John's coda to the history of my family is this:

"In reviewing K's ancestors for four generations it is highly significant that there was not a weakling, nor even a mildly psychotic or neurotic individual in the lot. Taken together they provided K with a rich bank of genes upon which to draw. How this genetic background was influenced by K's adolescent conditioning is for him to say. But with respect to his ancestors who came to America from their homeland, let him observe the counsel of the poet Goethe:

'WAS DU ERERBET VON DEINEN VATERN HAST, ERWIRB ES; UM EST ZU BESITZEN.'

"WE WILL LET HIM TELL HIS OWN STORY."

The German quotation means this, and I take it seriously: "Whatever it is that you have inherited from your father, you are going to have to earn it if it is to *really* belong to you."

III

WHEN I
LOST MY
INNOCENCE

*a*ND my story seems to be this to me:

I left Indianapolis, where my ancestors had prepared so many comforts and privileges for me, because those comforts and privileges were finally based on money, and the money was gone.

I might have stayed if I had done what my father had done, which was to marry one of the richest women in town. But I married a poor one instead. I might have stayed if my father had not told me this: be anything but an architect. He and my older brother, who had become a chemist, urged me to study chemistry instead. I would have liked to be an architect, and an architect in Indianapolis at that. I would have become a third-generation Indianapolis architect. There can't be very many of those around.

But Father was so full of anger and sorrow about having had no work as an architect during the Great Depression that he persuaded me that I, too, would be that unhappy if I studied architecture.

❦

So I entered Cornell University in 1940 as a chemistry student. I had in high school been an editor of *The Shortridge Daily Echo,* one of two high school dailies in the country at the time, so I also qualified easily for the staff of *The Cornell Daily Sun.*

The children now running the *Sun* invited me to speak at their annual banquet in Ithaca, New York, on May 3, 1980. The *Sun,* by the way, a corporation entirely separate from the university, will be one hundred years old when this book is published—in 1981.

This doddering alumnus, who drinks no more, had this to say above the rattling of the ice cubes:

"Good evening, fellow Americans.

"You should have invited a more sentimental speaker, I think. This is surely a sentimental occasion, and I am sentimental about faithful dogs sometimes, but that is as far as it goes.

"The most distinguished living writer who was also a *Sun* man is, of course, Elwyn Brooks White of the class of 1921. He will be eighty-one on July eleventh of this year. You might want to send him a card. His mind is as clear as a bell, and he is not only sentimental about dogs but about Cornell.

"I myself liked only two things about this place: the *Sun* and the horse-drawn artillery. Yes—there was horse-drawn artillery here in my time. I suppose I should tell you how old I am, too. I will be fifty-eight in November of this year. You might want to send me a card, too. We never hooked up the horses to caissons, because we knew that was no way to frighten Hitler. So we just put saddles on the horses, and pretended we were at war with Indians, and rode around all afternoon.

"It was not Cornell's fault that I did not like this place much, in case some alumni secretary or chaplain is about to burst into tears. It was my father's fault. He said I should become a chemist like my brother, and not waste my time and his money on subjects he considered so much junk jewelry—literature, history, philosophy. I had no talent for science. What was infinitely worse: all my fraternity brothers were engineers.

"I probably would have adored this hellhole, if I had been allowed to study and discuss the finer things in life. Also: I would not have become a writer.

"I eventually wound up on academic probation. I was accelerating my course at the time—because of the war. My instructor in organic chemistry was my lab partner in biochemistry. He was fit to be tied.

"And one day I came down with pneumonia. It is such a dreamy disease. Pneumonia used to be called 'the old people's friend.' It can be a young person's friend, too. All that you feel is that you are sleepy and that it is time to go. I did not die, so far as I know—but I left Cornell, and I've never come back until now.

"Good evening, fellow Cornellians. I am here to congratulate *The Cornell Daily Sun* on its one-hundredth anniversary. To place this event in historical perspective: the *Sun* is now forty years younger than the saxophone, and sixty years older than the electric guitar.

"It was a family to me—one that included women. Once a week we allowed coeds to put together a woman's page, but I never got to know any of them. They always seemed so burned up about something. I never did find out what it was. It must have been something over at the sorority house.

"I pity you *Sun* people of today for not having truly great leaders to write about—Roosevelt and Churchill and Chiang Kai-shek and Stalin on the side of virtue, and Hitler and Mussolini and Emperor Hirohito on the side of sin.

"Oh, sure, we have another world war coming, and another great depression, but where are the leaders this time? All you have is a lot of ordinary people standing around with their thumbs up their ass.

"Here is what we must do, if glamour is to be restored to those who lead us into catastrophes, out of catastrophes, and then back into catastrophes again: We must outlaw television and set an example for our children by worshiping the silver screens in motion picture palaces every week.

"We should see moving and talking images of leaders only once a week in newsreels. This is the only way we can get leaders all balled up in our heads with movie stars again.

"When I was a freshman here, I didn't know or care where the life of Ginger Rogers ended and the life of General Douglas MacArthur began. The senior senator from California was Mickey Mouse, who would serve with great distinction as a bombardier in the Pacific during the Second World War. Commander Mouse dropped a bomb right down the smokestack of a Japanese battleship. The captain of the battleship was Charlie Chan. Boy, was he mad.

"What a shame that there are so many young people here

who never saw J. Edgar Hoover on the silver screen. This was a man fourteen feet high who could not be bribed. Imagine a man who loved this country so much that he could not be bribed, except for some minor carpentry on his house. You can't adore such integrity without the magic of the silver screen.

"Was the *Sun* any good when I was here? I don't know, and I am afraid to find out. I remember I spelled the first name of Ethel Barrymore 'E-T-H-Y-L' one time—in a headline.

"In preparation for this event, I had lunch last week with the best editor in chief I worked under here. That was Miller Harris, who is one year older than I am. I would sure hate to be as old as he is. I wouldn't mind being as old as E. B. White, if I could actually be E. B. White. Miller Harris is president of the Eagle Shirtmakers now. I ordered a shirt from him one time, and he sent me a bill for one one-hundred-forty-fourth of a gross.

"He said at lunch that the *Sun* in our day was without question the finest student paper in the United States of America. It would be nice if that were true. Eagle shirts, I know, are the greatest shirts in the world.

"I was shattered, I remember, during my sophomore year here, when a world traveler said that Cornell was the forty-ninth greatest university in the world. I had hoped we would at least be in the high teens somewhere. Little did I realize that going to an only marginally great university would also make me a writer.

"That is how you get to be a writer, incidentally: you feel somehow marginal, somehow slightly off-balance all the time. I spent an awful lot of time here buying gray flannel. I never could find the right shade.

"I finally gave up on gray flannel entirely, and went to the University of Chicago, the forty-eighth greatest university in the world.

"Do I know Thomas Pynchon? No. Did I know Vladimir Nabokov? No. I know and knew Miller Harris, the president of Eagle Shirtmakers.

"Well—I am more sentimental about this occasion than I have so far indicated. We chemists can be as sentimental as anybody. Our emotional lives, probably because of the A-bomb and the H-bomb, and the way we spell 'Ethel,' have been much maligned.

"I found a family here at the *Sun,* or I no doubt would have invited pneumonia into my thorax during my freshman year. Those of you who have been kind enough to read a book of mine, any book of mine, will know of my admiration for large families, whether real or artificial, as the primary supporters of mental health.

"And it is surely curious that I, as an outspoken enemy of the disease called loneliness, should now remember as my happiest times in Ithaca the hours when I was most alone.

"I was happiest here when I was all alone—and it was very late at night, and I was walking up the hill after having helped to put the *Sun* to bed.

"All the other university people, teachers and students alike, were asleep. They had been playing games all day long with what was known about real life. They had been repeating famous arguments and experiments, and asking one another the sorts of hard questions real life would be asking by and by.

"We on the *Sun* were already in the midst of real life. By God, if we weren't! We had just designed and written and caused to be manufactured yet another morning newspaper for a highly intelligent American community of respectable size—yes, and not during the Harding administration, either, but during 1940, '41, and '42, with the Great Depression ending, and with World War Two well begun.

"I am an agnostic as some of you may have gleaned from my writings. But I have to tell you that, as I trudged up the hill so late at night and all alone, I knew that God Almighty approved of me."

❧

I make my living as a writer in New York City, the capital of the world, and am, so far as I know, now the only person from Indianapolis who is a member of the American Academy and Institute of Arts and Letters. Until last year, there were two of us. The other one was Janet Flanner, who, writing under the name of "Genêt," was *The New Yorker*'s Paris correspondent for thirty years or more. I got to know her some in recent years, and once wrote in a book I gave her, "Indianapolis needs you!"

She read that, and she said to me, "How little you know."

She used to know my father, too, when she was a young woman—before she lit out for the sunrise and never went home again. Her family in Indianapolis was best known for the mortuaries some of its members ran.

Janet Flanner was the most deft and charming literary stylist Indianapolis has so far produced, and the one who came closest to being a planetary citizen, too. She was not a local writer. Neither was she, like another Hoosier writer, Ernie Pyle, a globe-trotting rube.

So when she died here in New York, I wanted to make sure that her native city knew about it. I telephoned the city desk

of *The Indianapolis Star,* a morning paper being put to bed.
Nobody in the city room had ever heard of her. Neither was
anybody much interested when I told of all she had done.

But then I found a way to excite them, to get them to run
a front page obituary, which was a rewrite of the obituary
that had appeared in that morning's *New York Times.*

What did the trick? I told them that she was somehow
related to the people who ran the funeral homes.

❦

I myself will get an obituary in an Indianapolis paper when
I die because I am related to people who used to own a chain
of hardware stores. The chain was wrecked by discount
stores after the Second World War. It had a manufacturing
division, which made door hardware, and that was bought
by a conglomerate. It beat the mortuary business, at any rate.

I used to work in the main store of the Vonnegut Hardware Company in the summertime, when I was high school
age. I ran a freight elevator. I made up packages in the
shipping room, and so on. I liked what we sold. It was all so
honest and practical.

And I discovered only the other day how sentimental I still
was about the hardware business—when I was asked by one
Gunilla Boëthius of *Aftonbladet,* a Swedish newspaper, to
write for one thousand crowns a short essay on this subject:
"When I Lost My Innocence."

On May 9, 1980, I wrote this letter:

Dear Gunilla Boëthius—

I thank you for your letter of April 25, received by me only
this morning.

An enthusiasm for technological cures for almost all forms of human discontent was the only religion of my family during the Great Depression, when I first got to know that family well. It was religion enough for me, and one branch of the family owned the largest hardware store in Indianapolis, Indiana. I still do not believe that I was wrong to adore the cunning devices and compounds on sale there, and when I feel most lost in this world, I comfort myself by visiting a hardware store. I meditate there. I do not buy anything. A hammer is still my Jesus, and my Virgin Mary is still a cross-cut saw.

But I learned how vile that religion of mine could be when the atomic bomb was dropped on Hiroshima. The date of that event can be found in almost any good reference book. How profound had my innocence been? Only six months before, as a captured American foot soldier, I had been in Dresden when it was burned to the ground by a purposely set firestorm. I was still innocent after that. Why? Because the technology which created that firestorm was so familiar to me. I understood it entirely, and so had no trouble imagining how the same amount of ingenuity and determination could benefit mankind once the war was over. I could even help. There was nothing in the bombs or the airplanes, after all, which could not, essentially, be bought at a small hardware store.

As for fire: Everybody knows what you do with unwanted fire. You put water on it.

But the bombing of Hiroshima compelled me to see that a trust in technology, like all the other great religions of the world, had to do with the human soul. I will bet you the one thousand crowns you have offered me for this piece that every one of the tales of lost innocence you receive will embody not only the startling discovery of the human soul, but of how diseased it can be.

How sick was the soul revealed by the flash at Hiroshima? And I deny that it was a specifically American soul. It was the soul of every highly industrialized nation on earth, whether at war or at peace. How sick was it? It was so sick that it did not want to live anymore. What other sort of soul would create a new physics based on nightmares, would place into the hands of mere politicians a planet so "destabilized," to borrow a CIA term, that the briefest fit of stupidity could easily guarantee the end of the world?

It is supposed to be good to lose one's innocence. I do not read them, but I think that is what my novels say, so it must be true. I, for one, now know what is *really* going on, so I can plan more shrewdly and be less open to surprise. But my morale has been lowered a good deal, so I am probably not any stronger than I used to be. Since Hiroshima, I have increased my amperes but decreased my volts, and wound up with the same number of watts, so to speak.

It is quite awful, really, to realize that perhaps most of the people around me find lives in the service of machines so tedious and exasperating that they would not mind much, even if they have children, if life were turned off like a light switch at any time. How many of your readers will deny that the movie *Dr. Strangelove* was so popular because its ending was such a happy one?

❦

I am invited to all sorts of neo-Luddite gatherings, of course, and am sometimes asked to speak. I had this to say between rock and roll numbers at an antinuke rally in Washington, D.C., on May 6, 1979:

"I am embarrassed. We are all embarrassed. We Americans have guided our destinies so clumsily, with all the world watching, that we must now protect ourselves against our own government and our own industries.

"Not to do so would be suicide. We have discovered a brand-new method for committing suicide—family style, Reverend Jim Jones style, and by the millions. What is the method? To say nothing and do nothing about what some of our businessmen and military men are doing with the most unstable substances and the most persistent poisons to be found anywhere in the universe.

"The people who play with such chemicals are so *dumb!*

"They are also vicious. How vicious it is of them to tell us as little as possible about the hideousness of nuclear weapons and power plants!

"And, among all the dumb and vicious people, who jeopardizes all life on earth with hearts so light? I suggest to you that it is those who will lie for the nuclear industries, or who will teach their executives how to lie convincingly —*for a fee.* I speak of certain lawyers and communicators, and *all* public relations experts. The so-called profession of public relations, an American invention, stands entirely disgraced today.

"The lies we have been fed about nuclear energy have been as cunningly handcrafted as the masterpieces of Benvenuto Cellini. They have been a damned sight better built, I must say, than the atomic energy plants themselves.

"I say to you that the makers of such lies are filthy little monkeys. I hate them. They may think they are cute. They are not cute. They stink. If we let them, they will kill everything on this lovely blue-green planet with their rebuttals to what we say here today—with their vicious, stupid lies."

10

TRIAGE

I was educated some in chemistry, and in biology and physics, too, at Cornell University. I did badly, and I soon forgot all they tried to teach me. The Army sent me to Carnegie Tech and the University of Tennessee to study mechanical engineering—thermodynamics, mechanics, the actual use of machine tools, and so on. I did badly again. I am very used to failure, to being at the bottom of every class.

An Indianapolis cousin of mine, who was also a high school classmate, did very badly at the University of Michigan while I did badly at Cornell. His father asked him what the trouble was, and he made what I consider an admirable reply: "Don't you know, Father? I'm dumb!" It was the truth.

I did badly in the Army, remaining a preposterously tall private for the three years I served. I was a good soldier, an especially deadly marksman, but nobody thought to promote me. I learned all the dances of close-order drill. Nobody in the Army could dance better than I could in ranks. If a third world war comes, I am still spry enough to dance again.

❧

YES, and I was a mediocrity in the anthropology department of the University of Chicago after the Second World War. Triage was practiced there as it is practiced everywhere. There were those students who would surely be anthropologists, and the most winsome faculty members gave them intensive care. A second group of students, in the opinion of the faculty, just might become so-so anthropologists, but more probably, would use what they had learned about *Homo sapiens* to good advantage in some other field, such as medicine or law, say.

The third group, of which I was a member, might as well have been dead—or studying chemistry. We were given as a thesis advisor the least popular faculty member, untenured and justifiably paranoid. His position paralleled that of the waiter Mespoulets in the stories of Ludwig Bemelmans about the fictitious Hotel Splendid. Mespoulets had the table next to the kitchen, and his specialty was making sure that certain sorts of guests at the hotel restaurant never came back again.

This terrible faculty advisor of mine was surely the most exciting and instructive teacher I have ever had. He gave courses whose lectures were chapters in books he was writing about the mechanics of social change, and which no one, as it turned out, would ever publish.

After I left the university, I would visit him whenever business brought me to Chicago. He never remembered me, and seemed annoyed by my visits—especially, I suppose, when I brought the wonderful news of my having been published here and there.

One night on Cape Cod, when I was drunk and reeking of mustard gas and roses, and calling up old friends and enemies, as used to be my custom, I called up my beloved old thesis advisor. I was told he was dead—at the age of about fifty, I think. He had swallowed cyanide. He had not published. He had perished instead.

And I wish I had an unpublished essay of his on the mechanics of social change to paste into this collage of mine now.

I do not give his name, because I do not think he would like to see it here.

Or anywhere.

❦

My mother, who was also a suicide and who never saw even the first of her eleven grandchildren, is another one, I gather, who would not like to see her name anywhere.

❦

Am I angry at having had triage practiced on me? I am glad it was practiced on me at a university rather than at a battalion aid station behind the front lines. I might have wound up as a preposterously tall private expiring in a snowbank outside the tent, while the doctors inside operated on those who had at least a fifty-fifty chance to survive. Why waste time and plasma on a goner?

And I myself have since practiced triage in university settings—in writing classes at the University of Iowa, at Harvard, at City College.

One third of every class was corpses as far as I was concerned. What's more, I was right.

That would certainly be a better name for this planet than Earth, since it would give people who just got here a clearer idea of what they were in for: Triage.

Welcome to Triage.

❧

WHAT good is a planet called Earth, after all, if you own no land?

❧

AND let us end on a sunnier note, with an essay I wrote in May of 1980 at the behest of the International Paper Company. That company, for obvious reasons, hopes that Americans will continue to read and write. And so it has asked various well-known persons to write leaflets for free distribution to anyone hankering to read and write some—about how to increase one's vocabulary, how to write an effective business letter, about how to do library research, and so on.

In view of the fact that I had nearly flunked chemistry, mechanical engineering, and anthropology, and had never taken a course in literature or composition, I was elected to write about literary style. I was more than glad to do this.

But I must bring up the joyless subject of triage again, for I intended my essay not for the bottom third of would-be writers, the warm corpses, nor for the top third—those who are or could be brilliant writers anyway.

My essay is for the middle third, and it goes like this:

Newspaper reporters and technical writers are trained to reveal almost nothing about themselves in their writings. This makes them freaks in the world of writers, since almost all of the other ink-stained wretches in that world reveal a lot about themselves to readers. We call these revelations, accidental and intentional, elements of literary style.

These revelations are fascinating to us as readers. They tell us what sort of person it is with whom we are spending time. Does the writer sound ignorant or informed, crazy or sane, stupid or bright, crooked or honest, humorless or playful—? And on and on.

When you yourself put words on paper, remember that the most damning revelation you can make about yourself is that you do not know what is interesting and what is not. Don't you yourself like or dislike writers mainly for what they choose to show you or make you think about? Did you ever admire an empty-headed writer for his or her mastery of the language? No.

So your own winning literary style must begin with interesting ideas in your head. Find a subject you care about and which you in your heart feel others should care about. It is this genuine caring, and not your games with language, which will be the most compelling and seductive element in your style.

I am not urging you to write a novel, by the way—although I would not be sorry if you wrote one, provided you genuinely cared about something. A petition to the mayor about a pothole in front of your house or a love letter to the girl next door will do.

Do not ramble, though.

As for your use of language: Remember that two great masters of our language, William Shakespeare and James Joyce, wrote sentences which were almost childlike when their subjects were most profound. "To be or not to be?" asks Shakespeare's Hamlet. The longest word is three letters long. Joyce, when he was frisky, could put together a sentence as intricate and glittering as a necklace for Cleopatra, but my favorite sentence in his short story "Eveline" is this one: "She was tired." At that point in the story, no other words could break the heart of a reader as those words do.

Simplicity of language is not only reputable, but perhaps even sacred. The Bible opens with a sentence well within the writing skills of a lively fourteen-year-old: "In the beginning God created the heavens and the earth."

It may be that you, too, are capable of making necklaces for Cleopatra, so to speak. But your eloquence should be the servant of the ideas in your head. Your rule might be this: If a sentence, no matter how excellent, does not illuminate my subject in some new and useful way, scratch it out. Here is the same rule paraphrased to apply to storytelling, to fiction: Never include a sentence which does not either remark on character or advance the action.

The writing style which is most natural for you is bound to echo speech you heard when a child. English was the novelist Joseph Conrad's third language, and much that seems piquant in his use of English was no doubt colored by his first language, which was Polish. And lucky indeed is the writer who has grown up in Ireland, for the English spoken there is so amusing and musical. I myself grew up in Indianapolis, Indiana, where common speech sounds like a band saw cutting galvanized tin, and employs a vocabulary as unornamental as a monkey wrench.

In some of the more remote hollows of Appalachia, children still grow up hearing songs and locutions of Elizabethan times. Yes, and many Americans grow up hearing a language other than English, or an English dialect a majority of Americans cannot understand.

All these varieties of speech are beautiful, just as the varieties of butterflies are beautiful. No matter what your first language, you should treasure it all your life. If it happens not to be standard English, and if it shows itself when you write standard English, the result is usually delightful, like a very pretty girl with one eye that is green and one that is blue.

I myself find that I trust my own writing most, and others seem to trust it most, too, when I sound most like a person from Indianapolis, which is what I am. What alternatives do I have? The one most vehemently recommended by teachers has no doubt been pressed on you, as well: that I write like cultivated Englishmen of a century or more ago.

I used to be exasperated by such teachers, but am no more. I understand now that all those antique essays and stories with which I was to compare my own work were not magnificent for their datedness or foreignness, but for saying precisely what their authors meant them to say. My teachers wished me to write accurately, always selecting the most effective words, and relating the words to one another unambiguously, rigidly, like parts of a machine. The teachers did not want to turn me into an Englishman after all. They hoped that I would become understandable—and therefore understood.

And there went my dream of doing with words what Pablo Picasso did with paint or what any number of jazz idols did with music. If I broke all the rules of punctuation, had words mean whatever I wanted them to mean, and strung them together higgledy-piggledy, I would simply not be understood. So you, too, had better avoid Picasso-style or jazz-style writing, if you have something worth saying and wish to be understood.

If it were only teachers who insisted that modern writers stay close to literary styles of the past, we might reasonably ignore them. But readers insist on the very same thing. They want our pages to look very much like pages they have seen before.

Why? It is because they themselves have a tough job to do, and they need all the help they can get from us. They have to identify thousands of little marks on paper, and make sense of them immediately. They have to *read,* an art so difficult that most people do not really master it even after having studied it all through grade school and high school —for twelve long years.

So this discussion, like all discussions of literary styles, must finally acknowledge that our stylistic options as writers are neither numerous nor glamorous, since our readers are bound to be such imperfect artists. Our audience requires us to be sympathetic and patient teachers, ever willing to simplify and clarify—whereas we would rather soar high above the crowd, singing like nightingales.

That is the bad news. The good news is that we Americans are governed under a unique Constitution, which allows us to write whatever we please without fear of punishment. So the most meaningful aspect of our styles, which is what we choose to write about, is unlimited.

Also: we are members of an egalitarian society, so there is no reason for us to write, in case we are not classically educated aristocrats, as though we were classically educated aristocrats.

For a discussion of literary style in a narrower sense, in a more technical sense, I commend to your attention *The Elements of Style* by William Strunk, Jr., and E. B. White (Macmillan, 1979). It contains such rules as this: "A participial phrase at the beginning of a sentence must refer to the grammatical subject," and so on. E. B. White is, of course, one of the most admirable literary stylists this country has so far produced.

You should realize, too, that no one would care how well or badly Mr. White expressed himself, if he did not have perfectly enchanting things to say.

SELF-INTERVIEW

t HIS self-interview from *The Paris Review* No. 69, 1977, appears here with the permission of The Viking Press, which gets out collections of *Paris Review* interviews and owns the copyrights to all of them.

Sentences spoken by writers, unless they have been written out first, rarely say what writers wish to say. Writers are unlucky speakers, by and large, which accounts for their being in a profession which encourages them to stay at their desks for years, if necessary, pondering what to say next and how best to say it. Interviewers propose to speed up this process by trepaning writers, so to speak, and fishing around in their brains for unused ideas which otherwise might never get out of there. Not a single idea has ever been discovered by means of this brutal method—and still the trepaning of authors goes on every day.

I now refuse all those who wish to take the top off my skull yet again. The only way to get anything out of a writer's brains is to leave him or her alone until he or she is damn well ready to write it down.

This interview is purely written. Not a word of it was spoken aloud. The prefatory material in italics was not written by me, however, but by *The Paris Review,* to wit:

The introduction to the first of the incorporated interviews (done in West Barnstable, Massachusetts, when Vonnegut was 44) reads: "He is a veteran and a family man, large-boned, loose-jointed, at ease. He camps in an armchair in a shaggy tweed jacket, Cambridge gray flannels, a blue Brooks Brothers shirt, slouched down, his hands stuffed into his pockets. He shells the interview with explosive coughs and sneezes, windages of an autumn cold and a lifetime of heavy cigarette smoking. His voice is a resonant baritone, Midwestern, wry in its inflections. From time to time he issues the open alert smile of a man who has seen and reserved within himself almost everything: depression, war, the possibility of violent death, the inanities of corporate public relations, six children, an irregular income, long-delayed recognition."

The last of the interviews which made up the composite was conducted during the summer of 1976, years after the first. The description of him at this time reads: ". . . he moves with the low-keyed amiability of an old family dog. In general, his appearance is tousled: the long curly hair, moustache and sympathetic smile suggest a man at once amused and saddened by the world around him. He has rented the Gerald

Murphy house for the summer. He works in the little bedroom at the end of a hall where Murphy, artist, bon vivant, and friend to the artistic great, died in 1964. From his desk Vonnegut can look out onto the front lawn through a small window; behind him is a large, white canopy bed. On the desk next to the typewriter is a copy of Andy Warhol's Interview, Clancy Sigal's Zone of the Interior, *and several discarded cigarette packs.*

"Vonnegut has chain-smoked Pall Malls since 1936 and during the course of the interview he smokes the better part of one pack. His voice is low and gravelly, and as he speaks, the incessant procedure of lighting the cigarettes and exhaling smoke is like punctuation in his conversation. Other distractions such as the jangle of the telephone, and the barking of a small, shaggy dog named 'Pumpkin,' do not detract from Vonnegut's good-natured disposition. Indeed, as Dan Wakefield once said of his fellow Shortridge High School alumnus: 'He laughed a lot and was kind to everyone.'"

❦

INTERVIEWER: You are a veteran of the Second World War?

VONNEGUT: Yes. I want a military funeral when I die—the bugler, the flag on the casket, the ceremonial firing squad, the hallowed ground.

INTERVIEWER: Why?

VONNEGUT: It will be a way of achieving what I've always wanted more than anything—something I could have had, if only I'd managed to get myself killed in the war.

INTERVIEWER: Which is—?

VONNEGUT: The unqualified approval of my community.

INTERVIEWER: You don't feel that you have that now?

VONNEGUT: My relatives say that they are glad I'm rich, but that they simply cannot read me.

INTERVIEWER: You were an infantry battalion scout in the war?

VONNEGUT: Yes, but I took my basic training on the 240-millimeter howitzer.

INTERVIEWER: A rather large weapon.

VONNEGUT: The largest mobile field piece in the Army at that time. This weapon came in six pieces, each piece dragged wallowingly by a Caterpillar tractor. Whenever we were told to fire it, we had to build it first. We practically had to invent it. We lowered one piece on top of another, using cranes and jacks. The shell itself was about nine-and-a-half inches in diameter and weighed three hundred pounds. We constructed a miniature railway which would allow us to deliver the shell from the ground to the breech, which was about eight feet above grade. The breech-block was like the door on the vault of a savings and loan association in Peru, Indiana, say.

INTERVIEWER: It must have been a thrill to fire such a weapon.

VONNEGUT: Not really. We would put the shell in there, and then we would throw in bags of very slow and patient explosives. They were damp dog biscuits, I think. We would close the breech, and then trip a hammer which hit a fulminate of mercury percussion cap, which spit fire at the damp dog biscuits. The main idea, I think, was to generate steam. After a while, we could hear these cooking sounds. It was a lot like cooking a turkey. In utter safety, I think, we could have opened the breechblock from time to time, and basted the shell. Eventually, though, the howitzer always got restless. And finally it would heave back on its recoil mechanism, and it would have to expectorate the shell. The shell would come floating out like the Goodyear blimp. If we had had a stepladder, we could have painted "Fuck Hitler" on the shell as it left the gun. Helicopters could have taken after it and shot it down.

INTERVIEWER: The ultimate terror weapon.

VONNEGUT: Of the Franco-Prussian War.

INTERVIEWER: But you were ultimately sent overseas not with this instrument but with the 106th Infantry Division?

VONNEGUT: "The Bag Lunch Division." They used to feed us a lot of bag lunches. Salami sandwiches. An orange.

INTERVIEWER: In combat?

VONNEGUT: When we were still in the States.

INTERVIEWER: While they trained you for the infantry?

VONNEGUT: I was never trained for the infantry. Battalion scouts were elite troops, see. There were only six in each battalion, and nobody was very sure about what they were supposed to do. So we would march over to the rec room every morning, and play Ping-Pong and fill out applications for Officer Candidate School.

INTERVIEWER: During your basic training, though, you must have been familiarized with weapons other than the howitzer.

VONNEGUT: If you study the 240-millimeter howitzer, you don't have time for other weapons. You don't even have time left over for a venereal disease film.

INTERVIEWER: What happened when you reached the front?

VONNEGUT: I imitated various war movies I'd seen.

INTERVIEWER: Did you shoot anybody in the war?

VONNEGUT: I thought about it. I did fix my bayonet once, fully expecting to charge.

INTERVIEWER: Did you charge?

VONNEGUT: No. If everybody else had charged, I would have charged, too. But we decided not to charge. We couldn't see anybody.

INTERVIEWER: This was during the Battle of the Bulge, wasn't it? It was the largest defeat of American arms in history.

VONNEGUT: Probably. My last mission as a scout was to find our own artillery. Usually, scouts go out and look for enemy stuff. Things got so bad that we were finally looking for our own stuff. If I'd found our own battalion commander, everybody would have thought that was pretty swell.

INTERVIEWER: Do you mind describing your capture by the Germans?

VONNEGUT: Gladly. We were in this gully about as deep as a World War I trench. There was snow all around. Somebody said we were probably in Luxembourg. We were out of food.

INTERVIEWER: Who was "we"?

VONNEGUT: Our batallion scouting unit. All six of us. And about fifty people we'd never met before. The Germans could see us, because they were talking to us through a loudspeaker. They told us our situation was hopeless, and so on. That was when we fixed bayonets. It was nice there for a few minutes.

INTERVIEWER: How so?

VONNEGUT: Being a porcupine with all those steel quills. I pitied anybody who had to come in after us.

INTERVIEWER: But they came in anyway?

VONNEGUT: No. They sent in eighty-eight-millimeter shells instead. The shells burst in the treetops right over us. Those were very loud bangs right over our heads. We were showered with splintered steel. Some people got hit. Then the Germans told us again to come out. We didn't yell "nuts" or anything like that. We said, "Okay," and "Take it easy," and so on. When the Germans finally showed themselves, we saw they were wearing white camouflage suits. We didn't have anything like that. We were olive drab. No matter what season it was, we were olive drab.

INTERVIEWER: What did the Germans say?

VONNEGUT: They said the war was all over for us, that we were lucky, that we could now be sure we would live through the war, which was more than they could be sure of. As a matter of fact, they were probably killed or captured by Patton's Third Army within the next few days. Wheels within wheels.

INTERVIEWER: Did you speak any German?

VONNEGUT: I had heard my parents speak it a lot. They hadn't taught me how to do it, since there had been such bitterness in America against all things German during the First World War. I tried a few words I knew on our captors, and they asked me if I was of German ancestry, and I said, "Yes." They wanted to know why I was making war against my brothers.

INTERVIEWER: And you said—?

VONNEGUT: I honestly found the question ignorant and comical. My parents had separated me so thoroughly from my Germanic past that my captors might as well have been Bolivians or Tibetans, for all they meant to me.

INTERVIEWER: After you were captured, you were shipped to Dresden?

VONNEGUT: In the same boxcars that had brought up the troops that captured us—probably in the same boxcars that had delivered Jews and Gypsies and Jehovah's Witnesses and so on to the extermination camps. Rolling stock is rolling stock. British mosquito bombers attacked us at night a few times. I guess they thought we were strategic materials of some kind. They hit a car containing most of the officers from our battalion. Every time I say I hate officers, which I still do fairly frequently, I have to remind myself that practically none of the officers I served under survived. Christmas was in there somewhere.

INTERVIEWER: And you finally arrived in Dresden.

VONNEGUT: In a huge prison camp south of Dresden first. The privates were separated from the noncoms and officers. Under the articles of the Geneva Convention, which is a very Edwardian document, privates were required to work for their keep. Everybody else got to languish in prison. As a private, I was shipped to Dresden.

INTERVIEWER: What were your impressions of the city itself before the bombing?

VONNEGUT: The first fancy city I'd ever seen. A city full of statues and zoos, like Paris. We were living in a slaughter-house, in a nice new cement-block hog barn. They put bunks and straw mattresses in the barn, and we went to work every morning as contract labor in a malt syrup factory. The syrup was for pregnant women. The damned sirens would go off and we'd hear some other city getting it—*whump a whump a whumpa whump.* We never expected to get it. There were very few air raid shelters in town and no war industries, just cigarette factories, hospitals, clarinet factories. Then a siren went off—it was February 13, 1945—and we went down two stories under the pavement into a big meat locker. It was cool there, with cadavers hanging all around. When we came up the city was gone.

INTERVIEWER: You didn't suffocate in the meat locker?

VONNEGUT: No. It was quite large, and there weren't very many of us. The attack didn't sound like a hell of a lot either. *Whump.* They went over with high explosives first to loosen things up, and then scattered incendiaries. When the war started, incendiaries were fairly sizeable, about as long as a shoebox. By the time Dresden got it, they were tiny little things. They burnt the whole damn town down.

INTERVIEWER: What happened when you came up?

VONNEGUT: Our guards were noncoms—a sergeant, a corporal, and four privates—and leaderless. Cityless, too, because they were Dresdeners who'd been shot up on the front and sent home for easy duty. They kept us at attention for a couple of hours. They didn't know what else to do. They'd go over and talk to each other. Finally we trekked across the rubble and they quartered us with some South Africans in a suburb. Every day we walked into the city and dug into basements and shelters to get the corpses out, as a sanitary measure. When we went into them, a typical shelter, an ordinary basement usually, looked like a streetcar full of people who'd simultaneously had heart failure. Just people sitting there in their chairs, all dead. A fire storm is an amazing thing. It doesn't occur in nature. It's fed by the tornadoes that occur in the midst of it and there isn't a damned thing to breathe. We brought the dead out. They were loaded on wagons and taken to parks, large open areas in the city which weren't filled with rubble. The Germans got funeral pyres going, burning the bodies to keep them from stinking and from spreading disease. 130,000 corpses were hidden underground. It was a terribly elaborate Easter egg hunt. We went to work through cordons of German soldiers. Civilians didn't get to see what we were up to. After a few days the city began to smell, and a new technique was invented. Necessity is the mother of invention. We would bust into the shelter, gather up valuables from people's laps without attempting identification, and turn the valuables over to guards. Then soldiers would come with a flame thrower and stand in the door and cremate the people inside. Get the gold and jewelry out and then burn everybody inside.

INTERVIEWER: What an impression on someone thinking of becoming a writer!

VONNEGUT: It was a fancy thing to see, a startling thing. It was a moment of truth, too, because American civilians and ground troops didn't know American bombers were engaged in saturation bombing. It was kept a secret until very close to the end of the war. One reason they burned down Dresden is that they'd already burned down everything else. You know: "What're we going to do tonight?" Here was everybody all set to go, and Germany still fighting, and this machinery for burning down cities was being used. It was a secret, burning down cities—boiling pisspots and flaming prams. There was all this hokum about the Norden bombsight. You'd see a newsreel showing a bombardier with an MP on either side of him holding a drawn .45. That sort of nonsense, and hell, all they were doing was just flying over cities, hundreds of airplanes, and dropping everything. When I went to the University of Chicago after the war the guy who interviewed me for admission had bombed Dresden. He got to that part of my life story and he said, "Well, we hated to do it." The comment sticks in my mind.

INTERVIEWER: Another reaction would be, "We were ordered to do it."

VONNEGUT: His was more humane. I think he felt the bombing was necessary, and it may have been. One thing everybody learned is how fast you can rebuild a city. The engineers said it would take 500 years to rebuild Germany. Actually it took about 18 weeks.

INTERVIEWER: Did you intend to write about it as soon as you went through the experience?

VONNEGUT: When the city was demolished I had no idea of the scale of the thing. . . . Whether this was what Bremen looked like or Hamburg, Coventry . . . I'd never seen Coventry, so I had no scale except for what I'd seen in movies. When I got home (I was a writer since I had been on the *Cornell Sun* except that was the extent of my writing) I thought of writing my war story, too. All my friends were home; they'd had wonderful adventures, too. I went down to the newspaper office, *The Indianapolis News,* and looked to find out what they had about Dresden. There was an item about half an inch long, which said our planes had been over Dresden and two had been lost. And so I figured, well, this really was the most minor sort of detail in World War II. Others had so much more to write about. I remember envying Andy Rooney who jumped into print at that time; I didn't know him, but I think he was the first guy to publish his war story after the war; it was called *Tail Gunner.* Hell, I never had any classy adventure like that. But every so often I would meet a European and we would be talking about the war and I would say I was in Dresden; he'd be astonished that I'd been there, and he'd always want to know more. Then a book by David Irving was published about Dresden, saying it was the largest massacre in European history. I said, By God, I saw something after all! I would try to write my war story, whether it was interesting or not, and try to make something out of it. I describe that process a little in the beginning of *Slaughterhouse-Five;* I saw it as starring John Wayne and Frank Sinatra. Finally, a girl called Mary O'Hare, the wife of a friend of mine who'd been there with me, said, "You were just children then. It's not fair to pretend that you were men like Wayne and Sinatra and it's not fair to future generations because you're going to make war look good." That was a very important clue to me.

INTERVIEWER: That sort of shifted the whole focus. . .

VONNEGUT: She freed me to write about what infants we really were: 17, 18, 19, 20, 21. We were baby-faced, and as a prisoner of war I don't think I had to shave very often. I don't recall that that was a problem.

INTERVIEWER: One more question; do you still think about the fire-bombing of Dresden at all?

VONNEGUT: I wrote a book about it, called *Slaughterhouse-Five.* The book is still in print, and I have to do something about it as a businessman now and then. Marcel Ophuls asked me to be in his film, *A Memory of Justice.* He wanted me to talk about Dresden as an atrocity. I told him to talk to my friend Bernard V. O'Hare, Mary's husband, instead, which he did. O'Hare was a fellow battalion scout, and then a fellow prisoner of war. He's a lawyer in Pennsylvania now.

INTERVIEWER: Why didn't you wish to testify?

VONNEGUT: I had a German name. I didn't want to argue with people who thought Dresden should have been bombed to hell. All I ever said in my book was that Dresden, willy-nilly, *was* bombed to hell.

INTERVIEWER: It was the largest massacre in European history?

VONNEGUT: It was the fastest killing of large numbers of people—one hundred and thirty-five thousand people in a matter of hours. There were slower schemes for killing, of course.

INTERVIEWER: The death camps.

VONNEGUT: Yes—in which millions were eventually killed. Many people see the Dresden massacre as correct and quite minimal revenge for what had been done by the camps. Maybe so. As I say, I never argue that point. I do note in passing that the death penalty was applied to absolutely anybody who happened to be in the undefended city —babies, old people, the zoo animals, and thousands upon thousands of rabid Nazis, of course, and, among others, my best friend Bernard V. O'Hare and me. By all rights, O'Hare and I should have been part of the body count. The more bodies, the more correct the revenge.

INTERVIEWER: The Franklin Library is bringing out a deluxe edition of *Slaughterhouse-Five,* I believe.

VONNEGUT: Yes. I was required to write a new introduction for it.

INTERVIEWER: Did you have any new thoughts?

VONNEGUT: I said that only one person on the entire planet benefited from the raid, which must have cost tens of millions of dollars. The raid didn't shorten the war by half a second, didn't weaken a German defense or attack anywhere, didn't free a single person from a death camp. Only one person benefited—not two or five or ten. Just one.

INTERVIEWER: And who was that?

VONNEGUT: Me. I got three dollars for each person killed. Imagine that.

INTERVIEWER: How much affinity do you feel toward your contemporaries?

VONNEGUT: My brother and sister writers? Friendly, certainly. It's hard for me to talk to some of them, since we seem to be in very different sorts of businesses. This was a mystery to me for a while, but then Saul Steinberg—

INTERVIEWER: The graphic artist?

VONNEGUT: Indeed. He said that in almost all arts there were some people who responded strongly to art history, to triumphs and fiascoes and experiments of the past, and others who did not. I fell into the second group, and had to. I couldn't play games with my literary ancestors, since I had never studied them systematically. My education was as a chemist at Cornell and then an anthropologist at the University of Chicago. Christ—I was thirty-five before I went crazy about Blake, forty before I read *Madame Bovary,* forty-five before I'd even heard of Céline. Through dumb luck, I read *Look Homeward, Angel* exactly when I was supposed to.

INTERVIEWER: When?

VONNEGUT: At the age of eighteen.

INTERVIEWER: So you've always been a reader?

VONNEGUT: Yes. I grew up in a house crammed with books. But I never had to read a book for academic credit, never had to write a paper about it, never had to prove I'd understood it in a seminar. I am a hopelessly clumsy discusser of books. My experience is nil.

INTERVIEWER: Which member of your family had the most influence on you as a writer?

VONNEGUT: My mother, I guess. Edith Lieber Vonnegut. After our family lost almost all of its money in the Great Depression, my mother thought she might make a new fortune by writing for the slick magazines. She took short

95

story courses at night. She studied magazines the way gamblers study racing forms.

INTERVIEWER: She'd been rich at one time?

VONNEGUT: My father, an architect of modest means, married one of the richest girls in town. It was a brewing fortune based on Lieber Lager Beer and then Gold Medal Beer. Lieber Lager became Gold Medal after winning a prize at some Paris exposition.

INTERVIEWER: It must have been a very good beer.

VONNEGUT: Long before my time. I never tasted any. It had a secret ingredient, I know. My grandfather and his brewmaster wouldn't let anybody watch while they put it in.

INTERVIEWER: Do you know what it was?

VONNEGUT: Coffee.

INTERVIEWER: So your mother studied short story writing?

VONNEGUT: And my father painted pictures in a studio he'd set up on the top floor of the house. There wasn't much work for architects during the Great Depression—not much work for anybody. Strangely enough, though, Mother was right: Even mediocre magazine writers were making money hand over fist.

INTERVIEWER: So your mother took a very practical attitude toward writing.

VONNEGUT: Not to say crass. She was a highly intelligent, cultivated woman, by the way. She went to the same high school I did, and was one of the few people who got nothing but A-plusses while she was there. She went east to a finishing school after that, and then traveled all over Europe. She was fluent in German and French. I still have her high school report cards somewhere. "A-plus, A-plus, A-plus . . ." She was a good writer, it turned out, but she had no talent for the vulgarity the slick magazines required. Fortunately, I was loaded with vulgarity, so, when I grew up, I was able to make her dream come true. Writing for *Collier's* and *The Saturday Evening Post* and *Cosmopolitan* and *Ladies' Home Journal* and so on was as easy as falling off a log for me. I only wish she'd lived to see it. I only wish she'd lived to see all her grandchildren. She has ten. She didn't even get to see the first one. I made another one of her dreams come true: I lived on Cape Cod for many years. She always wanted to live on Cape Cod. It's probably very common for sons to try to make their mothers' impossible dreams come true. I adopted my sister's sons after she died, and it's spooky to watch them try to make her impossible dreams come true.

INTERVIEWER: What were your sister's dreams like?

VONNEGUT: She wanted to live like a member of *The Swiss Family Robinson,* with impossibly friendly animals in impossibly congenial isolation. Her oldest son, Jim, has been a goat farmer on a mountain top in Jamaica for the past eight years. No telephone. No electricity.

INTERVIEWER: The Indianapolis high school you and your mother attended—

VONNEGUT: And my father. Shortridge High.

INTERVIEWER: It had a daily paper, I believe.

VONNEGUT: Yes. *The Shortridge Daily Echo.* There was a print shop right in the school. Students wrote the paper. Students set the type. After school.

INTERVIEWER: You just laughed about something.

VONNEGUT: It was something dumb I remembered about high school. It doesn't have anything to do with writing.

INTERVIEWER: You care to share it with us anyway?

VONNEGUT: Oh—I just remembered something that happened in a high school course on civics, on how our government worked. The teacher asked each of us to stand up in turn and tell what we did after school. I was sitting in the back of the room, sitting next to a guy named J. T. Alburger. He later became an insurance man in Los Angeles. He died fairly recently. Anyway—he kept nudging me, urging me, daring me to tell the truth about what I did after school. He offered me five dollars to tell the truth. He wanted me to stand up and say, "I make model airplanes and jerk off."

INTERVIEWER: I see.

VONNEGUT: I also worked on *The Shortridge Daily Echo*.

INTERVIEWER: Was that fun?

VONNEGUT: Fun and easy. I've always found it easy to write. Also, I learned to write for peers rather than for teachers. Most beginning writers don't get to write for peers—to catch hell from peers.

INTERVIEWER: So every afternoon you would go to the *Echo* office—

VONNEGUT: Yeah. And one time, while I was writing, I happened to sniff my armpits absent-mindedly. Several people saw me do it, and thought it was funny—and ever after that I was given the name "Snarf." In the Annual for my graduating class, the Class of 1940, I'm listed as "Kurt Snarfield Vonnegut, Jr." Technically, I wasn't really a snarf. A snarf was a person who went around sniffing girls' bicycle saddles. I didn't do that. "Twerp" also had a very specific meaning, which few people know now. Through careless usage, "twerp" is a pretty formless insult now.

INTERVIEWER: What is a twerp in the strictest sense, in the original sense?

VONNEGUT: It's a person who inserts a set of false teeth between the cheeks of his ass.

INTERVIEWER: I see.

VONNEGUT: I beg your pardon; between the cheeks of his or *her* ass. I'm always offending feminists that way.

INTERVIEWER: I don't quite understand why someone would do that with false teeth.

VONNEGUT: In order to bite the buttons off the back seats of taxicabs. That's the only reason twerps do it. It's all that turns them on.

INTERVIEWER: You went to Cornell University after Shortridge?

VONNEGUT: I imagine.

INTERVIEWER: You imagine?

VONNEGUT: I had a friend who was a heavy drinker. If somebody asked him if he'd been drunk the night before, he would always answer off-handedly, "Oh, I imagine." I've always liked that answer. It acknowledges life as a dream. Cornell was a boozy dream, partly because of booze itself, and partly because I was enrolled exclusively in courses I had no talent for. My father and brother agreed that I should study chemistry, since my brother had done so well with chemicals at M.I.T. He's eight years older than I am. Funnier, too. His most famous discovery is that silver iodide will sometimes make it rain or snow.

INTERVIEWER: Was your sister funny, too?

VONNEGUT: Oh, yes. There was an odd cruel streak to her sense of humor, though, which didn't fit in with the rest of her character somehow. She thought it was terribly funny whenever anybody fell down. One time she saw a woman come out of a streetcar horizontally, and she laughed for weeks after that.

INTERVIEWER: Horizontally?

VONNEGUT: Yes. This woman must have caught her heels

somehow. Anyway, the streetcar door opened, and my sister happened to be watching from the sidewalk, and then she saw this woman come out horizontally—as straight as a board, facedown, and about two feet off the ground.

INTERVIEWER: Slapstick?

VONNEGUT: Sure. We loved Laurel and Hardy. You know what one of the funniest things is that can happen in a film?

INTERVIEWER: No.

VONNEGUT: To have somebody walk through what looks like a shallow little puddle, but which is actually six feet deep. I remember a movie where Cary Grant was loping across lawns at night. He came to a low hedge, which he cleared ever so gracefully, only there was a twenty-foot drop on the other side. But the thing my sister and I loved best was when somebody in a movie would tell everybody off, and then make a grand exit into the coat closet. He had to come out again, of course, all tangled in coathangers and scarves.

INTERVIEWER: Did you take a degree in chemistry at Cornell?

VONNEGUT: I was flunking everything by the middle of my junior year. I was delighted to join the Army and go to war. After the war, I went to the University of Chicago, where I was pleased to study anthropology, a science that was mostly poetry, that involved almost no math at all. I was married by then, and soon had one kid, who was Mark. He would later go crazy, of course, and write a fine book about it—*The Eden Express.* He has just fathered a kid himself, my first grandchild, a boy named Zachary.

Mark is finishing his second year in Harvard Medical School, and will be about the only member of his class not to be in debt when he graduates—because of the book. That's a pretty decent recovery from a crackup, I'd say.

INTERVIEWER: Did the study of anthropology later color your writings?

VONNEGUT: It confirmed my atheism, which was the faith of my fathers anyway. Religions were exhibited and studied as the Rube Goldberg inventions I'd always thought they were. We weren't allowed to find one culture superior to any other. We caught hell if we mentioned races much. It was highly idealistic.

INTERVIEWER: Almost a religion?

VONNEGUT: Exactly. And the only one for me. So far.

INTERVIEWER: What was your dissertation?

VONNEGUT: *Cat's Cradle.*

INTERVIEWER: But you wrote that years after you left Chicago, didn't you?

VONNEGUT: I left Chicago without writing a dissertation— and without a degree. All my ideas for dissertations had been rejected, and I was broke, so I took a job as a P.R. man for General Electric in Schenectady. Twenty years later, I got a letter from a new dean at Chicago, who had been looking through my dossier. Under the rules of the university, he said, a published work of high quality could be substituted for a dissertation, so I was entitled to an M.A. He had shown *Cat's Cradle* to the Anthropology Department, and they had said it was halfway decent anthropology, so they were mailing me my degree. I'm Class of 1972 or so.

INTERVIEWER: Congratulations.

VONNEGUT: It was nothing, really. A piece of cake.

INTERVIEWER: Some of the characters in *Cat's Cradle* were based on people you knew at G.E., isn't that so?

VONNEGUT: Dr. Felix Hoenikker, the absent-minded scientist, was a caricature of Dr. Irving Langmuir, the star of the G.E. Research Laboratory. I knew him some. My brother worked with him. Langmuir was wonderfully absent-minded. He wondered out loud one time whether, when turtles pulled in their heads, their spines buckled or contracted. I put that in the book. One time he left a tip under his plate after his wife served him breakfast at home. I put that in. His most important contribution, though, was the idea for what I called "Ice-9," a form of frozen water that was stable at room temperature. He didn't tell it directly to me. It was a legend around the Laboratory—about the time H. G. Wells came to Schenectady. That was long before my time. I was just a little boy when it happened—listening to the radio, building model airplanes.

INTERVIEWER: Yes?

VONNEGUT: Anyway—Wells came to Schenectady, and Langmuir was told to be his host. Langmuir thought he might entertain Wells with an idea for a science-fiction story—about a form of ice that was stable at room temperature. Wells was uninterested, or at least never used the idea. And then Wells died, and then, finally, Langmuir died. I thought to myself: "Finders, keepers—the idea is mine." Langmuir, incidentally, was the first scientist in private industry to win a Nobel Prize.

INTERVIEWER: How do you feel about Bellow's winning the Nobel Prize for Literature?

VONNEGUT: It was the best possible way to honor our entire literature.

INTERVIEWER: Do you find it easy to talk to him?

VONNEGUT: Yes. I've had about three opportunities. I was his host one time at the University of Iowa, where I was teaching and he was lecturing. It went very well. We had one thing in common, anyway—

INTERVIEWER: Which was—?

VONNEGUT: We were both products of the Anthropology Department of the University of Chicago. So far as I know, he never went on any anthropological expeditions, and neither did I. We invented pre-industrial peoples instead—I in *Cat's Cradle* and he in *Henderson the Rain King.*

INTERVIEWER: So he is a fellow scientist.

VONNEGUT: I'm no scientist at all. I'm glad now, though, that I was pressured into becoming a scientist by my father and my brother. I understand how scientific reasoning and playfulness work, even though I have no talent for joining in. I enjoy the company of scientists, am easily excited and entertained when they tell me what they're doing. I've spent a lot more time with scientists than with literary people, my brother's friends, mostly. I enjoy plumbers and carpenters and automobile mechanics, too. I didn't get to know any literary people until the last ten years, starting with two years of teaching at Iowa. There at Iowa, I was suddenly friends with Nelson Algren and José Donoso and Vance Bourjaily and Donald Justice and George Starbuck and Marvin Bell, and so on. I was amazed. Now, judging from the review my latest book, *Slapstick,* has received, people would like to bounce me out of the literary establishment—send me back where I came from.

INTERVIEWER: There were some bad reviews?

VONNEGUT: Only in *The New York Times, Time, Newsweek,*

The New York Review of Books, The Village Voice, and *Rolling Stone.* They loved me in Medicine Hat.

INTERVIEWER: To what do you attribute this rancor?

VONNEGUT: *Slapstick* may be a very bad book. I am perfectly willing to believe that. Everybody else writes lousy books, so why shouldn't I? What was unusual about the reviews was that they wanted people to admit now that I had never been any good. The reviewer for the Sunday *Times* actually asked critics who had praised me in the past to now admit in public how wrong they'd been. My publisher, Sam Lawrence, tried to comfort me by saying that authors were invariably attacked when they became fabulously well-to-do.

INTERVIEWER: You needed comforting?

VONNEGUT: I never felt worse in my life. I felt as though I were sleeping standing up on a boxcar in Germany again.

INTERVIEWER: That bad?

VONNEGUT: No. But bad enough. All of a sudden, critics wanted me squashed like a bug. And it wasn't just that I had money all of a sudden, either. The hidden complaint was that I was barbarous, that I wrote without having made a systematic study of great literature, that I was no gentleman, since I had done hack writing so cheerfully for vulgar magazines—that I had not paid my academic dues.

INTERVIEWER: You had not suffered?

VONNEGUT: I had suffered, all right—but as a badly-educated person in vulgar company and in a vulgar trade. It was dishonorable enough that I perverted art for money. I then topped that felony by becoming, as I say, fabulously well-to-do. Well, that's just too damn bad for me and for everybody. I'm completely in print, so we're all stuck with me and stuck with my books.

INTERVIEWER: Do you mean to fight back?

VONNEGUT: In a way. I'm on the New York State Council for the Arts now, and every so often some other member talks about sending notices to college English departments about some literary opportunity, and I say, "Send them to the chemistry departments, send them to the zoology departments, send them to the anthropology departments and the astronomy departments and physics departments, and all the medical and law schools. That's where the writers are most likely to be."

INTERVIEWER: You believe that?

VONNEGUT: I think it can be tremendously refreshing if a creator of literature has something on his mind other than the history of literature so far. Literature should not disappear up its own asshole, so to speak.

INTERVIEWER: Let's talk about the women in your books.

VONNEGUT: There aren't any. No real women, no love.

INTERVIEWER: Is this worth expounding upon?

VONNEGUT: It's a mechanical problem. So much of what happens in storytelling is mechanical, has to do with the technical problems of how to make a story work. Cowboy stories and policeman stories end in shoot-outs, for example, because shoot-outs are the most reliable mechanisms for making such stories end. There is nothing like death to say what is always such an artificial thing to say: "The end." I try to keep deep love out of my stories because, once that particular subject comes up, it is almost impossible to talk about anything else. Readers don't want to hear about anything else. They go gaga about love. If a lover in a story wins his true love, that's the end of the tale, even if World War III is about to begin, and the sky is black with flying saucers.

INTERVIEWER: So you keep love out.

VONNEGUT: I have other things I want to talk about. Ralph Ellison did the same thing in *Invisible Man*. If the hero in that magnificent book had found somebody worth loving, somebody who was crazy about him, that would have been the end of the story. Céline did the same thing in *Journey to the End of the Night:* He excluded the possibility of true and final love—so that the story could go on and on and on.

INTERVIEWER: Not many writers talk about the mechanics of stories.

VONNEGUT: I am such a barbarous technocrat that I believe they can be tinkered with like Model T Fords.

INTERVIEWER: To what end?

VONNEGUT: To give the reader pleasure.

INTERVIEWER: Will you ever write a love story, do you think?

VONNEGUT: Maybe. I lead a loving life. I really do. Even when I'm leading that loving life, though, and it's going so well, I sometimes find myself thinking, "My goodness, couldn't we talk about something else for just a little while?" You know what's really funny?

INTERVIEWER: No.

VONNEGUT: My books are being thrown out of school libraries all over the country—because they're supposedly obscene. I've seen letters to small town newspapers that put *Slaughterhouse-Five* in the same class with *Deep Throat* and *Hustler* magazine. How could anybody masturbate to *Slaughterhouse-Five*?

INTERVIEWER: It takes all kinds.

VONNEGUT: Well, that kind doesn't exist. It's my religion the censors hate. They find me disrespectful toward their idea of God Almighty. They think it's the proper business of government to protect the reputation of God. All I can say is, "Good luck to them, and good luck to the government, and good luck to God." You know what H.L. Mencken said one time about religious people? He said he'd been greatly misunderstood. He said he didn't hate them. He simply found them comical.

INTERVIEWER: When I asked you a while back which member of your family had influenced you most as a writer, you said your mother. I had expected you to say your sister, since you talked so much about her in *Slapstick*.

VONNEGUT: I said in *Slapstick* that she was the person I wrote for—that every successful creative person creates with an audience of one in mind. That's the secret of artistic unity. Anybody can achieve it, if he or she will make something with only one person in mind. I didn't realize that she was the person I wrote for until after she died.

INTERVIEWER: She loved literature?

VONNEGUT: She wrote wonderfully well. She didn't read much—but, then again, neither in later years did Henry David Thoreau. My father was the same way: he didn't read much, but he could write like a dream. Such letters my father and sister wrote! When I compare their prose with mine, I am ashamed.

INTERVIEWER: Did your sister try to write for money, too?

VONNEGUT: No. She could have been a remarkable sculptor, too. I bawled her out one time for not doing more with the talents she had. She replied that having talent doesn't carry with it the obligation that something has to be done with it. This was startling news to me. I thought people were supposed to grab their talents and run as far and fast as they could.

INTERVIEWER: What do you think now?

VONNEGUT: Well—what my sister said now seems a peculiarly feminine sort of wisdom. I have two daughters who are as talented as she was, and both of them are damned if they are going to lose their poise and senses of humor by snatching up their talents and desperately running as far and as fast as they can. They saw me run as far and as fast as I could—and it must have looked like quite a crazy performance to them. And this is the worst possible metaphor, for what they actually saw was a man sitting still for decades.

INTERVIEWER: At a typewriter.

VONNEGUT: Yes, and smoking his fool head off.

INTERVIEWER: Have you ever stopped smoking?

VONNEGUT: Twice. Once I did it cold turkey, and turned into Santa Claus. I became roly-poly. I was approaching 250 pounds. I stopped for almost a year, and then the University of Hawaii brought me to Oahu to speak. I was drinking out of a coconut on the roof of the Ili Kai one night, and all I had to do to complete the ring of my happiness was to smoke a cigarette. Which I did.

INTERVIEWER: The second time?

VONNEGUT: Very recently—last year. I paid SmokEnders 150 dollars to help me quit, over a period of six weeks. It was exactly as they had promised—easy and instructive. I won my graduation certificate and recognition pin. The only trouble was that I had also gone insane. I was supremely happy and proud, but those around me found me unbearably opinionated and abrupt and boisterous. Also: I had stopped writing. I didn't even write letters anymore. I had made a bad trade, evidently. So I started smoking again. As the National Association of Manufacturers used to say—

INTERVIEWER: I'm not sure I know what they used to say.

VONNEGUT: "There's no such thing as a free lunch."

INTERVIEWER: Do you really think creative writing can be taught?

VONNEGUT: About the same way golf can be taught. A pro can point out obvious flaws in your swing. I did that well, I think, at the University of Iowa for two years. . . . I taught creative writing badly at Harvard—because my marriage was breaking up, and because I was commuting every week to Cambridge from New York. I taught even worse at City College a couple of years ago. I had too many other projects going on at the same time. I don't have the will to teach anymore. I only know the theory.

INTERVIEWER: Could you put the theory into a few words?

VONNEGUT: It was stated by Paul Engle—the founder of the Writers' Workshop at Iowa. He told me that, if the Workshop ever got a building of its own, these words should be inscribed over the entrance: "Don't take it all so seriously."

INTERVIEWER: And how would that be helpful?

VONNEGUT: It would remind the students that they were learning to play practical jokes.

INTERVIEWER: Practical jokes?

VONNEGUT: If you make people laugh or cry about little black marks on sheets of white paper, what is that but a practical joke? All the great story lines are great practical jokes that people fall for over and over again.

INTERVIEWER: Can you give an example?

VONNEGUT: The Gothic novel. Dozens of the things are published every year, and they all sell. My friend Borden Deal recently wrote a Gothic novel for the fun of it, and I asked him what the plot was, and he said, "A young woman takes a job in an old house and gets the pants scared off her."

INTERVIEWER: Some more examples?

VONNEGUT: The others aren't that much fun to describe: Somebody gets into trouble, and then gets out again; somebody loses something and gets it back; somebody is wronged and gets revenge; Cinderella; somebody hits the skids and just goes down, down, down; people fall in love with each other, and a lot of other people get in the way; a virtuous person is falsely accused of sin; a sinful person is believed to be virtuous; a person faces a challenge bravely, and succeeds or fails; a person lies, a person steals, a person kills, a person commits fornication.

INTERVIEWER: If you will pardon my saying so, these are very old-fashioned plots.

VONNEGUT: I guarantee you that no modern story scheme, even plotlessness, will give a reader genuine satisfaction, unless one of those old fashioned plots is smuggled in somewhere. I don't praise plots as accurate representations of life, but as ways to keep readers reading. When I used to teach creative writing, I would tell the students to make their characters want something right away—even if it's only a glass of water. Characters paralyzed by the meaningless of modern life still have to drink water from time to time. One of my students wrote a story about a nun who got a piece of dental floss stuck between her lower left molars, and who couldn't get it out all day long. I thought that was wonderful. The story dealt with issues a lot more important than dental floss, but what kept readers going was anxiety about when the dental floss would finally be removed. Nobody could read that story without fishing around in his mouth with a finger. Now, there's an admirable practical joke for you. When you exclude plot, when you exclude anyone's wanting anything, you exclude the reader, which is a mean-spirited thing to do. You can also exclude the reader by not telling him immediately where the story is taking place, and who the people are—

INTERVIEWER: And what they want.

VONNEGUT: Yes. And you can put him to sleep by never having characters confront each other. Students like to say that they stage no confrontations because people avoid confrontations in modern life. "Modern life is so lonely," they say. This is laziness. It's the writer's job to stage confrontations, so the characters will say surprising and revealing things, and educate and entertain us all. If a writer can't or won't do that, he should withdraw from the trade.

INTERVIEWER: Trade?

VONNEGUT: Trade. Carpenters build houses. Storytellers use a reader's leisure time in such a way that the reader will not feel that his time has been wasted. Mechanics fix automobiles.

INTERVIEWER: Surely talent is required?

VONNEGUT: In all those fields. I was a Saab dealer on Cape Cod for a while, and I enrolled in their mechanic's school, and they threw me out of their mechanic's school. No talent.

INTERVIEWER: How common is storytelling talent?

VONNEGUT: In a creative writing class of twenty people anywhere in this country, six students will be startlingly talented. Two of those might actually publish something by and by.

INTERVIEWER: What distinguishes those two from the rest?

VONNEGUT: They will have something other than literature itself on their minds. They will probably be hustlers, too. I mean that they won't want to wait passively for somebody to discover them. They will insist on being read.

INTERVIEWER: You have been a public relations man and an advertising man—

VONNEGUT: Oh, I imagine.

INTERVIEWER: Was this painful? I mean—did you feel your talent was being wasted, being crippled?

VONNEGUT: No. That's romance—that work of that sort damages a writer's soul. At Iowa, Dick Yates and I used to give a lecture each year on the writer and the free enterprise system. The students hated it. We would talk about all the hack jobs writers could take in case they found themselves starving to death, or in case they wanted to accumulate enough capital to finance the writing of a book. Since publishers aren't putting money into first novels anymore, and since the magazines have died, and since television isn't buying from young freelancers anymore, and since the foundations give grants only to old poops like me, young writers are going to have to support themselves as shameless hacks. Otherwise, we are soon going to find ourselves without a contemporary literature. There is only one genuinely ghastly thing hack jobs do to writers, and that is to waste their precious time.

INTERVIEWER: No joke.

VONNEGUT: A tragedy. I just keep trying to think of ways, even horrible ways, for young writers to somehow hang on.

INTERVIEWER: Should young writers be subsidized?

VONNEGUT: Something's got to be done, now that free enterprise has made it nearly impossible for them to support themselves through free enterprise. I was a sensational businessman in the beginning—for the simple reason that there was so much business to be done. When I was working for General Electric, I wrote a story, "Report on the

Barnhouse Effect," the first story I ever wrote. I mailed it off to *Collier's.* Knox Burger was fiction editor there. Knox told me what was wrong with it and how to fix it. I did what he said, and he bought the story for seven hundred and fifty dollars, six weeks' pay at G.E. I wrote another, and he paid me ninehundred and fifty dollars, and suggested that it was perhaps time for me to quit G.E. Which I did. I moved to Provincetown. Eventually, my price for a short story got up to twenty-nine hundred dollars a crack. Think of that. And Knox got me a couple of agents who were as shrewd about storytelling as he was —Kenneth Littauer, who had been his predecessor at *Collier's,* and Max Wilkinson, who had been a story editor for MGM. And let it be put on the record here that Knox Burger, who is about my age, discovered and encouraged more good young writers than any other editor of his time. I don't think that's ever been written down anywhere. It's a fact known only to writers, and one that could easily vanish, if it isn't somewhere written down.

INTERVIEWER: Where is Knox Burger now?

VONNEGUT: He's a literary agent. He represents my son Mark, in fact.

INTERVIEWER: And Littauer and Wilkinson?

VONNEGUT: Littauer died ten years ago or so. He was a colonel in the Lafayette Escadrille, by the way, at the age of twenty-three—and the first pilot to strafe a trench. He was my mentor. Max Wilkinson has retired to Florida. It always embarrassed him to be an agent. If some stranger asked him what he did for a living, he always said he was a cotton planter.

INTERVIEWER: Do you have a new mentor now?

VONNEGUT: No. I guess I'm too old to find one. Whatever

I write now is set in type without comment by my publisher, who is younger than I am, by editors, by anyone. I don't have my sister to write for anymore. Suddenly, there are all these unfilled jobs in my life.

INTERVIEWER: Do you feel as though you're up there without a net under you?

VONNEGUT: And without a balancing pole, either. It gives me the heebie-jeebies sometimes.

INTERVIEWER: Is there anything else you'd like to add?

VONNEGUT: You know the panic bars they have on the main doors of schools and theaters? If you get slammed into the door, the door will fly open?

INTERVIEWER: Yes.

VONNEGUT: The brand name on most of them is "Vonduprin." The "Von" is for Vonnegut. A relative of mine was caught in the Iroquois Theater Fire in Chicago a long time ago, and he invented the panic bar along with two other guys. "Prin" was Prinz. I forget who "Du" was.

INTERVIEWER: O.K.

VONNEGUT: And I want to say, too, that humorists are very commonly the youngest children in their families. When I was the littlest kid at our supper table, there was only one way I could get anybody's attention, and that was to be funny. I had to specialize. I used to listen to radio comedians very intently, so I could learn how to make jokes. And that's what my books are, now that I'm a grownup—mosaics of jokes.

INTERVIEWER: Do you have any favorite jokes?

VONNEGUT: My sister and I used to argue about what the funniest joke in the world was—next to a guy storming into a coat closet, of course. When the two of us worked together, incidentally, we could be almost as funny as Laurel and Hardy. That's basically what *Slapstick* was about.

INTERVIEWER: Did you finally agree on the world's champion joke?

VONNEGUT: We finally settled on one. It's sort of hard to tell it just flat-footed like this.

INTERVIEWER: Do it anyway.

VONNEGUT: Well—you won't laugh. Nobody ever laughs. But one is an old "Two Black Crows" joke. The "Two Black Crows" were white guys in blackface—named Moran and Mack. They made phonograph records of their routines, two supposedly black guys talking lazily to each other. Anyway, one of them says, "Last night I dreamed I was eating flannel cakes." The other one says, "Is that so?" And the first one says, "And when I woke up, the blanket was gone."

INTERVIEWER: Um.

VONNEGUT: I told you you wouldn't laugh.

INTERVIEWER: You seem to prefer Laurel and Hardy over Chaplin. Is that so?

VONNEGUT: I'm crazy about Chaplin, but there's too much distance between him and his audience. He is too obviously a genius. In his own way, he's as brilliant as Picasso, and this is intimidating to me.

INTERVIEWER: Will you ever write another short story?

VONNEGUT: Maybe. I wrote what I thought would be my last one about eight years ago. Harlan Ellison asked me to contribute to a collection he was making. The story's called "The Big Space Fuck." I think I am the first writer to use "Fuck" in a title. It was about firing a space ship with a warhead full of jizzum at Andromeda. Which reminds me of my good Indianapolis friend, about the only Indianapolis friend I've got left—William Failey. When we got into the Second World War, and everybody was supposed to give blood, he wondered if he couldn't give a pint of jizzum instead.

INTERVIEWER: If your parents hadn't lost all their money, what would you be doing now?

VONNEGUT: I'd be an Indianapolis architect—like my father and grandfather. And very happy, too. I still wish that had happened. One thing, anyway: One of the best young architects out there lives in a house my father built for our family the year I was born—1922. My initials, and my sister's initials, and my brother's initials are all written in leaded glass in the three little windows by the front door.

INTERVIEWER: So you have good old days you hanker for.

VONNEGUT: Yes. Whenever I go to Indianapolis, the same question asks itself over and over again in my head: "Where's my bed, where's my bed?" And if my father's and grandfather's ghosts haunt that town, they must be wondering where all their buildings have gone to. The center of the city, where most of their buildings were, has been turned into parking lots. They must be wondering where all their relatives went, too. They grew up in a huge extended family which is no more. I got the slightest taste of that—the big family thing. And when I went to the University of Chicago, and I heard the head of the Department of Anthropology, Robert Redfield, lecture on the folk society, which was essentially a stable, isolated extended family, he did not have to tell me how nice that could be.

INTERVIEWER: Anything else?

VONNEGUT: Yes. *Slapstick* is the first American novel to employ units from the metric system throughout. Nobody noticed, so now I have to toot my own horn about it.

INTERVIEWER: Anything else?

VONNEGUT: Well—I just discovered a prayer for writers. I'd

heard of prayers for sailors and kings and soldiers and so on
—but never of a prayer for writers. Could I put that in here?

INTERVIEWER: Certainly.

VONNEGUT: It was written by Samuel Johnson on April 3,
1753, the day on which he signed a contract which required him to write the first complete dictionary of the
English language. He was praying for himself. Perhaps
April third should be celebrated as "Writers' Day." Anyway, this is the prayer: "O God, who hast hitherto supported me, enable me to proceed in this labor, and in the
whole task of my present state; that when I shall tender up,
at the last day, an account of the talent committed to me, I
may receive pardon, for the sake of Jesus Christ. Amen."

INTERVIEWER: That seems to be a wish to carry his talent
as far and as fast as he can.

VONNEGUT: Yes. He was a notorious hack.

INTERVIEWER: And you consider yourself a hack?

VONNEGUT: Of a sort.

INTERVIEWER: What sort?

VONNEGUT: A child of the Great Depression.

INTERVIEWER: I see. Our last question. If you were Commis-
sar of Publishing in the United States, what would you do
to alleviate the present deplorable situation?

VONNEGUT: There is no shortage of wonderful writers. What
we lack is a dependable mass of readers.

INTERVIEWER: So—?

VONNEGUT: I propose that every person out of work be
required to submit a book report before he or she gets his
or her welfare check.

INTERVIEWER: Thank you.

VONNEGUT: Thank *you.*

VI

THE
PEOPLE
ONE KNOWS

F ROM *Politics Today,* January/February 1979:

"Who in America is truly happy?" my offspring used to ask me in one way or another as they entered adolescence, which is children's menopause. I was silent then, but need not have been. There was an answer then which holds good today: "William F. Buckley, Jr." I have his fifteenth solo book at hand, a collection of 130 or so pieces published elsewhere (with one interesting exception) since 1975 began. Norman Mailer has said of himself that he is one of the best "fast writers" around. Buckley is at least twice as fast. He can do a column in 20 minutes, he tells us, and turn out 150 a year, plus a book and many reviews and speeches and articles, and television introductions besides. The fast writings collected in this volume are uniformly first rate—not only in terms of unbridled happiness (where Mailer surely falls short), but as shrewd comedies and celebrations of the English language.

He is a superb sailor and skier as well—and multilingual, and a musician, and an airplane pilot, and a family man, and polite and amusing to strangers. More: He is, like the Yale-educated hero of his novel *Saving the Queen,* startlingly good-looking. His distinctly American features are animated, but tempered with a certain shyness, a reserve. (The last nine words are Buckley's own gloss on the good looks of the hero, Bradford Oakes.)

So whenever I see Mr. Buckley, I think this, and, word of honor, without an atom of irony: "There is a man who has won the decathlon of human existence."

I also marvel at how much he resembles a far more lop-sided genius, the comedian Stanley Laurel. Laurel also managed to imply, despite his beauty and seriousness, that something screamingly funny was going on. People cannot earn or cultivate that look, in my opinion. Peer through the window of any hospital nursery, and you will find that one infant in fifty has it. The difficult part for many, but easy as pie for Laurel and Buckley, is living up to such a face.

I would give a million dollars to look like that.

I wonder, too, when I see Buckley: Would he have known that it was possible to be genuinely funny and conservative at the same time, if it had not been for the pioneering work of H. L. Mencken? Probably so. That face of his, when coupled with his fine mind and high social position, would have made him sound like a spiritual son of Mencken's, even if he had never heard of the Sage of Baltimore.

How serious is he about conservatism? Well—serious enough to devote his life to it, surely, but beyond that? The ideals he defends, conventional Republicanisms, really, were logically his from birth. He was rich and brilliant with congenial and enterprising relatives before he wore his first diaper—and he had the rare gift of being happy a lot, as I say. And nothing changed much except, perhaps, that life kept getting better and better.

Most important: there has never been anything to be ashamed of. It is a quite unusual experience in America to have never been ashamed. Buckley's intellectual voyage has been one of confirmations rather than discoveries. So there is the chance that he is more playful about conservatism than many who have come to it the hard way—than Aleksandr Solzhenitsyn, say. Buckley has not come to conservatism through rage and pain.

Solzhenitsyn could never say at the beginning of a book, and neither could Mencken, for that matter, what Buckley says at the beginning of this one, that he must subtitle it as being controversial for this reason: ". . . for almost everything that is said here, there is an opposite, if intellectually unequal, reaction set down somewhere. This is of course a pity, but on the other hand I have not expected to bring around the world by acclamation."

These are, I submit, the nearly weightless words of an undefeatable debater rather than of a passionate advocate—a debater who, because he is so good at debating, is about to make ninnies of the opposition yet again, knowing that nobody is going to be particularly burned up afterward. He continues to do what he did as a Yale undergraduate, which was to engage in badinage with registered Democrats, and always genially. He tells us that ". . . one of the reasons I was so happy at Yale was that geniality is . . . as natural to Yale as laughter is to Dublin, song to Milan, or angst to *The New York Review of Books.*"

I, for one, am grateful that Buckley, serious or not, has volunteered to be as consistent in his responses to outside stimuli as a pinball machine, a machine designed to teach conservative ideals—5,000 points for the electric chair, 10,-000 for right-to-work laws, 50,000 for more sympathy with the CIA, a cool million for individual excellence and daring, and so on. If we did not have such an intelligent and genial man (as compared with General Goldwater, for instance) to argue in favor of social Darwinism, some of us might be too appalled and confused to listen, to learn for our own good how uncharitable we had better be.

❦

WILLIAM F. Buckley, Jr., is a friend of mine. Ours is a New York friendship. A New York friendship is a friendship with a person you have met at least once. If you have met a person only once, and you are a New Yorker, you are entitled to say, whenever that person's name comes up in conversation, "Yes —so-and-so is a friend of mine."

I have met Mr. Buckley, or Bill, as his friends call him, maybe thrice, for a grand total of sixty seconds. I am intimidated by his cultural and athletic accomplishments, and by his social rank—but especially by his skills as a debater. I have no idea how to win an argument, or even to hold my own in one.

If I am to say what I believe, I must do so without opposition, or I am mute. I have been on the Irv Kupcinet Show, a talk show originating in Chicago, four times. I have never said a word. I ran into Mr. Kupcinet recently, and he said he would certainly like to have me on again. Why not?

❦

I spoke one time at the Library of Congress, in 1972, or so. A man stood up in the middle of the audience, when I was about halfway through, and he said, "What right have you, as a leader of America's young people, to make those people so cynical and pessimistic?"

I had no good answer, so I left the stage.

Talk about profiles in courage!

❦

THE beliefs I have to defend are so soft and complicated, actually, and, when vivisected, turn into bowls of undifferentiated mush. I am a pacifist, I am an anarchist, I am a planetary citizen, and so on.

But the subject of this chapter is friendship, and, thanks to a routine miracle of this age of computers, I am able to submit an alphabetized list of writers who are or, in the case of the dead, were friends of mine. My wife, Jill Krementz, you see, has over the years photographed hundreds of writers, and has given their names and negative numbers to a computer, in order that she may deliver a picture of any one of them in a twinkling or two.

So I simply go down her list with my index finger, stopping at the name of each person I have met at least once, and, hey presto, my friends are Chinua Achebe, Richard Adams, Renata Adler, Ghingiz Aitmatov, Edward Albee, Nelson

Algren, Lisa Alther, Robert Anderson, Maya Angelou, Hannah Arendt, Michael Arlen, John Ashbery, Isaac Asimov, Richard Bach, Russell Baker, James Baldwin, Marvin Barrett, John Barth, Donald Barthelme, Jacques Barzun, Steve Becker, Saul Bellow, Ingrid Benjis, Robert Benton, Tom Berger, Charles Berlitz, Carl Bernstein, Michael Bessie, Ann Birstein, William Blatty, Heinrich Böll, Vance Bourjaily, Ray Bradbury, John Malcolm Brinnin, Jimmy Breslin, Harold Brodkey, C.D.B. Bryan, Art Buchwald, and, yes, William F. Buckley, Jr., William Burroughs, Lynn Caine, Erskine Caldwell, Hortense Calisher, Vincent Canby, Truman Capote, Schuyler Chapin, John Cheever, Marchette Chute, John Ciardi, Eleanor Clark, Ramsey Clark, Arthur C. Clarke, James Clavell, Arthur Cohen, William Cole, Dr. Alex Comfort, Richard Condon, Evan Connell, Frank Conroy, Malcolm Cowley, Harvey Cox, Robert Creighton, Michael Crichton, Judith Crist, John Crosby, Charlotte Curtis, Gwen Davis, Peter Davison, Peter de Vries, Borden Deal, Midge Decter, Lester Del Rey, Barbaralee Diamonstein, Monica Dickens, James Dickey, Joan Didion, E. L. Doctorow, Betty Dodson, J. P. Donleavy, José Donoso, Rosalyn Drexler, John Dunne, Richard Eberhart, Leon Edel, Margareta Ekström, Stanley Elkin, Ralph Ellison, Richard Elman, Amos Elon, Gloria Emerson, Hans Magnus Enzensberger, Nora Ephron, Edward Epstein, Jason Epstein, Willard Espy, Fred Exley, Oriana Fallaci, James T. Farrell, Lawrence Ferlinghetti, Frances Fitzgerald, Joe Flaherty, Janet Flanner, Thomas Fleming, Peter Forbath, William Price Fox, Gerald Frank, Michael Frayne, Eliot Fremont-Smith, Betty Friedan, Bruce Jay Friedman, Otto Friedrich, Max Frisch, Erich Fromm, Carlos Fuentes, William Gaddis, Nicholas Gage, Charles Gaines, John Kenneth Galbraith,

Mavis Gallant, John Gardner, William Gass, Barbara Gelb, Dan Gerber, Brendan Gill, Penelope Gilliatt, Allen Ginsberg, Nikki Giovanni, Gail Godwin, William Goldman, Nadine Gordimer, Edward Gorey, Lois Gould, Günter Grass, Francine du Plessix Gray, Adolph Green, Gael Greene, Germaine Greer, Winston Groom, Alex Haley, Daniel Halpern, Pete Hamill, Elizabeth Hardwick, Curtis Harnack, Michael Harper, Jim Harrison, Molly Haskell, John Hawkes, Joseph Heller, Lillian Hellman, Nat Hentoff, John Hersey, Rust Hills, Warren Hinkle, Sandra Hochman, Townsend Hoopes, A. E. Hotchner, Barbara Howar, Jane Howard, William Inge, Clifford Irving, John Irving, Christopher Isherwood, Roman Jakobson, Jill Johnston, James Jones, Erica Jong, Pauline Kael, E. J. Kahn, Garson Kanin, Justin Kaplan, Sue Kaufman, Elia Kazan, Alfred Kazin, Murray Kempton, Galway Kinnell, Judy Klemesrud, John Knowles, Hans Koning, Jerzy Kosinski, Robert Kotlowitz, Joe Kraft, Paul Krassner, Stanley Kunitz, Lewis Lapham, Jack Leggett, Siegfried Lenz, John Leonard, Max Lerner, Doris Lessing, Ira Levin, Meyer Levin, Robert Jay Lifton, Jakov Lind, Loyd Little, Anita Loos, Anthony Lukas, Alison Lurie, Leonard Lyons, Peter Maas, Dwight MacDonald, John D. MacDonald, Ross Macdonald, Archibald MacLeish, Eugene McCarthy, Mary McCarthy, Tom McGuane, Marshall McLuhan, Larry McMurtry, Terrance McNally, John McPhee, James McPherson, Norman Mailer, Bernard Malamud, Marya Mannes, Peter Matthiessen, Armistead Maupin, Rollo May, Margaret Mead, William Meredith, James Merrill, Arthur Miller, Jonathan Miller, Merle Miller, Kate Millett, James Mills, Jessica Mitford, Honor Moore, Elsa Morante, Alberto Moravia, Hans Morgenthau, Willie Morris, Wright Morris, Toni Morrison, Penelope Mortimer, Ray

Mungo, Albert Murray, William Murray, V. S. Naipaul, Victor Navasky, Edwin Newman, Leslie Newman, Anais Nïn, William A. Nolen, Marsha Norman, Edna O'Brien, Joyce Carol Oates, Sidney Offit (best friend!), Iris Owens, Amos Oz, Cynthia Ozick, Grace Paley, Gordon Parks, Jonathan Penner, S. J. Perelman, Eleanor Perry, Frank Perry, Jayne Anne Phillips, George Plimpton, Robert Pisig, Peter Prescott, V. S. Pritchett, Dotson Rader, Ishmael Reed, Rex Reed, Richard Reeves, James Reston, Jr., Adrienne Rich, Jill Robinson, Betty Rollins, Judith Rossner, Philip Roth, Mike Royko, Muriel Rukeyser, John Sack, William Safire, Carl Sagan, Harrison Salisbury, William Saroyan, Andrew Sarris, Nora Sayre, Dick Schaap, Susan Fromberg Schaeffer, Arthur Schlesinger, Jr., Steve Schlesinger, Bud Schulberg, Ellen Schwamm, Barbara Seaman, Erich Segal, Anne Sexton, Ntozake Shange, Harvey Shapiro, Adam Shaw, Irwin Shaw, Wilfrid Sheed, Neil Sheehan, Susan Sheehan, Lynn Sherr, Alix Kates Shulman, Andre Simenov, John Simon, Isaac B. Singer, Hedrick Smith, W. D. Snodgrass, C. P. Snow, Barbara Probst Soloman, Susan Sontag, Terry Southern, Wole Soyinka, Stephen Spender, Benjamin Spock, Jean Stafford, Gloria Steinem, Shane Stevens, I. F. Stone, Irving Stone, Robert Stone, Dorothea Straus, Rose Styron, William Styron, Jacqueline Susann, Gay Talese, James Tate, Peter Taylor, Studs Terkel, Hunter S. Thompson, Lionel Tiger, Hannah Tillich, Alvin Toffler, Lazlo Toth, Michael Tournier, Willard Trask, Calvin Trillin, Diana Trilling, Barbara Tuchman, Kenneth Tynan, Amy Vanderbilt, Gore Vidal, Esther Vilar, Roman Vishniac, Mark Vonnegut, Andrei Voznesensky, Alice Walker, Joseph Wambaugh, Wayne Warga, Robert Penn Warren, Per Wästberg, Peter Weiss, Eudora Welty, Glenway Wescott, Morris West, E. B. White,

Theodore White, William Whitworth, Tom Wicker, Elie Wiesel, Richard Wilbur, Paul Wilkes, Joy Williams, Tennessee Williams, Garry Wills, Larry Woiwode, Tom Wolfe, Geoffrey Wolff, Herman Wouk, Christopher Wren, Charles Wright, James Wright, Lois Wyse, and Richard Yates.

Would you like an introduction?

❧

WHAT stories I must have to tell in Indianapolis about all these celebrities! Not really. Most writers are not quick-witted when they talk. Novelists in particular, as I have said before, drag themselves around in society like gut-shot bears. The good ones do.

Some people say that my friend Gore Vidal, who once suggested in an interview that I was the worst writer in the United States, is witty. I myself think he wants an awful lot of credit for wearing a three-piece suit.

❧

AFTER meeting all these people, I have only a single shapely anecdote to tell. It took place at the University of Iowa in Iowa City, where I taught in the famed Writers' Workshop in 1965 and 1966. My most famous colleagues were the novelists Vance Bourjaily, Nelson Algren, and Richard Yates, and the Chilean José Donoso, and the poets George Starbuck, James Tate, Marvin Bell, Donald Justice—and the poet-founder of the Workshop, of course, who is Paul Engle.

Among those students of ours who would really amount to something as writers by and by, incidentally, were Jane Barnes and John Casey and Bruce Dobler and Andre Dubus and Gail Godwin and John Irving and Jonathan Penner.

So Algren and Donoso and I were new arrivals, and we went together to the first autumn meeting of the English department, against whose treasury our paychecks were drawn. We thought we should be there. Nobody had told us that lecturers in the Writers' Workshop traditionally ignored all such bureaucratic, sesquipedalian sniveling and obfuscation.

So Algren and Donoso and I were going down a staircase afterward. Algren had come late, and so had sat separate from Donoso and me. He and Donoso had never met before, so I introduced them on the staircase, explaining to Algren that Donoso was from Chile, but a graduate of Princeton University.

Algren shook Donoso's hand, but said nothing to him until we reached the bottom. He at last thought of something to say to a Chilean novelist: "It must be nice," he said, "to come from a country that long and narrow."

❦

ARE many novelists schizophrenic—at least marginally so? Do they hallucinate, seeing and hearing things that healthy people cannot sense? Do they turn disordered perceptions into gold in the literary marketplace? If writers are usefully crazy, what is the medical name for their disease? Or, if writers themselves aren't lunatics, perhaps a lot of their ancestors were.

The psychiatric department of the University of Iowa's hospital, it turns out, has wondered some about these questions, which have their roots in folklore. It has taken advantage of the large numbers of reputable writers who come to

Iowa City, usually down on their luck, to teach at the Writers' Workshop. So they have questioned us about our mental health and about that of our ancestors and siblings, too.

It is apparent to them, I am told, that we are not hallucinators, nor are many of us descended from those who saw or heard things which weren't really there. Overwhelmingly, we are depressed, and are descended from those who, psychologically speaking, spent more time than anyone in his or her right mind would want to spend in gloom.

❦

I would add that novelists are not only unusually depressed, by and large, but have, on the average, about the same IQs as the cosmetics consultants at Bloomingdale's department store. Our power is patience. We have discovered that writing allows even a stupid person to seem halfway intelligent, if only that person will write the same thought over and over again, improving it just a little bit each time. It is a lot like inflating a blimp with a bicycle pump. Anybody can do it. All it takes is time.

❦

I heard a Frenchman in a Madison Avenue bookstore say in English the other day that nobody in America had produced a book in forty years or more. I knew what he meant. He was talking about planetary literary treasures on the order of *Moby Dick* or *Huckleberry Finn* or *Leaves of Grass* or *Walden,* say. I had to agree with him. No book from this country during my lifetime (1922–?) has been in scale with *Ulysses* or *Remembrance of Things Past* or *The Tin Drum* or *One Hundred Years of Solitude* or *A Day in the Life of Ivan Denisovitch.*

Still, now that I contemplate all the Americans on my list of friends, I wish the Frenchman were here so that I could say to him frostily: "You are quite right, mon-sewer, we have not produced a book. All we poor Americans could do was produce a literature."

❦

AND here is how I spoke well of my friend Joseph Heller's contributions to that literature in *The New York Times Book Review* of Sunday, October 6, 1974:

The company that made a movie out of Joseph Heller's first novel, *Catch-22,* had to assemble what became the 11th or 12th largest bomber force on the planet at the time. If somebody wants to make a movie out of his second novel, *Something Happened,* he can get most of his props at Bloomingdale's—a few beds, a few desks, some tables and chairs.

Life is a whole lot smaller and cheaper in this second book. It has shrunk to the size of a grave, almost.

Mark Twain is said to have felt that his existence was all pretty much downhill from his adventures as a Mississippi riverboat pilot. Mr. Heller's two novels, when considered in sequence, might be taken as a similar statement about an entire white, middle-class generation of American males, my generation, Mr. Heller's generation, Herman Wouk's generation, Norman Mailer's generation, Irwin Shaw's generation, Vance Bourjaily's generation, James Jones's generation, and on and on—that for them everything has been downhill since World War II, as absurd and bloody as it often was.

Both books are full of excellent jokes, but neither one is funny. Taken together they tell a tale of pain and disappointments experienced by mediocre men of good will.

Mr. Heller is a first-rate humorist who cripples his own jokes intentionally—with the unhappiness of the characters who perceive them. He also insists on dealing with only the most hackneyed themes. After a thousand World War II airplane novels had been published and pulped, he gave us yet another one, which was gradually acknowledged as a sanely crazy masterpiece.

Now he offers us the thousand and first version of *The Hucksters* or *The Man in the Gray Flannel Suit.*

There is a nattily dressed, sourly witty middle-management executive named Robert Slocum, he tells us, who lives in a nice house in Connecticut with a wife, a daughter, and two sons. Slocum works in Manhattan in the communications racket. He is restless. He mourns the missed opportunities of his youth. He is itchy for raises and promotions, even though he despises his company and the jobs he does. He commits unsatisfying adulteries now and then at sales conferences in resort areas, during long lunch hours, or while pretending to work late at the office.

He is exhausted.

He dreads old age.

Mr. Heller's rewriting of this written-to-death situation took him 12 years. It comes out as a monologue by Slocum. Nobody else gets to talk, except as reported by Slocum. And Slocum's sentences are so alike in shape and texture from the beginning to the end of the book, that I imagined a man who was making an enormous statue out of sheet metal. He was shaping it with millions of identical taps from a ball-peen hammer.

Each dent was a fact, a depressingly ordinary fact.

"My wife is a good person, really, or used to be," says Slocum near the beginning, "and sometimes I'm sorry for her. She drinks during the day and flirts, or tries to, at parties we go to in the evening, although she doesn't know how."

"I have given my daughter a car of her own," he says near the end. "Her spirits seem to be picking up."

Slocum does his deadly best to persuade us, with his tap-tap-tapping of facts, that he is compelled to be as unhappy as he is, not because of enemies or flaws in his own character, but because of the facts.

What have these tedious facts done to him? They have required that he respond to them, since he is a man of good will. And responding and responding and responding to them has left him petrified with boredom and drained of any capacity for joyfulness, now that he is deep into middle age.

Only one fact among the millions is clearly horrible. Only one distinguishes Slocum's bad luck from that of his neighbors. His youngest child is an incurable imbecile.

Slocum is heartless about the child. "I no longer think of Derek as one of my children," he says. "Or even as mine. I try not to think of him at all. This is becoming easier, even at home when he is nearby with the rest of us, making noise with some red cradle toy or making unintelligible sounds as he endeavors to speak. By now I don't even know his name. The children don't care for him either."

Mr. Heller might have here, or at least somewhere in his book, used conventional, Chekhovian techniques for making us love a sometimes wicked man. He might have said that Slocum was drunk or tired after a bad day at the office when he spoke so heartlessly, or that he whispered his heartlessness only to himself or to a stranger he would never see again.

But Slocum is invariably sober and deliberate during his monologue, and does not seem to give a damn who hears what he says. Judging from his selection of unromantic episodes and attitudes it is his wish that we dislike him.

And we gratify that wish.

Is this book any good? Yes. It is splendidly put together and hypnotic to read. It is as clear and hard-edged as a cut diamond. Mr. Heller's concentration and patience are so evident on every page that one can only say that *Something Happened* is at all points precisely what he hoped it would be.

The book may be marketed under false pretenses, which is all right with me. I have already seen British sales promotion materials which suggest that we have been ravenous for a new Heller book because we want to laugh some more. This is as good a way as any to get people to read one of the unhappiest books ever written.

Something Happened is so astonishingly pessimistic, in fact, that it can be called a daring experiment. Depictions of utter hopelessness in literature have been acceptable up to now only in small doses, in short-story form, as in Franz Kafka's "The Metamorphosis," Shirley Jackson's "The Lottery," or John D. MacDonald's "The Hangover," to name a treasured few. As far as I know, though, Joseph Heller is the first major American writer to deal with unrelieved misery at novel length. Even more rashly, he leaves his chief character, Slocum, essentially unchanged at the end.

A middle-aged woman who had just finished *Something Happened* in galleys said to me the other day that she thought it was a reply to all the recent books by women about the unrewardingness of housewives' lives. And Slocum does seem to argue that he is entitled to at least as much unhappiness as any woman he knows. His wife, after all, has to adapt to only one sort of hell, the domestic torture chamber in Connecticut, in which he, too, must writhe at night and on weekends, when he isn't committing adultery. But he must go regularly to his office, where pain is inflicted on all the nerve centers which were neglected by the tormentors at home.

(The place where Slocum works, incidentally, is unnamed, and its products and services are undescribed. But I had a friend of a friend of an acquaintance ask Mr. Heller if he minded naming Slocum's employers. Mr. Heller replied with all possible speed and openness, "Time, Incorporated." So we have a small scoop.)

Just as Mr. Heller is uninterested in tying a tin can to anything as localized as a company with a familiar name, so is he far above the complaining contests going on between men and women these days. He began this book way back in 1962, and there have been countless gut-ripping news items and confrontations since then. But Heller's man Slocum is deaf and blind to them. He receives signals from only three sources: his office, his memory and home.

And, on the basis of these signals alone, he is able to say, apparently in all seriousness: "The world just doesn't work. It's an idea whose time is gone."

This is black humor indeed—with the humor removed.

Robert Slocum was in the Air Force in Italy during World War II, by the way. He was especially happy there while demonstrating his unflagging virility to prostitutes. So it was also with John Yossarian, the hero of *Catch-22*, whose present whereabouts are unknown.

There will be a molasses-like cautiousness about accepting this book as an important one. It took more than a year for

Catch-22 to gather a band of enthusiasts. I myself was cautious about that book. I am cautious again.

The uneasiness which many people will feel about liking *Something Happened* has roots which are deep. It is no casual thing to swallow a book by Joseph Heller, for he is, whether he intends to be or not, a maker of myths. (One way to do this, surely, is to be the final and most brilliant teller of an oft-told tale.) *Catch-22* is now the dominant myth about Americans in the war against fascism. *Something Happened,* if swallowed, could become the dominant myth about the middle-class veterans who came home from that war to become heads of nuclear families. The proposed myth has it that those families were pathetically vulnerable and suffocating. It says that the heads of them commonly took jobs which were vaguely dishonorable or at least stultifying, in order to make as much money as they could for their little families, and they used that money in futile attempts to buy safety and happiness. The proposed myth says that they lost their dignity and their will to live in the process.

It says they are hideously tired now.

To accept a new myth about ourselves is to simplify our memories—and to place our stamp of approval on what might become an epitaph for our era in the shorthand of history. This, in my opinion, is why critics often condemn our most significant books and poems and plays when they first appear, while praising feebler creations. The birth of a new myth fills them with primitive dread, for myths are so effective.

Well—I have now suppressed my own dread. I have thought dispassionately about *Something Happened* and I am now content to have it shown to future generations as a spooky sort of summary of what my generation of nebulously clever white people experienced, and what we, within the cage of those experiences, then did with our lives.

And I am counting on a backlash. I expect younger readers to love Robert Slocum—on the grounds that he couldn't possibly be as morally repellent and socially useless as he claims to be.

People a lot younger than I am may even be able to laugh at Slocum in an affectionate way, something I am unable to do. They may even see comedy in his tragic and foolish belief that he is totally responsible for the happiness or unhappiness of the members of his tiny family.

They may even see some nobility in him as an old soldier who has been brought to emotional ruin at last by the aging process and civilian life.

As for myself: I can't crack a smile when he says, ostensibly about the positions in which he sleeps, "I have exchanged the position of the fetus for the position of the corpse." And I am so anxious for Slocum to say something good about life that I read hope into lines meant to be supremely ironical, such as when he says this: "I know at last what I want to be when I grow up. When I grow up I want to be a little boy."

What is perhaps Slocum's most memorable speech mourns not his own generation but the one after his, in the person of his sullen, teen-age daughter. "There was a cheerful baby girl in a high chair in my house once," he says, "who ate and drank with a hearty appetite and laughed a lot with spontaneous zest; she isn't here now, and there is no trace of her anywhere."

We keep reading this overly long book, even though there is no rise and fall in passion and language, because it is structured as a suspense novel. The puzzle which seduces us is this one: Which of several possible tragedies will result from so much unhappiness? The author picks a good one.

I say that this is the most memorable, and therefore the most permanent variation on a familiar theme, and that it says baldly what the other variations only implied, what the other variations tried with desperate sentimentality not to imply: That many lives, judged by the standards of the people who live them, are simply not worth living.

❧

WAS it unethical of me to review a book by a friend of mine for *The New York Times*? I did not know Heller all that well back then. We had taught at City College together, and had exchanged greetings in the halls. If I had known him well, I would have refused the assignment.

But then, after I accepted it, I rented a summer house close to his on Long Island—and I got to know him better and better at precisely the time I was reviewing *Something Happened*. He was especially concerned, it turned out, about who was going to do that job for the *Times*.

I told him that I had heard a strong rumor, one which satisfied him entirely, that the *Times* had hired Robert Penn Warren, who was, even as we spoke, probably ransacking the book for its deepest meanings in his leafy hideaway in Vermont.

❧

As for literary criticism in general: I have long felt that any reviewer who expresses rage and loathing for a novel or a play or a poem is preposterous. He or she is like a person who has put on full armor and attacked a hot fudge sundae or a banana split.

I admire anybody who finishes a work of art, no matter how awful it may be. A drama critic from a news magazine, speaking to me on the opening night of a play of mine, said that he liked to remind himself from time to time that Shakespeare was standing right behind him, so that he had to be very responsible and wise whenever he expressed an opinion about a play.

I told him that he had it exactly ass backwards—that Shakespeare was standing behind me and every other playwright who was foolhardy enough to face an opening night, no matter how bad our plays might be.

❦

AND here is how I praised my friend Irwin Shaw at a banquet in his honor at The Players club here in New York, a so-called pipe night, on October 7, 1979. My friend Frank Sinatra was there, and my friends Adolph Green and Betty Comden, and my friend Joseph Heller, and my friend Willie Morris, and my friend Martin Gabel, and on and on. I had this to say:

"I apologize for reading from a piece of paper. Writers are pitiful people in a way. They have to write everything out.

"This is an actors' club, and I must admit that actors are far superior to writers when it comes to public speaking. They have somebody else write whatever it is they're going to say, and then they memorize it.

"This is a club for memorizers, and I think it's nice that they have a club. Everybody who wants a club should have one. That's what America is all about.

"That, and fighting different diseases, and so on.

"We are here principally to honor Irwin Shaw as an artist and human being. I would like to thank him, too, for his demonstration of what a lifetime of vigorous athletics can do to the human body.

"He likes to be thought of as a very tough guy. And it's true that he has turned skiing into a contact sport.

"So, Irwin, I salute you now as the Rocky Graziano of American letters—because that is the way I think you want to be saluted. And you will be happy to know that I often get taxi drivers who don't talk just a little like you. Irwin, they talk exactly like you.

"They've also all turned out to be gentlemen like you.

"And how can you claim to be so tough anyway, when you have written one of the most innocent and beautiful stories I ever hope to read? I refer to 'The Girls in Their Summer Dresses.' This story says that even men in love will look longingly at every beautiful girl who comes along when the weather is warm, but concludes that there is no harm in this.

"Irwin, how innocent can you be?

"Well, I hate to say this with Joseph Heller present. . . .

"Actually, it's sort of elating to say it with Joseph Heller present. . . .

"Irwin Shaw wrote the best American novel about World War Two, which was *The Young Lions.* He was the only one of us who had enough wisdom and nerve to write about the European part of that war from both sides of the lines. As a German-American, of course, I was sorry to see him make the Nazis the bad guys.

"But by and large *The Young Lions* was such a good book that it made Ernest Hemingway mad. He thought he had copyrighted war.

"But the Ernest Hemingway story is a tragic one, and the Irwin Shaw story is anything but that. Look how happy Irwin is.

"I know where a lot of that happiness is coming from, but some of it should surely be attributed to the fact that the publication of Irwin's collected short stories last year confirmed beyond a doubt that he is one of the greatest storytellers of all time.

"Oh, I know it is cruel on a man's ninety-second birthday to talk about nothing but the work he did as a youngster. But I have done that tonight for selfish reasons, to celebrate my own youth, when I was so enthusiastic about so many things. That's what it was to be young—to be enthusiastic rather than envious about the good work other people could do.

"And I was so enthusiastic about everything written by Irwin Shaw. He continues to write as well as ever, but I can no longer take pleasure in reading him, since he is my colleague now. I simply can't afford to like anybody but me. When I read anybody else now, I see his or her words only dimly, as though through a finely divided mist of sulfuric acid or mustard gas.

"I can see this much in Irwin's present work, though: Despite all the high living he has done far away from us, in Europe and the Hamptons and so on, he still knows how Americans talk and feel. This is highly unusual in our literary history. Almost every other important American writer who has lived elsewhere has soon lost touch with how we talk and feel.

"How has he worked this miracle? I will have to guess, but I am almost sure I'm right about this. Every time Irwin comes to New York, I think, he takes a job driving a taxicab.

"Now that I have let you in on his little secret, you won't

be surprised if you find him driving you home after this banquet in his honor.

"I thank you for your attention."

❦

AND here is what I said about my friends Bob Elliott and Ray Goulding, perhaps the most significant and ridiculous American comedy team alive today, as an introduction to their book *Write If You Get Work: The Best of Bob & Ray* (Random House, 1975):

It is the truth: Comedians and jazz musicians have been more comforting and enlightening to me than preachers or politicians or philosophers or poets or painters or novelists of my time. Historians in the future, in my opinion, will congratulate us on very little other than our clowning and our jazz.

And if they know what they are doing, they will have especially respectful words for Bob and Ray, whose book this is. They will say, among other things, that Bob and Ray's jokes were remarkably literary, being fun to read as well as to hear. They may note, too, that Bob and Ray had such energy and such a following that they continued to create marvelous material for radio at a time when radio creatively was otherwise dead.

I have listened to Bob and Ray for years and years now —in New England, in New York City. We are about the same age, which means that we were inspired by roughly the same saints—Jack Benny, Fred Allen, W. C. Fields, Stoopnagle and Bud, and on and on. And my collected works would fill Oliver Hardy's derby, whereas theirs would fill the Astrodome.

This book contains about one ten-thousandth of their output, I would imagine. And it might be exciting to say that it represents the cream of the cream of the cream of their jokes. But the truth is that there has been an amazing evenness to their performances. I recall a single broadcast of ten years ago, for example, which might have made a book nearly as elating as this one.

I was in the studio when I heard it—and saw it, too. I was supposedly applying for a job as a writer for Bob and Ray. We meant to talk about the job in between comedy bits, when the microphones were dead. One of the bits I remember was about selling advertising space on the sides of the Bob and Ray Satellite, which was going to be orbited only twenty-eight feet off the ground.

There was an announcement, too, about the Bob and Ray Overstocked Surplus Warehouse, which was crammed with sweaters emblazoned with the letter "O." If your name didn't begin with "O," they said, they could have it legally changed for you.

And so on.

There was an episode from Mary Backstayge. Mary's actor husband, Harry, was trying to get a part in a play. His big talent, according to his supporters, was that he was wonderful at memorizing things.

There was an animal imitator who said that a pig went "oink oink," and a cow went "moo," and that a rooster went "cock-a-doodle-doo."

I very nearly popped a gut. I am pathetically vulnerable to jokes such as these. I expect to be killed by laughter sooner or later. And I told Bob and Ray that I could never write anything as funny as what I had heard on what was for them a perfectly ordinary day.

I was puzzled that day by Bob's and Ray's melancholy. It seemed to me that they should be the happiest people on earth, but looks of sleepy ruefulness crossed their faces like clouds from time to time. I have seen those same clouds at subsequent encounters—and only now do I have a theory to explain them:

I surmise that Bob and Ray feel accursed sometimes—like crewmen on the *Flying Dutchman* or caged squirrels on an exercise wheel. They are so twangingly attuned to their era and to each other that they can go on being extremely funny almost indefinitely.

Such an unlimited opportunity to make people happy must become profoundly pooping by and by.

It occurs to me, too, as I look through this marvelous book, that Bob and Ray's jokes are singularly burglar-proof. They aren't like most other comedians' jokes these days, aren't rooted in show business and the world of celebrities and news of the day. They feature Americans who are almost always fourth-rate or below, engaged in enterprises which, if not contemptible, are at least insane.

And while other comedians show us persons tormented by bad luck and enemies and so on, Bob and Ray's characters threaten to wreck themselves and their surroundings with their own stupidity. There is a refreshing and beautiful innocence in Bob's and Ray's humor.

Man is not evil, they seem to say. He is simply too hilariously stupid to survive.

And this I believe.

Cheers.

❦

AND here is what I said at a funeral here for my friend James T. Farrell on August 24, 1979, whose body was taken afterward to a Catholic cemetery in his native Chicago:

"I am here at the request of a member of the family—perhaps as a representative of the generation of American writers most influenced by James T. Farrell. I was not a close friend. Many of you were, and I envy you that. I knew him some. I found him easy to love and admire. He was eighteen years my senior.

"Here is what he did for me and many like me when I was very young: He showed me through his books that it was perfectly all right, perhaps even useful and beautiful, to say what life really looked like, what was really said and felt and done—what really went on. Until I read him, I wished only to be well received in polite company.

"We were both University of Chicago people.

"I note that there is a cross over his casket. That is a nice try by whoever put it there, but it is surely known in heaven that James T. Farrell of Chicago and New York was not among our leaders in organized tub-beating for Jesus Christ. He took his chances that way. If he is being scolded at this moment at the Pearly Gates, it may be for his overemphasis of rationality and compassion and honor at the expense of piety. I fear not for him. This is an argument he has won before.

"The last time I was in this melancholy depot, it was to say farewell to Janet Flanner, another midwesterner who became a planetary patriot. Ms. Flanner and Mr. Farrell were members of the American Academy and Institute of Arts and Letters. Ms. Flanner came regularly to the annual spring meeting of that organization. So do many of our leading culture heroes. James T. Farrell never came. One time I asked him why not. He said that he did not care to come face to face with some of the critics, fellow writers, who had damned his work years ago—had damned it ostensibly for bad writing, but actually for the supposedly incorrect political opinions he was known to hold. He was a premature anti-Stalinist. He was, and remained so to his death, a left-wing thinking man.

"The malicious attacks did not humble him, could not humble him, since he was Irish. They did, however, so muddy his reputation that a dispassionate appraisal of his life's work remains to be made. It is a huge work. It is Balzacian in scale. I spoke at his seventy-third birthday, two years ago, and I suggested that, if only James T. Farrell had produced such a body of work in a smaller country, he would have won a Nobel prize by then. That was a strong statement. It had the added force of ringing true.

"The ancient Greeks believed, or some of them did, anyway, that a person could not be said to have lived well if he or she died in unhappy circumstances. This is a deservedly unpopular opinion in America, where so many lives end abominably, almost as a matter of routine. But let us suppose that the Greeks were right. By their hard standards we can say that the American writer James T. Farrell had a wonderful life. He died in his sleep, in the presence of deep love such as the world has seldom seen—and owing no one an apology for anything.

"He was a sports nut, of course—and once an athlete of great and varied skills. So it is appropriate if we now address our memories of him in this fashion: 'You won, you won.' "

VII

PLAYMATES

I delivered a speech at the University of Virginia maybe eight years ago, which mercifully has been lost, so I do not have to paste it in here somewhere. I said, I remember, that Thomas Jefferson in his mansion called Monticello, with an artificial trout pool in its front yard, and its dumbwaiters for bringing wine and cider up from the basement, and its secret staircases and so on, was the Hugh Hefner of his time. Jefferson didn't have for servants young women with great balls of cotton stuck to their behinds. He owned honest-to-God slaves instead.

A history professor explained to me afterward that Jefferson was so slow to free his slaves because he did not really own them. He had mortgaged them. Like this mortgaged house in which I write now, they belonged to the bank.

Author's note: No entirely white descendent of Thomas Jefferson is alive today.

❧

BUT the best part of that visit was finding out what had happened to a childhood playmate of mine. He was two years my junior, and had lived right next door to me in Indianapolis. We were playmates during the 1930s. His father and mine had both built grandiose houses during the boom of the 1920s. But during the 1930s they were both going broke. His father owned a furniture store which was bankrupt, and my father could find no work as an architect, and my mother and father were becoming widely known as deadbeats who would run huge charge accounts and never pay. This playmate sent me a note while I was in Charlottesville, and by God if he hadn't become head of the astronomy department at the university. Sam Goldstein was his name.

So Sam and I had a good talk about the work he was doing, which was mainly with radio telescopes, and the work I was doing. We told about our children. Things were going well.

We refreshed our memories about neighborhood dogs we had known, dogs which had known us, too. We remembered two bulldogs named Boots and Beans, who were owned by a family named Wales. Boots and Beans used to catch cats and small dogs and pull them in two. I personally witnessed their doing that to a cat of ours.

Sam and I laughed when I told about my father's sending the message to Mr. Wales that he would shoot Boots and Beans if they ever came into our yard again. Mr. Wales sent back the message that he would shoot Father if Father shot Boots and Beans.

Psychoanalysts are missing important clues about patients' childhoods if they do not ask about dogs the patients knew. As I have said elsewhere, dogs still seem as respectable and interesting as people to me. Any day.

❦

DOG poisoning is still the most contemptible crime I can think of. Boots and Beans were poisoned finally, but I couldn't celebrate that, and our family certainly had nothing to do with it. If we were going to poison anybody, it would have been Mr. Wales.

❦

THE dogs of our childhood were dead when Sam Goldstein and I were reunited in Charlottesville, so we would have been crazy to speculate about what they might be doing nowadays. We could speculate about children we had known, though, since human beings live so long. We would say things like, "What do you suppose ever happened to Nancy Briggs?" or "Where do you think Dick Martin is now?" and on and on. Sometimes one or the other of us had a stale clue or two. Nancy Briggs married a sailor and moved to Texas during the Second World War. How's that for a clue?

❦

I have played that game so often in this jerry-built society of ours—"Whatever Became of So-and-so?" It becomes a truly sad game only if someone actually knows in detail what became of several so-and-sos. Several ordinary life stories, if told in rapid succession, tend to make life look far more pointless than it really is, probably.

The people I am most eager to have news of, curiously enough, are those I worked with in the General News Bureau of the General Electric Company in Schenectady, New York —from 1948 to 1951, from the time I was twenty-six until I was twenty-nine. They were all men I worked with, but when I think of that good old gang of mine, I include their wives.

As the song from the Gay Nineties, "That Old Gang of Mine," would have it:

> So long forever, old fellows and pals,
> So long forever, old sweethearts and gals. . . .

My persisting concern about all those General Electric people is so irrational and deep that I have to suspect that it may have genetic roots of some sort. I may have been born with some sort of clock in me which required me to love those working alongside of me so much at that time. We were just getting our footing as adult citizens, and in other times we might have been correct in thinking that we had better like and trust each other a lot, since we would be together for life.

It was the Darwinian wish of General Electric, of the Free Enterprise System, of course, that we compete instead.

I have heard other people say that they, too, remain irrationally fond of those who were with them when they were just starting out. It's a common thing.

❦

ONE of my closest friends from General Electric is Ollie M. Lyon, who became a vice-president at Young and Rubicam advertising for a while, and then went back to his home state of Kentucky to sell sophisticated silos to farmers. The silos were so airtight that almost no silage was lost to fermentation and vermin and rot.

I loved Ollie's wife Lavina exactly as much as I loved him, and she died fast of cancer of the pancreas out there in Kentucky. One of her last requests was that I speak at her funeral. "I want him to say good-bye to me," she said. So I did. I said this:

"Lavina asked me to be up here.

"This is the hardest thing Lavina ever asked me to do, but then she never asked anyone to do anything hard. Her only instructions were that I was to say good-bye to her as an old friend—as *all* old friends.

"I say it now. If I had to say it at the end, to build up to saying it, I would go all to pieces, I think. I would bark like a dog. So I say it now: 'Good-bye, darling Lavina.'

"There—that is behind me now. That is behind us, now.

"It is common at funerals for survivors to regret many things that were said and done to the departed—to think, 'I wish I had said this instead of this, I wish I had done that instead of that.' This is not that sort of funeral. This is not a church filled with regrets.

"Why not? We *always* treated Lavina with love and decency. Why did we do that? It was Lavina's particular genius to so behave that the only possible responses on our part were love and decency. That is her richest legacy to us, I think: Her lessons in how to treat others so that their only possible responses are, again, love and decency.

149

"There is at least one person here who does not need to learn what Lavina knew. He is Lavina's spiritual equal, although he was so much in love with her that perhaps he never knew it. He is Ollie Morris Lyon.

"Ollie and Lavina are country people, by the way.

"I have seen them achieve success and happiness in the ugly factory city of Schenectady, New York, where I first met them. They were not much older than Mary and Philip then. Think of that. Yes, and when they lived in New York City, they had as much fun as any jazz-age babies ever did. Good for them! But they were always a farmer and his wife.

"Now the farmer's wife has died. I'm glad they got back here before she died.

"The wife died first.

"It happens all the time—but it always seems like such a terrible violation of the natural order when the wife dies first. Is there anyone here, even a child, who did not believe that Lavina would survive us all? She was so healthy, so capable, so beautiful, so strong. She was supposed to come to *our* funerals—not the other way around.

"Well—she may come to them yet. She will, if she can. She will talk to God about it, I'm sure. If anybody can stretch the rules of heaven a little, Lavina can.

"I say she was strong. We all say she was strong. Yes, and in this bicentennial springtime we can say that she was like a legendary pioneer woman in her seeming strengths. We know now that she was only pretending to be strong—which is the best any of us can do. Of course, if you can pretend to be strong all your life, which is what Lavina did, then you can be very comforting to those around you. You can allow them to be childlike now and then.

"Good job, Lavina, darling. And remember, too, Lavina, the times we let you be a little girl.

"When she was a little girl in Palmyra, Illinois, being the youngest of a large family, she was expected to leave a note in the kitchen saying where she had gone after school. One day the note that was found said 'I have gone where I have decided.'

"We loved you.

"We love you.

"We will always love you.

"We will meet again."

❦

I now confess that the American poems which move me most are those which marvel most, simply and clearly, at the queer shapes which the massive indifference of America gives to lives. So *The Spoon River Anthology* by Edgar Lee Masters seems a very great book to me.

That is a barbarous opinion. So I have nothing to lose by blurting moreover that I find much to celebrate in the shrewd innocence of many of the poems now being set to country music.

Pay attention, please, to the words of "The Class of '57," a big country hit of a few years ago:

> Tommy's sellin' used cars,
> Nancy's fixin' hair,
> Harvey runs a groc'ry store
> And Marg'ret doesn't care,
> Jerry drives a truck for Sears

and Charlotte's on the make.
And Paul sells life insurance
And part-time real estate.

And the Class of Fifty Seven had its dreams.
But we all thought we'd changed the world
With our great works and deeds;
Or maybe we just thought the world
Would change to fit our needs.
The Class of Fifty Seven had its dreams.

Betty runs a trailer park,
Jan sells Tupperware,
Randy's on an insane ward,
And Mary's on welfare,
Charley took a job with Ford,
Joe took Freddy's wife,
Charlotte took a millionaire,
And Freddy took his life.

And the Class of Fifty Seven had its dreams,
But livin' life from day to day
Is never like it seems.
Things get complicated
When you get past eighteen,
But the Class of Fifty Seven had its dreams.

Helen is a hostess,
Frank works at the mill,
Janet teaches grade school
And prob'ly always will,
Bob works for the city,

PALM SUNDAY

And Jack's in lab research,
And Peggy plays the organ
At the Presbyterian Church.

And the Class of Fifty Seven had its dreams.
But we all thought we'd change the world
With our great works and deeds;
Or maybe we just thought the world
Would change to fit our needs.
The Class of Fifty Seven had its dreams.

John is big in cattle,
Ray is deep in debt,
Where Mavis fin'ly wound up
Is anybody's bet,
Linda married Sonny,
Brenda married me,
and the class of all of us
Is just part of history.

And the Class of Fifty Seven had its dreams,
But livin' life from day to day
Is never like it seems.
Things get complicated
When you get past eighteen,
But the Class of Fifty Seven had its dreams.
Ah, the Class of Fifty Seven had its dreams.

The authors are Don and Harold Reid, the only actual brothers in the country-music quartet that calls itself the Statler Brothers. Nobody in the quartet is named Statler. The quartet named itself after a roll of paper towels.

❦

MY wife Jill and I admire the Statler Brothers so much that we went all the way to the Niagara Falls International Convention Center in April of 1980 to hear them and to shake their hands. We had our pictures taken with them, too.

Yes, and they announced from the stage that they were honored that night to have in the audience "the famous writer Kurt Vonnegut and his wife, Jill Krementz, the famous photographer." We got a terrific hand, although we did not stand up and identify ourselves, and although nobody, I'm sure, had ever heard of us before.

A woman came up to us afterward, and she said that we must be the famous people the brothers had mentioned, since we didn't look like anybody else in the auditorium. She said that from now on she was going to read everything we wrote.

Jill and I stayed in the same Holiday Inn as the Statler Brothers, but they slept all afternoon. Their bus was parked outside where we could see it from our room. Right after their performance, around midnight, they got on the bus, and it started up with that fruity, burbling, soft purple rumble that bus engines have. The bus left without any lights showing inside. Nobody waved from a window. It headed for Columbus, Ohio, for another performance the next night. I forget where it was supposed to go after that—Saginaw, Michigan, I think.

❦

I would actually like to have "The Class of '57" become our national anthem for a little while. Everybody knows that "The Star Spangled Banner" is a bust as music and poetry, and is as representative of the American spirit as the Taj Mahal.

I can see Americans singing in a grandstand at the Olympics somewhere, while one of our athletes wins a medal—for the decathlon, say. I can see tears streaming down the singers' cheeks when they get to these lines:

> Where Mavis fin'ly wound up
> Is anybody's bet.

❦

"THE Class of '57" could be an anthem for my generation, at least. Many people have said that we already have an anthem, which is my friend Allen Ginsberg's "Howl," which starts off like this:

I saw the best minds of my generation destroyed
  by madness, starving hysterical naked,
dragging themselves through the negro streets
  at dawn looking for an angry fix,
angelheaded hipsters burning for the ancient
  heavenly connection to the starry dynamo
  in the machinery of night.

And so on.

I like "Howl" a lot. Who wouldn't? It just doesn't have much to do with me or what happened to my friends. For one thing, I believe that the best minds of my generation were probably musicians and physicists and mathematicians and biologists and archaeologists and chess masters and so on, and Ginsberg's closest friends, if I'm not mistaken, were undergraduates in the English department of Columbia University.

No offense intended, but it would never occur to me to look for the best minds in any generation in an undergraduate English department anywhere. I would certainly try the physics department or the music department first—and after that biochemistry.

Everybody knows that the dumbest people in any American university are in the education department, and English after that.

❦

ALSO, and again I intend no offense, the most meaningful and often harrowing adventures which I and many like me have experienced have had to do with the rearing of children. "Howl" does not deal with such adventures.

Truly great poems never do, somehow.

❦

ALLEN Ginsberg and I were inducted into the National Institute of Arts and Letters in the same year, 1973. Somebody from *Newsweek* called me up to ask what I had to say about two such antiestablishment writers being embraced by such a conservative organization.

I said this, and I meant it, and my comment was not printed: "My goodness, if Mr. Ginsberg and I aren't already members of the establishment, I don't know who is."

❧

To return to the subject of childhood playmates: In the Vonnegut house, with its charge-account deadbeats, and in the Goldstein house next door, with its bankruptcy, there were many books. As luck would have it, the Goldstein children and I, and the Marks children three doors down, whose father would soon die quite suddenly, could all read about as easily as we could eat chocolate ice cream. Thus, at a very tender age and in utter silence, disturbing no one, being children as good as gold, we were comforted and nourished by human minds which were calmer and more patient and amusing and unafraid than our parents could afford to be.

❧

Years later, on October 1, 1976, I would pay this circuitous tribute to the art of reading at the dedication of a new library at Connecticut College, New London:

"The name of this speech is 'The Noodle Factory.'

"Like life itself, this speech will be over before you know it. Life is so short!

"I was born only yesterday morning, moments after daybreak—and yet, this afternoon, I am fifty-four years old. I am a mere baby, and yet here I am dedicating a library. Something has gone wrong.

"I have a painter friend named Syd Solomon. He was also born only yesterday. And the next thing he knew, it was time for him to have a retrospective exhibition of his paintings going back thirty-five years. Syd asked a woman claiming to be his wife what on earth had happened. She said, 'Syd, you're fifty-eight years old now.'

"You can imagine how he felt.

"Another thing Syd found out was that he was a veteran of something called the Second World War. Somebody said I was in that war, too. Maybe so. I don't argue when people tell me things like that.

"I decided to read up on that war some. I went to a library a lot like this one. It was a building full of books. I learned that the Second World War was so terrible that it caused Adolf Hitler himself to commit suicide. Think of that: He had just been born, and suddenly it was time for him to shoot himself.

"That's history for you. You can read about it yourself.

"My friend Syd Solomon was certainly luckier than Hitler. All Syd had to do was put on a retrospective exhibition. So I tried to help him out—by writing an essay for the front of his catalogue.

"That is certainly one of the nice things about this planet, I think—the way people will try to help other people sometimes.

"In the words of Barbra Streisand, which should perhaps be emblazoned on the facade of this building, along with a picture of an atomic submarine: 'People who need people are the luckiest people in the world.'

"In order to write the essay about Syd's paintings, I had to ask him what he thought he was doing with paint. He was an abstract expressionist, you see. His paintings looked like bright weather to me—neon thunderstorms and the like.

"Was I ever in for a shock! Syd could not tell me what he thought he was doing!

"This did not wobble my opinions of Syd or his work. Syd and his paintings remained as honorable and beautiful as ever. What I lost faith in was the English language—by far the largest language in the world, incidentally. We have more words than anybody.

"But our great language, when confronted by abstract expressionism, was failing Syd and me—and every art critic I ever read.

"The language was speechless!

"Until that moment of truth, I had agreed with the Nobel-prize chemist, the late Irving Langmuir, who once said within my hearing, 'Any person who can't explain his work to a fourteen-year-old is a charlatan.'

"I couldn't believe that anymore.

"So what I finally wrote for Syd's catalogue was your standard load of horse crap about modern art.

"It may be in your library here. Enjoy it in good health.

"But the puzzle has been on my mind ever since—and I have good news for you today. I can once again agree with Dr. Langmuir about charlatans. Here, in simple English, is what Syd Solomon does:

"He meditates. He connects his hand and paintbrush to the deeper, quieter, more mysterious parts of his mind—and he paints pictures of what he sees and feels down there.

"This accounts for the pleasurable shock of recognition we experience when we look at what he does.

"How nice!

"Hooray for Syd Solomon! I say. He is certainly more enterprising and useful than all the quack holy men who meditate deeply, who then announce smugly that it is impossible for them to express what they have seen and felt.

"The heck with inarticulate meditators! And three cheers for all artists who dare to show and tell.

"Since we are here to dedicate a library, let us especially applaud those artists we call writers. By golly, aren't writers wonderful? They don't just keep their meditations to themselves. They very commonly give themselves migraine headaches and ulcers, and destroy their livers and their marriages, too, doing their *best* to show and tell.

"I once learned how to be the other sort of meditator, the sort that doesn't show and tell. I paid Maharishi Mahesh Yogi eighty dollars to show me how.

"Maharishi Mahesh Yogi gave me a mantra, a nonsense word I was supposed to say over and over to myself as I sank deeper and deeper into my mind. I promised not to tell anybody what my mantra was. This was it: *Aye-eem.*

"I will now demonstrate. [*Going into a trance*] *Aye-eem, aye-eem, aye-eem. . . .*

[*Emerging from the trance*] "Where am I? Am I still fifty-four? Or am I eighty-six now? I wouldn't be surprised.

"All right—that was the socially fruitless sort of meditation. I feel mildly refreshed, but I don't see how that can be much use to anybody else in New London or anywhere.

"Now for the socially *fruitful* sort of meditation, which has filled this noble building here: When writers meditate, they don't pick bland, meaningless mantras to say over and over to themselves. They pick mantras that are hot and prickly, full of the sizzle and jingle-jangle of life. They jazz the heck out of their inner beings with the mantras they pick.

"I will give you some examples:

"*War and Peace.*

"*The Origin of Species.*

"*The Iliad.*

"*Decline and Fall of the Roman Empire.*

"*Critique of Pure Reason.*

"*Madame Bovary.*

"*Life on the Mississippi.*

"*Romeo and Juliet.*

"*The Red Badge of Courage.*

"I only wish I had your card catalogue here. I could go on and on with literary mantras that have changed the world for the better.

"About *The Red Badge of Courage,* by the way: That story by Stephen Crane is supposed to be a particularly salutary story for Americans to read—especially during the bicentennial. But I know another story by Crane which, in my opinion, is even more instructive for Americans of our time. Perhaps you know it, too. It is called 'The Blue Hotel.'

" 'The Blue Hotel' is about a foreigner who comes here and commits murder. He imagines that he is defending himself. He has scared himself out of his wits, thinking that Americans are much more dangerous than they really are.

"So he kills.

"So much for that.

"Ten percent of you may be wondering by now why I called this speech 'The Noodle Factory.' One hundred percent of me is delighted to explain:

"It is very simple. The title is an acknowledgment of the fact that most people can't read, or, in any event, don't enjoy it much.

"Reading is such a difficult thing to do that most of our time in school is spent learning how to do that alone. If we had spent as much time at ice skating as we have with reading, we would all be stars with the Hollywood Ice Capades instead of bookworms now.

"As you know, it isn't enough for a reader to pick up the little symbols from a page with his eyes, or, as is the case with a blind person, with his fingertips. Once we get those symbols inside our heads and in the proper order, then we must clothe them in gloom or joy or apathy, in love or hate, in anger or peacefulness, or however the author intended them to be clothed. In order to be good readers, we must even recognize irony—which is when a writer says one thing and really means another, contradicting himself in what he believes to be a beguiling cause.

"We even have to get *jokes*! God help us if we miss a joke.

"So most people give up on reading.

"So—for all the jubilation this new library will generate in the community at large, this building might as well be a noodle factory. Noodles are okay. Libraries are okay. They are rather neutral good news.

"Perhaps the central concept of this beautifully organized speech will enter the patois of Connecticut College.

"One student may say to another, 'You want to go out and drink some beer?'

"The other might reply: 'No. I'm about to flunk out, they tell me. In view of the heartbreaking sacrifices my parents have made to send me here, I guess I'd better go spend some time at the Noodle Factory instead.'

"A student might ask a particularly dumb question of a professor, and the professor might tell him, 'Go to the Noodle Factory and find out.'

"And so on.

"This noble stone-and-steel bookmobile is no bland noodle factory to us, of course, to this band of readers—we few, we happy few. Because we love books so much, this has to be one of the most buxom, hilarious days of our lives.

"Are we foolish to be so elated by books in an age of movies and television? Not in the least, for our ability to read, when combined with libraries like this one, makes us the freest of women and men—and children.

"(That is such a *strange* word on a printed page, incidentally: 'freest—f-r-e-e-s-t.' I'm glad I'm not a foreigner.)

"Anyway—because we are readers, we don't have to wait for some communications executive to decide what we should think about next—and how we should think about it. We can fill our heads with anything from aardvarks to zucchinis—at any time of night or day.

"Even more magically, perhaps, we readers can communicate with each other across space and time so cheaply. Ink and paper are as cheap as sand or water, almost. No board of directors has to convene in order to decide whether we can afford to write down this or that. I myself once staged the end of the world on two pieces of paper—at a cost of less than a penny, including wear and tear on my typewriter ribbon and the seat of my pants.

"Think of that.

"Compare that with the budgets of Cecil B. DeMille.

"Film is simply one more prosthetic device for human beings who are incomplete in some way. We live not only in the Age of Film, but in the Age of False Teeth and Glass Eyes and Toupees and Silicone Breasts—and on and on.

"Film is a perfect prescription for people who will not or cannot read, and have no imagination. Since they have no imaginations, those people can now be shown actors and scenery instead—with appropriate music and all that.

"But, again, film is a hideously expensive way to tell anybody anything—and I include television and all that. What is more: Healthy people exposed to too many actors and too much scenery may wake up some morning to find their own imaginations dead.

"The only cure I know of is a library—and the ability to read.

"Reading exercises the imagination—tempts it to go from strength to strength.

"So much for that.

"It would surely be shapely on an occasion like this if something holy were said. Unfortunately, the speaker you have hired is a Unitarian. I know almost nothing about holy things.

"The language is holy to me, which again shows how little I know about holiness.

"Literature is holy to me, which again shows how little I know about holiness.

"Our freedom to say or write whatever we please in this country is holy to me. It is a rare privilege not only on this planet, but throughout the universe, I suspect. And it is not something somebody gave us. It is a thing we give to ourselves.

"Meditation is holy to me, for I believe that all the secrets of existence and nonexistence are somewhere in our heads—or in other people's heads.

"And I believe that reading and writing are the most nourishing forms of meditation anyone has so far found.

"By reading the writings of the most interesting minds in history, we meditate with our own minds and theirs as well.

"This to me is a miracle.

"The motto of this noble library is the motto of all meditators throughout all time: 'Quiet, please.'

"Thus ends my speech.

"I thank you for your attention."

VIII

MARK TWAIN

I have meditated with Mark Twain's mind. I began doing it when a child. I do it still. It encouraged me when I was young to believe that there was so much that was amusing and beautiful on this continent that I need not be awed by persons from anywhere else. I should model myself after other Americans. I now have mixed feelings about such advice. It hasn't always been convenient or attractive to comport myself as the purely American person I am.

Since I am simultaneously a humorist and a serious novelist, I was asked to speak at the one hundredth anniversary of the completion of Mark Twain's fanciful house in Hartford, Connecticut. The celebration took place on April 30,

1979. As a special honor to me, balls had been racked up on Mark Twain's pool table on the third floor. I was to be allowed to break them with Mark Twain's own cue. I declined. I did not dare give Mark Twain's ghost the opportunity to tell me, by sending the cueball into a corner pocket without touching anything, say, what it thought of me.

My formal remarks on Twain were these:

"To every American writer this is a haunted house. My hair may turn white before this very short speech is done.

"I now quote a previous owner of this house: 'When I find a well-drawn character in fiction or biography, I generally take a warm personal interest in him, for the reason that I have known him before—met him on the river.'

"I submit to you that this is a profoundly Christian statement, an echo of the Beatitudes. It is constructed, as many jokes are, incidentally, with a disarmingly pedestrian beginning and an unexpectedly provoking conclusion.

"I will repeat it, for we are surely here to repeat ourselves. Lovers do almost nothing but repeat themselves.

" 'When I find a well-drawn character in fiction or biography, I generally take a warm personal interest in him, for the reason that I have known him before—met him on the river.'

"Three words, in my opinion, make this a holy joke. They are 'warm' and 'personal' and 'river.' The river, of course, is life—and not just to river pilots but even to desert people, to people who have never even seen water in that long and narrow form. Mark Twain is saying what Christ said in so many ways: that he could not help loving anyone in the midst of life.

"I am of course a skeptic about the divinity of Christ and a scorner of the notion that there is a God who cares how we are or what we do. I was raised this way—in the midst of what provincial easterners imagine to be a Bible Belt. I was confirmed in my skepticism by Mark Twain during my formative years, and by some other good people, too. I have since bequeathed this lack of faith and my love for the body of literature which supports it to my children.

"I am moved on this occasion to put into a few words the ideal my parents and Twain and the rest held before me, and which I have now passed on. The ideal, achieved by few, is this: 'Live so that you can say to God on Judgment Day, "I was a very good person, even though I did not believe in you." ' The word 'God,' incidentally, is capitalized throughout this speech, as are all pronouns referring to Him.

"We religious skeptics would like to swagger some in heaven, saying to others who spent a lot of time quaking in churches down here, 'I was never worried about pleasing or angering God—never took Him into my calculations at all.'

"Religious skeptics often become very bitter toward the end, as did Mark Twain. I do not propose to guess now as to why he became so bitter. I know why I will become bitter. I will finally realize that I have had it right all along: that I will not see God, that there is no heaven or Judgment Day.

"I have used the word 'calculations.' It is a relative of that elegant Missouri verb, 'to calculate.' In Twain's time, and on the frontier, a person who calculated this or that was asking that his lies be respected, since they had been arrived at by means of arithmetic. He wanted you to acknowledge that the arithmetic, the logic of his lies, was sound.

"I know a rowdy joke which is not fit to tell in mixed company in a Victorian home like this one. I can reveal the final line of it, however, without giving offense. This is it: 'Keep your hat on. We may wind up miles from here.' Any writer beginning a story might well say that to himself: 'Keep your hat on. We may wind up miles from here.'

"This is the secret of good storytelling: to lie, but to keep the arithmetic sound. A storyteller, like any other sort of enthusiastic liar, is on an unpredictable adventure. His initial lie, his premise, will suggest many new lies of its own. The storyteller must choose among them, seeking those which are most believable, which keep the arithmetic sound. Thus does a story generate itself.

"The wildest adventure with storytelling, with Missouri calculation, of which I know is *A Connecticut Yankee in King Arthur's Court.* It was written in this sacredly absurd monument—as were *The Adventures of Tom Sawyer, A Tramp Abroad, The Prince and the Pauper, Life on the Mississippi,* from which I have quoted, and the world masterpiece, *Huckleberry Finn.* Twain's most productive years were spent here —from the time he was thirty-nine until he was my age, which is fifty-six. He was my age when he left here to live in Europe and Redding and New York, his greatest work behind him.

"That is how far down the river of life he was when he left here. He could not afford to live here anymore. He was very bad at business.

"About *A Connecticut Yankee:* Its premise, its first lie, seemed to promise a lark. What could be more comical than sending back into the Dark Ages a late-nineteenth-century optimist and technocrat? Such a premise was surely the key to a treasure chest of screamingly funny jokes and situations. Mark Twain would have been wise to say to himself as he picked up that glittering key: 'Keep your hat on. We may wind up miles from here.'

"I will refresh your memories as to where he wound up,

with or without his hat. The Yankee and his little band of electricians and mechanics and what-have-you are being attacked by thousands of English warriors armed with swords and spears and axes. The Yankee has fortified his position with a series of electric fences and a moat. He also has several precursors to modern machine guns, which are Gatling guns.

"Comically enough, thousands of early attackers have already been electrocuted. Ten thousand of the greatest knights in England have been held in reserve. Now they come; I quote, and I invite you to chuckle along with me as I read:

" 'The thirteen Gatlings began to vomit death into the fated ten thousand. They halted, they stood their ground a moment against that withering deluge of fire, and then they broke, faced about, and swept toward the ditch like chaff before a gale. A full fourth part of their force never reached the top of the lofty embankment; the three-fourths reached it and plunged over—to death by drowning.

" 'Within ten short minutes after we had opened fire, armed resistance was totally annihilated, the campaign was ended, we fifty-four were masters of England! Twenty-five thousand men lay dead around us.'

"End quote.

"What a funny ending.

"Mark Twain died in 1910, at the age of seventy-five and four years before the start of World War One. I have heard it said that he predicted that war and all the wars after that in *A Connecticut Yankee*. It was not Twain who did that. It was his premise.

"How appalled this entertainer must have been to have his innocent joking about technology and superstition lead him inexorably to such a ghastly end. Suddenly and horrifyingly, what had seemed so clear throughout the book was not clear at all—who was good, who was bad, who was wise, who was foolish. I ask you, Who was most crazed by superstition and bloodlust, the men with the swords or the men with the Gatling guns?

"And I suggest to you that the fatal premise of *A Connecticut Yankee* remains a chief premise of Western civilization, and increasingly of world civilization, to wit: the sanest, most likeable persons, employing superior technology, will enforce sanity throughout the world.

"Shall I read the ending of *A Connecticut Yankee* to you yet again?

"No need.

"To return to mere storytelling, which never harmed anyone: It is the premise which shapes each story, yes, but the author must furnish the language and the mood.

"It seems clear to me, as an American writing one hundred years after this house was built, that we would not be known as a nation with a supple, amusing, and often beautiful language of our own, if it were not for the genius of Mark Twain. Only a genius could have misrepresented our speech and our wittiness and our common sense and our common decency so handsomely to ourselves and the outside world.

"He himself was the most enchanting American at the heart of each of his tales. We can forgive this easily, for he managed to imply that the reader was enough like him to be his brother. He did this most strikingly in the personae of the young riverboat pilot and Huckleberry Finn. He did this so well that the newest arrival to these shores, very likely a Vietnamese refugee, can, by reading him, begin to imagine that he has some of the idiosyncratically American charm of Mark Twain.

"This is a miracle. There is a name for such miracles, which is myths.

"Imagine, if you will, the opinion we would now hold of ourselves and the opinions others would hold of us, if it were not for the myths about us created by Mark Twain. You can then begin to calculate our debt to this one man.

"One man. Just one man.

"I named my firstborn son after him.

"I thank you for your attention."

FUNNIER ON PAPER THAN
MOST PEOPLE

I am better than most people in my trade at making jokes on paper.

For what it may be worth, I gave this graduation speech at Fredonia College, Fredonia, New York, on May 20, 1978, which contains, among other things, some of my theories about how jokes work, why jokes work:

"Your class spokesperson has just said that she is sick and tired of hearing people say, 'I'm glad I'm not a young person these days.' All I can say is, 'I'm glad I'm not a young person these days.'

"President Beal wished to exclude all negative thinking

from his own farewell to you, and so has asked me to make this announcement: 'All persons who still owe parking fees are to pay up before leaving the property, or there will be unpleasant monkey business with their transcripts.'

"When I was a boy in Indianapolis, there was a humorist there named Kin Hubbard. He wrote a few lines for *The Indianapolis News* every day. Indianapolis needs all the humorists it can get. He was often as witty as Oscar Wilde. He said, for instance, that Prohibition was better than no liquor at all. He said that whoever named near-beer was a poor judge of distance. He said that it was no disgrace to be poor, but that it might as well be. He went to a graduation ceremony one time, and he said afterward that he thought it would be better if all the really important stuff was spread out over four years instead of being saved up for the very end.

"Well—I assume that the really important stuff has been spread out over the years here at Fredonia, and that you have no need of anything much from me. This is lucky for me. I have only this to say, basically: This is the end—this is childhood's end for certain. 'Sorry about that,' as they used to say in the Vietnam War.

"Perhaps you have read the novel *Childhood's End* by Arthur C. Clarke, one of the few masterpieces in the field of science fiction. All of the others were written by me. In Clark's novel, mankind suddenly undergoes a spectacular evolutionary change. The children become very different from the parents, less physical, more spiritual—and one day they form up into a sort of column of light which spirals out into the universe, its mission unknown. The book ends there. You seniors, however, look a great deal like your parents, and I doubt that you will go radiantly into space as soon as you have your diplomas in hand. It is far more likely that you will go to Buffalo or Rochester or East Quogue—or Cohoes.

"And I suppose you will all want money and true love, among other things. I will tell you how to make money: Work very hard. I will tell you how to win love: Wear nice clothing and smile all the time. Learn the words to all the latest songs.

"What other advice can I give you? Eat lots of bran to provide necessary bulk in your diet. The only advice my father ever gave me was this: 'Never stick anything in your ear.' The tiniest bones in your body are inside your ears, you know—and your sense of balance, too. If you mess around with your ears, you could not only become deaf, but you could also start falling down all the time. So just leave your ears completely alone. They're fine, just the way they are.

"Don't murder anybody—even though New York State does not put people in the electric chair anymore.

"That's about it.

"One sort of optional thing you might do is to realize that there are six seasons instead of four. The poetry of four seasons is all wrong for this part of the planet, and this may explain why we are so depressed so much of the time. I mean, spring doesn't feel like spring a lot of the time, and November is all wrong for autumn, and so on. Here is the truth about the seasons: Spring is May and June. What could be springier than May and June? Summer is July and August. Really hot, right? Autumn is September and October. See the pumpkins? Smell those burning leaves? Next comes the season called Locking. That is when nature shuts everything down. November and December aren't winter. They're Locking. Next comes winter, January and February. Boy! Are they ever cold! What comes next? Not spring. 'Unlocking' comes next. What else could cruel March and only slightly less cruel April be? March and April are not spring. They are Unlocking.

"One more optional piece of advice: If you ever have to give a speech, start with a joke, if you know one. For years I have been looking for the best joke in the world. I think I know what it is. I will tell it to you, but you have to help me. You have to say, 'No,' when I hold up my hand like this. All right? Don't let me down.

"Do you know why cream is so much more expensive than milk?"

[AUDIENCE: "No."]

"It is because the cows hate to squat on those little bottles.

"That is the best joke I know. One time when I worked for the General Electric Company over in Schenectady, I had to write speeches for company officers. I put that joke about the cows and the little bottles in a speech for a vice-president. He was reading along, and he had never heard the joke before. He couldn't stop laughing, and he had to be led away from the podium with a nosebleed. I was fired the next day.

"How do jokes work? The beginning of each good one challenges you to think. We are such earnest animals. When I asked you about cream, you could not help yourselves. You really tried to think of a sensible answer. Why does a chicken cross the road? Why does a fireman wear red suspenders? Why did they bury George Washington on the side of a hill?

"The second part of the joke announces that nobody wants you to think, nobody wants to hear your wonderful answer. You are so relieved to at last meet somebody who doesn't demand that you be intelligent. You laugh for joy.

"I have in fact designed this entire speech so as to allow you to be as stupid as you like, without strain, and without penalties of any kind. I have even written a ridiculous song

176

for the occasion. It lacks music, but we are up to our necks
in composers here. One is sure to come along. The words go
like this:

> Oh, farewell, farewell to Fredonia,
> Adios to teachers and pneumonia.
> If I find out where the party is,
> I'll telephone ya.
> I love you so much, Sonya,
> That I am going to buy you a begonia.
> You love me, too, doan ya, Sonya?

"See—you were trying to guess what the next rhyme was
going to be. Nobody cares how smart you are. So laugh with
relief.

"I am being so silly because I pity you so much. I pity all
of us so much. Life is going to be very tough again, just as
soon as this is over. And the most useful thought we can hold
when all hell cuts loose again is that we are not members of
different generations, as unlike, as some people would have
us believe, as Eskimos and Australian aborigines. We are all
so close together in time that we should think of ourselves
as brothers and sisters. I have several children—six, to be
exact—too many children for an atheist, certainly. Whenever my children complain about the planet to me, I say:
'Shut up! I just got here myself. Who do you think I am—
Methuselah? You think I like the news of the day any better
than you do? You're wrong.'

"We are all experiencing more or less the same lifetime
now.

"What is it the slightly older people want from the slightly
younger people? They want credit for having survived so
long, and often imaginatively, under difficult conditions.

Slightly younger people are intolerably stingy about giving them credit for that.

"What is it the slightly younger people want from the slightly older people? More than anything, I think, they want acknowledgment and without further ado that they are, *without question,* women and men now. Slightly older people are intolerably stingy about making any such acknowledgment.

"Therefore, I take it upon myself to pronounce those about to graduate women and men. No one must ever treat them like children again. Neither must they ever act like children—ever again.

"This is what is known as a puberty ceremony.

"I realize that it is coming a little late, but better late than never. Every primitive society ever studied has had a puberty ceremony, at which former children became unchallengeably women and men. Some Jewish communities still honor this old practice, of course, and benefit from it, in my opinion. But, by and large, ultramodern, massively industrialized societies like ours have decided to do without puberty ceremonies—unless you want to count the issuance of driver's licenses at the age of sixteen. If you want to count that as a puberty ceremony, then it has a highly unusual feature: a judge can take your puberty away again, even if you're fifty-six, like me.

"Another event in the lives of American and European males which might be considered a puberty ceremony is war. If a male comes home from a war, especially with serious wounds, everybody agrees: Here indeed is a man. When I came home to Indianapolis from the Second World War in Germany, an uncle of mine said to me, 'By golly—you look like a man now.' I wanted to strangle him. If I had, he would have been the first German I'd killed. I was a man before I went to war, but he was damned if he would say so.

"I suggest to you that the withholding of a puberty cere-mony from young males in our society is a scheme, devised cunningly but subconsciously, to make those males eager to go to war, no matter how terrible or unjust a war may be. There are just wars, too, of course. The war I was eager to go to happened to be a just one.

"And when does a female stop being a little girl and be-come a woman, with all the rights and privileges appertain-ing thereto? We all know the answer in our bones: when she has a baby in wedlock, of course. If she has that first baby out of wedlock, she is still a child. What could be simpler or more natural and more obvious than that—or, in these days and in this society, at least, more unjust, irrelevant, and just plain stupid?

"I think we had better, for our own safety, reinstate pu-berty ceremonies.

"I not only declare those about to graduate women and men. With all the powers vested in me, I pronounce them clarks, as well. Most of you know, I'm sure, that all white people named Clark are descended from inhabitants of the British Isles who were remarkable for being able to read and write. A black person named Clark, of course, would be descended, most likely, from someone who was forced to work without pay or rights of any kind by a white person named Clark. An interesting family—the Clarks.

"I realize that you graduaters are all specialized in some way. But you have spent most of the past sixteen or more years learning to read and write. People who can read and write expertly, as you can, are miracles and, in my opinion, entitle us to suspect that we may be civilized after all. It is terribly hard to learn to read and write. It takes forever.

When we scold our schoolteachers about the low reading scores of their students, we pretend that it is the easiest thing in the world: to teach a person to read and write. Try it sometime, and you will discover that it is nearly impossible.

"What good is being a clark, now that we have computers and movies and television? Clarking, a wholly human enterprise, is sacred. Machinery is not. Clarking is the most profound and effective form of meditation practiced on this planet, and far surpasses any dream experienced by a Hindu on a mountaintop. Why? Because clarks, by reading well, can think the thoughts of the wisest and most interesting human minds throughout all history. When clarks meditate, even if they themselves have only mediocre intellects, they do it with the thoughts of angels. What could be more sacred than that?

"So much for puberty and clarking. Only two major subjects remain to be covered: loneliness and boredom. No matter how old we are, we are going to be bored and lonely during what remains of our lives.

"We are so lonely because we don't have enough friends and relatives. Human beings are supposed to live in stable, like-minded, extended families of fifty people or more. In Nigeria it's common for Ibos to have a thousand relatives who know them quite well. When a baby is born, it is taken on a long trip, so it can meet all its relatives. This sort of thing is still quite common in Europe today, although the number one-thousand is far too high for there. When we or our ancestors came to America, though, we were agreeing, among other things, to do without such families. It is a painful, unhuman agreement to make. Emotionally, it is hideously expensive.

"Your class spokesperson mourned the collapse of the institution of marriage in this country. Marriage is collapsing because our families are too small. A man cannot be a whole society to a woman, and a woman cannot be a whole society to a man. We try, but it is scarcely surprising that so many of us go to pieces.

"So I recommend that everybody here join all sorts of organizations, no matter how ridiculous, simply to get more people in his or her life. It does not matter much if all the other members are morons. Quantities of relatives of any sort are what we need.

"As for boredom: Friedrich Wilhelm Nietzsche, a German philosopher who died seventy-eight years ago, had this to say: 'Against boredom even the gods contend in vain.' We are supposed to be bored. It is a part of life. Learn to put up with it, or you will not be what I have declared the members of this graduating class to be: mature women and men.

"I come to a close now by noting that the news magazines, whose business is to know and understand everything, have found this year's graduates to be apathetic. This year's graduates have tired blood. They need Geritol. Well, as a member of a zippier generation, with sparkle in its eyes and a snap in its stride, let me tell you what kept us as high as kites a lot of the time: hatred. All my life I've had people to hate— from Hitler to Nixon, not that those two are at all comparable in their villainy. It is a tragedy, perhaps, that human beings can get so much energy and enthusiasm from hate. If you want to feel ten feet tall, as though you could run a hundred miles without stopping, hate beats pure cocaine any day. Hitler resurrected Germany, a beaten, bankrupt, half-starved nation, with hatred and nothing more. Imagine that.

"So it seems quite likely to me that the class of 1978 in the United States of America is not in fact apathetic, but only looks that way to people who are used to getting their ecstasies from hatred. The members of the class of 1978 are not sleepy, are not listless, are not apathetic. They are simply performing the experiment of doing without hate. Hate is the missing vitamin in their diet, and they have sensed correctly that hate, in the long run, is about as nourishing as cyanide.

"This is a very exciting thing they are doing, and I wish them well."

ONE reason I feel the need to be funnier on paper than most of my colleagues is that I have a German name, which can be counted on to remind almost any sort of American for at least a microsecond of German enemies in two world wars. I myself, a prisoner of war of the Germans, am so reminded for at least that microsecond when I hear a German name. I was on *our* side, remember?

So it is a good idea for me to tell a joke as soon as possible.

I have spoken to, and actually liked, several German veterans of the Second World War who live in America now. They, too, become screamingly funny as soon as possible.

And it may be that Mark Twain drew some of his comic energy from a similar uneasiness. He had served the Confederacy briefly, after all, in the bloodiest war in American history, and later faced paying audiences of, among others, Union veterans and their wives.

AN advantage of a writer's having a joke-making capability is that he or she can be really funny in case something really is funny. Most contemporary American novelists, especially those credited with greatness because their books are so huge, cannot be funny even when it is time to be funny. So they have to pretend to be dealing at all times with matters so serious, good and evil, for example, that there could not possibly be anything funny about them. Thus are their works as consistently lugubrious as bloodhounds appear to be.

The books of jokesters are short, which is a social disadvantage in an era when literary importance is measured by the pound. The problem is that jokes deal so efficiently with ideas that there is little more to be said after the punch line has been spoken. It is time to come up with a new idea—and another good joke.

❦

I once asked my friend Joe Heller what he was up to. He said that he had an idea for a new book. I said that one idea wasn't nearly enough for a whole book. I said this because he is a funny writer.

If he had been a serious writer, I would have said one idea was more than enough for a trilogy.

❦

THE worst thing about a writer's having a joke-making capability, of course, as James Thurber of Columbus, Ohio, pointed out in an essay years ago, is this: No matter what is being discussed, the jokester is going to head for a punch line every time.

❦

SOME smart young critic will soon quote that line above against me, imagining that I am too dumb to realize that I have condemned myself, too dense to know that I have accidentally put my finger on what is awfully wrong with me.

❦

I am often asked to give advice to young writers who wish to be famous and fabulously well-to-do. This is the best I have to offer:

While looking as much like a bloodhound as possible, announce that you are working twelve hours a day on a masterpiece. Warning: All is lost if you crack a smile.

EMBARRASSMENT

a friend of mine once spoke to me about what he
called the "existential hum," the uneasiness
which keeps us moving, which never allows us to feel entirely
at ease. He had tried heroin once. He said he understood at
once the seductiveness of that narcotic. For the first time in
his life, he was not annoyed by the existential hum.

I would describe the hum that is with me all the time as
embarrassment. I have somehow disgraced myself.

My Indianapolis relatives may actually feel that I have
done so. They are not enthusiastic about my work. I have
already described my Uncle John's distaste for it. As for my
Uncle Alex: I dedicated *The Sirens of Titan* to him, and he

said he could not read it. He supposed that beatniks would think it was wonderful. My Aunt Ella, who owned Stewart's Bookstore in Louisville, Kentucky, would not stock my books. She found them degenerate, and said so.

The only big write-up I have so far received in my home town appeared in the October 1976 issue of *Indianapolis Magazine,* a publication of the Chamber of Commerce. It began like this:

Whether they like his book or not (some don't), most of those who know Kurt Vonnegut, Jr., agree that he is a nice guy.

In Indianapolis his aunts, cousins and old friends call him Kay, and their memories of him are fond and lively. His Aunt, Irma Vonnegut Lindener, says warmly, "He's a dear, awfully nice," and her eyes light up with affection as she recounts thoughtful things he has done for the family over the years. He shared an enviable rapport with his uncle, Alex Vonnegut . . . though they were worlds apart in their convictions.

The tremendous gap between the old world gentility of Vonnegut's relatives and his own contemporary manner of living, thinking and writing has not dimmed the fondness that exists between them. Mrs. Lindener, an intellectual, articulate woman, admits that she has not read *Breakfast of Champions,* and doesn't intend to. She is also puzzled by some of his other books, but her pride in his achievement as a major novelist is not diminished by a difference in point of view . . .

More offensive to my relatives than my books, even, I think, is the fact of my being divorced. In the history of my family in America, I am only the second member to have been divorced. When I returned to Indianapolis for the funeral of Uncle Alex, at the Flanner and Buchanan funeral home, a girl cousin I had once been very close to turned her back on me—because I had not stuck with my first wife through thick and thin.

❧

THE only other Vonnegut to get divorced was my Uncle Walter—again, a first cousin of my father. He, too, had the hubris to seek his fortune in the arts in New York City—as an actor on the stage. He was a protégé of the then premiere novelist of Indianapolis, who was Booth Tarkington. I never met Mr. Tarkington, although I lived for a while only a block from his home on North Meridian Street, where he died in 1946. His use of black people for comic relief in some of his stories, no matter how kindly Mr. Tarkington's intentions, makes the stories sound somewhat dated today.

Be that as it may, Mr. Tarkington was a first-rate playwright on top of everything else, which I am not, and he saw Uncle Walter in amateur productions in Indianapolis, and urged him to come here in the late 1920s, which Uncle Walter did.

He was an instant success as a supporting actor, appearing, for example, with Humphrey Bogart in *The Petrified Forest.* His wife Marjorie also did well as a supporting actress, and Uncle Walter and Aunt Marjorie and their two children, Walter, Jr., and Irma Ruth, were all in the cast of Eugene O'Neill's only comedy, *Ah, Wilderness!,* starring George M. Cohan. Think of that: four Vonneguts all at once in a Broadway play.

When I first came to New York City as a working grown-up, as a public relations man for General Electric, based in Schenectady, older people would often ask me if I was related to Walter and Marjorie Vonnegut. They were remembered as actors and bon vivants. They drank a lot. They drank hard liquor in speakeasies, and had stories to tell about gangsters they had met.

They got divorced because Marjorie fell in love with Don Marquis, the creator of *Archie and Mehitabel*. Marquis was a bachelor then, and she married him.

Late in the 1930s Uncle Walter had trouble getting parts because of his drinking, and he came home to Indiana with a new wife, a pretty young actress named Rosalie, who was never really accepted by the family. They built a little house in an orchard in northern Indiana, which Uncle Walter's widowed mother owned. They lived there and drank a lot, and talked about starting a little repertory company there in the wilderness, as boozed-up former actors and actresses will do.

They died pretty soon.

❦

JANE Cox Vonnegut and I, childhood sweethearts in Indianapolis, separated in 1970 after a marriage which by conventional measurement was said to have lasted twenty-five years. We are still good friends, as they say. Like so many couples who are no longer couples these days, we have been through some terrible, unavoidable accident that we are ill-equipped to understand. Like our six children, we only just arrived on this planet and we were doing the best we could. We never saw what hit us. It wasn't another woman, it wasn't another man.

We woke up in ambulances headed for different hospitals, so to speak, and would never get together again. We were alive, yes, but the marriage was dead.

And it was no Lazarus.

It was a good marriage for a long time—and then it wasn't. The shock of having our children no longer need us happened somewhere in there. We were both going to have to find other sorts of seemingly important work to do and other compelling reasons for working and worrying so. But I am beginning to explain, which is a violation of a rule I lay down whenever I teach a class in writing: "All you can do is tell what happened. You will get thrown out of this course if you are arrogant enough to imagine that you can tell me why it happened. You do not know. You cannot know."

❦

So I am embarrassed about the failure of my first marriage. I am embarrassed by my older relatives' responses to my books. But I was embarrassed before I was married or had written a book. A bad dream I have dreamed for as long as I can remember may hold a clue. In that dream, I know that I have murdered an old woman a long time ago. I have led an exemplary life ever since.

But now the police have come to get me, with incontrovertible evidence of my crime. This is more or less the plot of Dostoevski's *Crime and Punishment,* of course. By coincidence, Dostoevski and I have the same birthday, too.

COULD that woman be my mother? I asked a psychiatrist that. She said that the woman might not even be a woman. She could be a man.

I went to a Hindu with occult powers, supposedly. I answered his ad in *The Village Voice,* in which he offered to tell people for a fee what they had been in previous lives. I asked him whether I had ever killed anybody in another life. He replied that I had lived only once before, and that my highest rank was as a squire to a knight in northern Europe. I had in fact killed a child accidentally. My knight and I and some others were riding through a village, and a child somehow fell under the hooves of my horse.

"It was not your fault," said the seer.

Even so.

❦

LONG after I started dreaming that dream, I did a story for *Life* magazine about a mass murderer in Provincetown, Massachusetts. He and my daughter Edith knew each other some. His name was Tony Costa.

He was adjudged guilty and insane. He was put into Bridgewater, a Massachusetts institution for the criminally insane—not all that far from Provincetown. That was where they put the Boston Strangler also. Tony Costa and the Strangler killed only women. Tony Costa killed women who were young and nubile and adventuresome, unafraid to go with presentable strangers almost anywhere. The Strangler killed any sort of woman he could catch alone.

Tony Costa and I exchanged a few letters after he was put away. He would eventually hang himself. The message of his letters to me was that a person as intent on being virtuous as he was could not possibly have harmed a fly. He believed it.

I know the feeling.

HAVE I ever really killed anybody, even in a war? Not that I know of. Maybe I have forgotten. I await the police.

xl

RELIGION

t OWARD the end of our marriage, it was mainly religion in a broad sense that Jane and I fought about. She came to devote herself more and more to making alliances with the supernatural in her need to increase her strength and understanding—and happiness and health. This was painful to me. She could not understand and cannot understand why that should have been painful to me, or why it should be any of my business at all.

And it is to suggest to her and to some others why it was painful that I chose for this book's epigraph a quotation from a thin book, *Instruction in Morals,* published in 1900 and written by my Free Thinker great-grandfather Clemens Von-negut, then seventy-six years old:

"Whoever entertains liberal views and chooses a consort that is captured by superstition risks his liberty and his happiness."

❧

I did not know that my great-grandfather had said such a thing, or even that he had written a book, until about ten days ago. My brother Bernard sent the book to me then, after picking it up on a recent trip to Indianapolis. Bernard also sent me a copy of Clemens Vonnegut's comments on life and death, which were read at his funeral. Clemens Vonnegut planned his own funeral in 1874, and actually died in 1906. His words to his mourners were these:

"Friends or Opponents: To all of you who stand here to deliver my body to the earth:

"To you, my next of kin:

"Do not mourn! I have now arrived at the end of the course of life, as you will eventually arrive at yours. I am at rest and nothing will ever disturb my deep slumber.

"I am disturbed by no worries, no grief, no fears, no wishes, no passions, no pains, no reproaches from others. All is infinitely well with me.

"I departed from life with loving, affectionate feelings for all mankind; and I admonish you: Be aware of this truth that the people on this earth could be joyous, if only they would live rationally and if they would contribute mutually to each others' welfare.

"This world is not a vale of sorrows if you will recognize discriminatingly what is truly excellent in it; and if you will avail yourself of it for mutual happiness and well-being. Therefore, let us explain as often as possible, and particularly at the departure from life, that we base our faith on firm foundations, on Truth for putting into action our ideas which do not depend on fables and ideas which Science has long ago proven to be false.

"We also wish Knowledge, Goodness, Sympathy, Mercy, Wisdom, Justice, and Truthfulness. We also strive for and venerate all of those attributes from which the fantasy of man has created a God. We also strive for the virtues of Temperance, Industriousness, Friendship, and Peace. We believe in pure ideas based on Truth and Justice.

"Therefore, however, we do not believe, cannot believe, that a Thinking Being existed for millions and millions of years, and eventually and finally out of nothing—through a Word—created this world, or rather this earth with its Firmament, its Sun and Moon and the Stars.

"We cannot believe that this Being formed a human being from clay and breathed into it an Immortal Soul, and then allowed this human being to procreate millions, and then delivered them all into unspeakable misery, wretchedness and pain for all eternity. Nor can we believe that the descendents of one or two human beings will inevitably become sinners; nor do we believe that through the criminal executions of an Innocent One may we be redeemed."

❦

SUCH is my ancestral religion. How it was passed on to me is a mystery. By the time I got to know them, my parents were both so woozy with Weltschmerz that they weren't passing anything on—not the German language, not their love for German music, not the family history, nothing. Everything was all over with. They were *kaput*.

So I must have questioned them, finally, about what our family believed. I must have noticed that the Goldsteins and the Waleses and others proudly believed one thing or another, and I wanted a belief to be proud of, too.

How proud I became of our belief, how pigheadedly proud, even, is the most evident thing in my writing, I think. Haven't I already attributed the breakup of my first marriage in part to my wife's failure to share my family belief with me?

And did I not speak in this Free Thinking manner to the graduating class at Hobart and William Smith Colleges in Geneva, New York, on May 26, 1974:

"Kin Hubbard was an Indianapolis newspaper humorist. He wrote under the name of Abe Martin. My father, who was an Indianapolis architect, knew him some. Kin Hubbard had fault to find with commencement addresses. He thought that all the really important information should be spread out over four years, instead of being saved up for one big speech at the very end.

"That is an elegant joke, although nobody here seems to be hemorrhaging with laughter. That is just as well. I want us to be serious. I want us to ponder seriously about commencement addresses, to realize what it is that is withheld from students until the very end. In the fiction game, we call a marvelous thing withheld until the very end the 'snapper' of a tale. O. Henry probably devised more snappers than any other writer in history. So what is the snapper of a college education? What is the thing colleges hire outsiders to deliver on commencement day?

"The outsider is expected to answer the questions: what is life all about, and what are new college graduates supposed to do with it now?

"This information has to be saved up until the very end for this good reason: No responsible, truth-loving teacher can answer those questions in class, or even in the privacy of his office or home. No respecter of evidence has ever found the least clue as to what life is all about, and what people should do with it.

"Oh, there have been lots of brilliant guesses. But honest, educated people have to identify them as such—as guesses. What are guesses worth? Scientifically and legally, they are not worth doodley-squat. As the saying goes: Your guess is as good as mine.

"The guesses we like best, as with so many things we like best, were taught to us in childhood—by people who loved us and wished us well. We are reluctant to criticize those guesses. It is an ultimate act of rudeness to find fault with anything which is given to us in a spirit of love. So a modern, secular education is often painful. By its very nature, it invites us to question the wisdom of the ones we love.

"Too bad.

"I have said that one guess is as good as another, but that is only roughly so. Some guesses are crueler than others— which is to say, harder on human beings, and on other animals as well. The belief that God wants heretics burned to death is a case in point. Some guesses are more suicidal than others. The belief that a true lover of God is immune to the bites of copperheads and rattlesnakes is a case in point. Some guesses are greedier and more egocentric than others. Belief

196

in the divine right of kings and presidents is a case in point.

"Those are all discredited guesses. But it is reasonable to suppose that other bad guesses are poisoning our lives today. A good education in skepticism can help us to discover those bad guesses, and to destroy them with mockery and contempt. Most of them were made by honest, decent people who had no way of knowing what we know, or what we can find out, if we want to. We have one hell of a lot of good information about our bodies, about our planet, and the universe—about our past. We don't have to guess as much as the old folks did.

"Bertrand Russell declared that, in case he met God, he would say to Him, 'Sir, you did not give us enough information.' I would add to that, 'All the same, Sir, I'm not persuaded that we did the best we could with the information we had. Toward the end there, anyway, we had tons of information.'

"Our most dismaying failure is in the use of our knowledge of what human beings need in the way of bodily and spiritual nourishment. And I suspect that some of the guesses made by our ancestors are partly responsible for the starved bodies and spirits we see everywhere.

"Shame on us. Less shame on our ancestors.

"I myself am an ancestor, having reproduced, having written books, being fifty-one years old. I come from simpler times. When I was a boy, all a commencement speaker had to say was, 'Go out and kill Hitler, boy. And then get married and have a lot of kids.'

"Some of you might still go looking for Hitler, in Paraguay, say. He might be there. He would be eighty-five years old now. He has probably shaved off his mustache.

"Some of you might go out and kill Communists, but that

is no longer a fashionable thing to do. And you wouldn't be killing real Communists anyway. This country has fulfilled more of the requirements of the Communist Manifesto than any avowedly Communist nation ever did. Maybe we're the Communists.

"Our politicians like to say that we have religion and the Communist countries don't. I think it is just the other way around. Those countries have a religion called Communism, and the Free World is where sustaining religions are in very short supply.

"I am about to make my own ancestral guess as to what life is all about, and what young people should do with it. I will again issue the caveat that I am as full of baloney as anybody, and that anybody who says for sure what life is all about might as well lecture on Santa Claus and the Easter Bunny, and tooth fairies, as well.

"I am, incidentally, the world's greatest authority on tooth fairies. That is how most of my life has been spent: in the study of tooth fairies. That should be carved on my tombstone. I was the one who discovered that tooth fairies are cannibals. Mostly, Tooth Fairies eat june bugs, of course. But under crowded conditions and in an atmosphere rich in carbon monoxide, tooth fairies eat each other, too.

"And who can blame them?

"Okay.

"What should young people do with their lives today? Many things, obviously. But the most daring thing is to create stable communities in which the terrible disease of loneliness can be cured. Young people should also identify and expound theories about life in which sane human beings almost everywhere can believe.

"I suggest that we need a new religion. If suggesting

that we need a new religion is sacrilege, then the emperor Constantine was guilty of sacrilege, and the emperor Nero was an admirably pious man. And I want to point out that it is impossible to discard an old religion entirely. The religion of Nero survives today, determining as it does the dates and even moods of so many of our so-called Christian holidays.

"Easter is a time for the renewal of life, and it always has been, apparently, even when people ate mastodon meat. Nothing is more human than to wish for renewal when springtime comes. And, out of respect for our ancestors, it is in the area of spiritual renewal that we are the most conservative. We must become less conservative.

"What makes me think we need a new religion? That's easy. An effective religion allows people to imagine from moment to moment what is going on and how they should behave. Christianity used to be like that. Our country is now jammed with human beings who say out loud that life is chaos to them, and that it doesn't seem to matter what anybody does next. This is worse than being seasick.

"Might not we do without religion entirely? Plenty of people have tried—not in Communist countries, as I've already said, but here. A lot of people have been forced to do without it—because the old-time religions they know of are too superstitious, too full of magic, too ignorant about biology and physics to harmonize with the present day.

"They are told to have faith. Faith in what? Faith in faith, as nearly as I can tell. That is as detailed as many contemporary preachers care to be, except when amazing audiences of cavemen. How can a preacher tell us about men and women who heard voices without raising questions about schizophrenia, a disease which we know is common in all places and all times.

"We know too much for old-time religion; and in a way, that knowledge is killing us.

"The Book of Genesis is usually taken to be a story about what happened a long time ago. The beginning of it, at least, can also be read as a prophecy of what is going on right now. It may be that Eden is this planet. If that is so, then we are still in it. It may be that we, poisoned by all our knowledge, are still crawling toward the gate.

"Can we spit out all our knowledge? I don't think that is possible. It is something I have often wanted to do. We are stuck with our knowledge, which has seeped into all of our tissues. We had better make the best of a bad situation, which is a wonderful human skill. We had better make use of what has poisoned us, which is knowledge.

"What can we use it for?

"Why don't we use it to devise realistic methods for preventing us from crawling out the gate of the Garden of Eden? We're such wonderful mechanics, maybe we can lock that gate with us inside.

"It is springtime here in Paradise. There is hope in the air!

"If I talk about the Loud family now, will all of you know who I mean? I don't mean everybody's noisy neighbors. I mean a family of prosperous human beings in California, whose last name is Loud. They were the willing subjects last year of a television documentary. Seemingly invisible cameramen and sound men were able to record for all time even the most disappointing and embarrassing moments in their lives.

"Most viewers, and the Louds themselves, claimed to be mystified by the tinhorn tragedies and unfunny comedies thus immortalized. I suggest to you that the Louds were healthy earthlings who had everything but a religion in which they could believe. There was nothing to tell them what they should want, what they should shun, what they should do next. Socrates told us that the unexamined life wasn't worth living. The Louds demonstrated that the morally unstructured life is a clunker, too.

"Christianity could not nourish the Louds. Neither could Buddhism or the profit motive or participation in the arts, or any other nostrum on America's spiritual smorgasbord. So the Louds were dying before our eyes.

"If my analysis is correct, then we have a formula for more such successful TV shows. Each show can feature an otherwise healthy family, from which a single life-sustaining element has been withheld. We might begin with the Watson family, which has everything but water. But no family could survive an entire television season without water, so we had better give the Watsons a diet absolutely devoid of Vitamin B complex, instead.

"We wouldn't tell the audience or the critics or the Watsons what was really wrong with the Watsons. We would pretend to be as puzzled as anybody about why they weren't happier with their quadraphonic sound system and their tap dancing lessons and their Pontiac Ventura and all. We would take part in symposia with ministers and sociologists, and so forth, reaching no firm conclusions—while the Watsons slowly died of beriberi.

"A microscopic quantity of vitamins could save the Watsons. But a ton of Billy Grahams couldn't save the Louds. They know too much.

"Now is as good a time as any to mention White House prayer breakfasts, I guess. I think we all know now that religion of that sort is about as nourishing to the human spirit as potassium cyanide. We have been experimenting with it. Every guinea pig died. We are up to our necks in dead guinea pigs.

"The lethal ingredient in those breakfasts wasn't prayer. And it wasn't the eggs or the orange juice or the hominy grits. It was a virulent new strain of hypocrisy which did everyone in.

"Talk about typhoid Mary!

"If I have offended anyone here by talking of the need of a new religion, I apologize. I am willing to drop the word religion, and substitute for it these three words: *heartfelt moral code*. We sure need such a thing, and it should be simple enough and reasonable enough for anyone to understand. The trouble with so many of the moral codes we have inherited is that they are subject to so many interpretations. We require specialists, historians and archaeologists and linguists and so on, to tell us where this or that idea may have come from, to suggest what this or that statement might actually mean. This is good news for hypocrites, who enjoy feeling pious, no matter what they do.

"If we were to try to grow recent strains of hypocrisy in the laboratory, what would we grow them in? I think they would grow like Jack's beanstalk in a mulch of ancient moral codes.

"It may be that moral simplicity is not possible in modern times. It may be that simplicity and clarity can come only from a new messiah, who may never come. We can talk about portents, if you like. I like a good portent as much as anyone. What might be the meaning of the comet Kahoutek, which was to make us look upward, to impress us with the paltriness of our troubles, to cleanse our souls with cosmic awe? Kahoutek was a fizzle, and what might this fizzle mean?

"I take it to mean that we can expect no spectacular miracles from the heavens, that the problems of ordinary human beings will have to be solved by ordinary human beings. The message of Kahoutek is: 'Help is not on the way. Repeat: help is not on the way.'

"What about visitors from other planets, who are supposed to be so smart? A lot of people believe that they have already been here, and that they taught us how to build pyramids. One thing that even the Egyptians can agree on, I think, is that we don't need any more pyramids.

"As an ordinary person, appalled as I am by the speed with which we are wrecking our topsoil, our drinking water, and our atmosphere, I will suggest an idea about good and evil which might fit into a modern and simple moral code. Evil disgusts us. Good fills us with joy and brings a sparkle to our eyes. That much remains the same. Might we not go farther, though, and say that anything which wounds the planet is evil, and anything which preserves it or heals it is good?

"Let me be the first to say that the idea is sappy, whatever that means. I think sappiness has something to do with being concerned about grandchildren, and the hell with them. But the worst thing about my moral code is that it invites people to have the fun of being glamorously wicked at first, which many of us feel is sexy, and then becoming almost swooningly virtuous at the end. This comes close to being the biography of Saint Augustine, and of several other famous holy men.

"On a larger scale, entire nations love to blow the hell out of other nations, and then to come like angels to pass out glass eyes and artificial limbs and Hershey bars and all that, to rebuild everything, to get everything going again.

"We would have to understand from the first the scientific fact that any wound we inflict on the life-support systems of this planet is likely to be quite permanent. So anyone who wounded the planet, and then pretended to heal it, would simply be another hypocrite. He would remain quite permanently an evil and therefore disgusting human being.

"I went to a Unitarian church for a while, and it might show. The minister said one Easter Sunday that, if we listened closely to the bell on his church, we would hear that it was singing, over and over again, 'No hell, no hell, no hell.' No matter what we did in life, he said, we wouldn't burn throughout eternity in hell. We wouldn't even fry for ten or fifteen minutes. He was just guessing, of course.

"Jimmy Breslin, on the other hand, told me one time that he sort of hankered to get back into Catholicism, because he thought there were a lot of people in the Nixon administration who deserved to roast in hell. Maybe so.

"At any rate, I don't think anybody ever dreaded hell as much as most of us dread the contempt of our fellowmen. Under our new and heartfelt moral code, we might be able to horrify would-be evildoers with just that: the contempt of their fellowmen.

"For that contempt to be effective, though, we would need cohesive communities, which are about as common as bald eagles these days. And it is curious that such communities should be so rare, since human beings are genetically such gregarious creatures. They need plenty of like-minded friends and relatives almost as much as they need B-complex vitamins and a heartfelt moral code.

"I know Sargent Shriver slightly. When he was campaigning for vice-president, he asked me if I had any ideas. You remember that there was plenty of money around, but as far as ideas went, both parties were in a state of destitution. So I told him, and I am afraid he didn't listen, that the number one American killer wasn't cardiovascular disease, but loneliness. I told him that he and McGovern could swamp the Republicans if they would promise to cure that disease. I even gave him a slogan to put on buttons and bumpers and flags and billboards: Lonesome No More!

"The rest is history.

"I was in Biafra several years ago, at the bitter end of the Nigerian civil war. The Biafrans had nothing to eat, you'll remember. They were blockaded, so no food got in. They had almost nothing to fight with, except for some Mauser rifles which were a good deal older than I was. And still they fought on. They had no recruiting program. There was no governmental scheme for the relief of refugees, and none was needed. The government did nothing to look out for the old, the sick, either. Biafra, for the short time it lasted, could be admired simultaneously by both anarchists and conservatives.

"The people could look out for each other, without any help from the central government, because every Biafran was a member of an extended family. He had hundreds of relatives he knew by name and reputation. Some Biafrans had thousands of relatives or more.

"Those families took care of their own wounded, their own lunatics, their own refugees. They shared equally whatever they had. The government didn't have to send a policeman to make sure the food was divided fairly. When the government needed new soldiers, it told each family how many recruits it was expected to send. The family decided then who was to go.

"And this admirable scheme was far from being an invention by the Biafrans. They were simply continuing to live as most human beings have lived until recently.

"I have seen the past, and it works.

"We should return to extended families as quickly as we can, and be lonesome no more, lonesome no more.

"Some of you will become leaders, although that is now thought to be a grungy destiny. Nobody wants to be Papa anymore. If you do have to lead, you may imagine that your mission is to help us find an amazing future. You should consider the possibility that you could serve the people better if you were to lead them intelligently and imaginatively back to some of the more humane and comforting institutions of the past.

"It seems certain that you will face plenty of social unrest in the future, and demands will continue to be made for economic justice. You will be very shrewd leaders indeed if you recognize that the people are in fact crying out not so much for money as for relief from loneliness.

"Let me beguile you just a little bit more about extended families. Let us talk about divorce, and the fact that one out of every three of us here has been or will be divorced. When we do it, we will very likely wrangle and wail and weep formlessly about money and sex, about treachery, about outgrowing one another, about how close love is to hate, and so on. Nobody ever gets anywhere near close to the truth, which is this: The nuclear family doesn't provide nearly enough companionship.

"I am going to write a play about the breakup of a marriage, and at the end of the play I am going to have a character say what people should say to each other in real life at the end of a marriage: 'I'm sorry. You, being human, need a hundred affectionate and like-minded companions. I'm only one person. I've tried, but I could never be a hundred people to you. You've tried, but you could never be a hundred people to me. Too bad. Good-bye.'

"Let's talk about incompatibility between parents and children, which happens often merely because of genetic rotten luck. In a nuclear family, children and parents can be locked in hellish close combat for twenty-one years and more. In an extended family, a child has scores of other homes to go to in search of love and understanding. He need not stay home and torture his parents, and he need not starve for love.

"In an extended family, anybody can bug out of his own house for months, and still be among relatives. Nobody has to go on a hopeless quest for friendly strangers, which is what most Americans have to do.

"Massage parlors come to mind—bus stations and bars.

"You graduates here are leaving an artificial extended family now. Even if you hated it here, you will find a nuclear family to be a very poor substitute for what you had here. As for those of us who have come to praise you for having graduated: we have fled here from loneliness, to be part of an artificial extended family for just a little while.

"And what we will all be seeking when we decamp, and for the rest of our lives, will be large, stable communities of like-minded people, which is to say relatives. They no longer exist. The lack of them is not only the main cause, but probably the only cause of our shapeless discontent in the midst of such prosperity.

"We thought we could do without tribes and clans. Well, we can't.

"There was a time when I was avid to invent new religions

and social orders. It has now penetrated my skull that such schemes will not work without the support of huge and gruesome police forces and prison systems, unless they are allowed to invent themselves. The emperor Constantine did not, after all, invent anything. He had many religions to choose from. He selected Christianity because it seemed to him to be the most refreshing.

"Hitler and Lenin and some others have also tried to refresh their people with ideas that had been around awhile. They chose abominably, as we know. It matters what we choose. And history and the deteriorating physical and moral environments are now telling us what we would rather not hear, what we would rather our children or grandchildren would hear: It is our turn to choose.

"At least we do not have to choose between various theories of magic, of ways to manipulate God and the devil and whatever, which is what our ancestors had to do. We no longer believe that God causes earthquakes and crop failures and plagues when He gets mad at us. We no longer imagine that He can be cooled off by sacrifices and festivals and gifts. I am so glad we don't have to think up presents for Him anymore. What's the perfect gift for someone who has everything?

"The perfect gift for somebody who has everything, of course, is nothing. Any gifts we have should be given to creatures right on the surface of the planet, it seems to me. If God gets angry about that, we can call in the Massachusetts Institute of Technology. There's a very good chance they can calm Him down.

"The new moral code we choose may already have martyrs. It is difficult to spot such things. One corpse tends to look pretty much like another one—until the historians sort them out with the benefit of hindsight.

"We shall see what we shall see.

"For two thirds of my life I have been a pessimist. I am astonished to find myself an optimist now. I feel now that I have been underestimating the intelligence and resourcefulness of man. I honestly thought that we were so stupid that we would continue to tear the planet to pieces, to sell it to each other, to burn it up. I've never expected thermonuclear war. What seemed certain to me was that we would simply gobble up the planet out of boredom and greed, not in centuries, but in ten or twenty years.

"Kilgore Trout wrote a science-fiction story called 'The Planet Gobblers' one time. It was about us, and we were the terrors of the universe. We were sort of interplanetary termites. We would arrive on a planet, gobble it up, and die. But before we died, we always sent out spaceships to start tiny colonies elsewhere. We were a disease, since it was not necessary to inhabit planets with such horrifying destructiveness. It is easy to take good care of a planet.

"Our grandchildren will surely think of us as the Planet Gobblers. Poorer nations than America think of America as a Planet Gobbler right now. But that is going to change. There is welling up within us a willingness to say 'No, thank you' to our factories. We were once maniacs for possessions, imagining that they would somehow moderate or somehow compensate us for our loneliness.

"The experiment has been tried in this most affluent nation in all of human history. Possessions help a little, but not as much as advertisers said they were supposed to, and we are now aware of how permanently the manufacture of some of those products hurts the planet.

"So there is a willingness to do without them.

"There is a willingness to do whatever we need to do in

order to have life on the planet go on for a long, long time. I didn't used to think that. And that willingness has to be a religious enthusiasm, since it celebrates life, since it calls for meaningful sacrifices.

"This is bad news for business, as we know it now. It should be thrilling news for persons who love to teach and lead. And thank God we have solid information in the place of superstition! Thank God we are beginning to dream of human communities which are designed to harmonize with what human beings really need and are.

"And now you have just heard an atheist thank God not once, but twice. And listen to this:

"God bless the class of 1974."

❦

SIX years later I would still be, outwardly at least, an unwobbled Free Thinker, for I said this at the First Parish Unitarian Church in Cambridge, Massachusetts, on January 27, 1980, approximately the 200th anniversary of the birth of William Ellery Channing:

"This will be very short. There will be almost no eye contact.

"This is only a dream. I know that this is only a dream. I have had it before. It is a dream of cosmic embarrassment. I stand before a large and nicely dressed audience. I have promised to speak on the most profound and poetic of all human concerns—the dignity of human nature.

"Only a maniac would make such a grandiose promise, but that is what I have done—in this dream.

"Now it is time for me to speak. I have nothing to say. Nothing.

"Dobedobedobedo.

"I will wake up at any moment now, and I will tell my wife about the dream. 'Where was it, honeybunch?' she will ask me. 'In a Yankee church on Harvard Square,' I will reply, and we will laugh and laugh.

"But every time I have had this dream before, I have been wearing nothing but olive drab, Army surplus undershorts. That detail is missing today—so this just might not be a dream after all. Who can say for certain?

"In this dream, if it is a dream, it is the two-hundredth anniversary of the birth of William Ellery Channing, a principal founder of Unitarianism in the United States. I wish that I had been born into a society like his—small and congenial and prosperous and self-sufficient. The people around here had ancestors in common then. They looked a lot like each other, dressed a lot like each other, enjoyed the same amusements and food. They were generally agreed as to what was good and what was evil—what God was like, who Jesus was.

"Channing grew up in what the late anthropologist Robert Redfield called a folk society, a relatively isolated community of like-thinking friends and relatives, a stable extended family of considerable size. Redfield said that we were all descended from persons who lived in such societies, and that we were likely to hanker to live in one ourselves from time to time. A folk society, in his imagination and in our imaginations, too, is an ideal scheme within which people can take really good care of one another, can share fairly, and can distribute honors to one and all.

211

"Maybe so. That could also be a dream, but I do not choose to think so.

"Channing's folk society, with Harvard at its center, was quite possibly the most intelligent and creative folk society the Western Hemisphere has ever known. I have to say 'possibly,' since we know so little about the Incas and the Aztecs and the Mayans—and some other tribes. I am tempted to include the Indianapolis of my grandfather's youth.

"But Channing's folk society is gone now. It has been drowned by tidal waves of strangers from simply everywhere —people like myself. Channing's folk society is now the American Atlantis, if you will.

"One of the most durable American legends has to do with the last days of the drowning of that Atlantis. It is the story of the arrest and trial and execution of Sacco and Vanzetti —of how the natives of Atlantis made war on the waves.

"That war on the waves came much too late. It happened only day before yesterday, practically. Sacco and Vanzetti were executed in Charlestown Prison in 1927. This part of New England had ceased to be a genuine folk society, had begun to admit strangers with unfamiliar ideas and customs in large numbers, one hundred years before that—when William Ellery Channing was nearly fifty years old.

"Channing did not live long enough to see the truly towering waves of immigrants come crashing in. But he did see, in my opinion, that the narrow, ethnocentric sermons suitable to a folk society should not be preached here anymore. Sermons deeply rooted in local history and sociology and politics are by and large harmless, and perhaps even charming in a relatively closed and isolated community. Why shouldn't a preacher in such a society raise the morale of his parishioners by implying that they are better servants of God than strangers are? That is a very old type of sermon—very old indeed. As old as the hills. Read the Old Testament. You can probably borrow a copy from the church next door.

"When Channing began preaching a new sort of sermon in this town, a sort of sermon we now perceive as Unitarian, he was urging his parishioners to credit with human dignity as great as their own persons not at all like their friends and relatives. The time to acknowledge the dignity of strangers, even black ones, had come.

"Couldn't strangers, even black ones, have human dignity without the acquiescence of Channing's congregation? No. Human dignity must be given by people to people. If you stand before me, and I do not credit you with dignity, then you have none. If I stand before you, and you do not credit me with dignity, then I have none. If Channing's parishioners felt that illiterate black slaves in the American South had negligible amounts of dignity, then those slaves would in fact be negligibly dignified—like chimpanzees, perhaps.

"It is easy to see dignity in relatives and friends. It is inevitable that we see it in relatives and friends. What is human dignity, then? It is the favorable opinion, respectful and uncritical, which we hold of those most familiar to us. It has been found that we can hold that same good opinion of strangers, if those who teach us and otherwise lead us tell us to.

"What could be more essential in a pluralistic society like ours than that every citizen see dignity in every other human being everywhere?

"And let us consider for a moment a society which was the exact opposite of what ours is supposed to be—which was Hitler's Germany. He trained a generation of warriors and police to be blind to human dignity, to never see it anywhere. So wherever he sent his warriors and police, there was no dignity. If he had conquered the world, there would have been no dignity anywhere. The penalty for crediting anyone with dignity in such a society? Death. And that, too, since there would be nobody to see dignity in it, would be undignified.

"Potter's field.

"Doesn't God give dignity to everybody? No—not in my opinion. Giving dignity, the sort of dignity that is of some earthly use, anyway, is something that only people do.

"Or fail to do.

"What happens if you credit a bum with human dignity —a drunken bum with his pants full of shit and snot dangling from his nose? At least you haven't made yourself poorer in a financial sense. And he can't take whatever it is that you have given him and spend it on Thunderbird wine.

"There is this drawback, though: If you give to that sort of a stranger the uncritical respect that you give to friends and relatives, you will also want to understand and help him. There is no way to avoid this.

"Be warned: If you allow yourself to see dignity in someone, you have doomed yourself to wanting to understand and help whoever it is.

"If you see dignity in anything, in fact—it doesn't have to be human—you will still want to understand it and help it. Many people are now seeing dignity in the lower animals and the plant world and waterfalls and deserts—and even in the entire planet and its atmosphere. And now they are helpless not to.want to understand and to help those things.

"Poor souls!

"I am descended from fairly recent immigrants. My first

214

American ancestor, an atheistic merchant from Münster, arrived here about five years after William Ellery Channing died. Channing died in 1842, a reluctant Abolitionist who did not live to see all the murdering in the Civil War. I am a drop of spray from one of the waves which swamped the American Atlantis.

"The faith of my ancestors, going back at least four generations, has been the most corrosive sort of agnosticism— or worse. When I was a child, all my relatives, male and female, agreed with H. L. Mencken when he said that he thought religious people were comical. Mencken said that he had been widely misunderstood as hating religious people. He did not hate them, he said. He merely found them comical.

"What is so comical about religious people in modern times? They believe so many things which science has proved to be unknowable or absolutely wrong.

"How on earth can religious people believe in so much arbitrary, clearly invented balderdash? For one thing, I guess, the balderdash is usually beautiful—and therefore echoes excitingly in the more primitive lobes of our brains, where knowledge counts for nothing.

"More important, though: the acceptance of a creed, any creed, entitles the acceptor to membership in the sort of artificial extended family we call a congregation. It is a way to fight loneliness. Any time I see a person fleeing from reason and into religion, I think to myself, There goes a person who simply cannot stand being so goddamned lonely anymore.

"I read an essay by Harvey Cox recently, in which he quoted an early Church father as having said, 'One Christian is no Christian.' Mr. Cox said that one of the most distinctive

215

and attractive features of Christianity for him was its insistence on forming congregations.

"We might also say that one human being is no human being.

"Many people have found a solution to loneliness by joining the paratroops. Membership in that particular family is gained and maintained by jumping out of airplanes and shouting 'Geronimo!' Not even the commanding general knows why everybody is supposed to shout 'Geronimo!' It does not matter.

"In a lonely society, the main thing is not to make sense. The main thing is to get rid of loneliness. I certainly sympathize.

"I have not mentioned love yet. I have been saving that for close to the end.

"Love was invented by a chef at the Brown Derby Restaurant in Hollywood, California, in 1939. It consists of overripe jumbo peaches with San Fernando Valley honey and chocolate jimmies on top. It is traditionally served in heated purple bowls.

"As every married person here knows, love is a rotten substitute for respect.

"I have spoken of the long tradition of religious skepticism in my family. One of my two daughters has recently turned her back on all that. Living alone and far from home, she has memorized an arbitrary Christian creed, Trinitarianism, by chance. She now has her human dignity regularly confirmed by the friendly nods of a congregation. I am glad that she is not so lonely anymore. This is more than all right with me.

"She believes that Jesus was the Son of God, or perhaps God Himself—or however that goes. I have had even more trouble with the Trinity than I had with college algebra. I refer those who are curious about it to what is known about the Council of Nicea, which took place in *anno Domini* 325. It was there that the Trinity was hammered into its present shape. Unfortunately, the minutes have been lost. It is known that the emperor Constantine was there, and probably spoke a good deal. He gave us the first Christian army. He may have given us the Holy Ghost as well.

"No matter. I do not argue with my Christian daughter about religion at all. Why should I? I have, however, begun to write a passion play for her which leaves God out entirely, but which manages to be spiritual anyway. It is still about Jesus Christ.

"I will tell you only about the last scene:

"The Roman soldiers, using ancient police methods, have done all they can to prove to Jesus that he has absolutely no dignity, so far as they can see. They have stripped him and whipped him. They have crowned him with thorns. They have made him drag his heavy cross through the streets. They have nailed his hands and feet to the cross. They have set the cross upright, so that he dangles in air.

"A group of ordinary people, who out of pity would like to take him from the cross and lay him down somewhere, and bandage his wounds and give him food and water and so on, approach the cross. The Roman soldiers stop them, tell them that they can go to the foot of the cross if they like but that they must not touch Jesus in any way, lest they give him comfort of some kind.

"That is the law.

"So the ordinary people—men, women, and children—gather beneath Jesus. They talk to him, sing to him, in the hopes that some of it will help a little. They say how sorry for him they are. They try to feel some of his pain—as though whatever they could feel of it he would not have to feel.

"They go down on their knees after a while. They are exhausted.

"Now a rich Roman tourist, a man, a successful speculator in Mesopotamian millet futures, comes upon the scene. I make him rich, because everybody hates rich people so much. He is blasé about crucifixions, since he has seen so many strangers crucified all over the Roman Empire. Crosses then were as common as lampposts are today.

"It seems to the tourist that the people on their knees, sighing and moaning, are worshiping this particular man on a cross. He says to them jocularly: 'My goodness! The way you are worshiping him, you would think he was the Son of your God.'

"A spokesperson for the kneelers, perhaps Mary Magdalene, says to him, 'Oh no, sir. If he were the Son of our God, he would not need us. It is because he is a common human being exactly like us that we are here—doing, as common people must, what little we can.'

"In this case this is not a dream. I thank you for your attention."

X‖

OBSCENITY

IAH Fagan Cox was a gallant and pretty little woman from Columbia City, Indiana, which is in the northeast corner of the state, about halfway between Fort Wayne and Winona Lake. She was born into a so-called "good family," but her father was an alcoholic. He could not hold a job.

So, although little more than a child, Riah set out to rescue herself and her brother and eventually their descendents from want and obscurity. She sent herself to the University of Wisconsin, and took a master's degree in the classics. Her thesis was a high school textbook on the Latin and Greek roots of common words in English. It was adopted by many school systems all over the country, and earned enough money to enable Riah to put her brother through medical school. He set up practice in Hollywood, and became the beloved obstetrician of many famous movie stars.

She married a lawyer in Indianapolis who did not make much money. She took jobs teaching Latin and Greek and English, and became the Indianapolis representative for touring lecturers and musicians. She also sold silly, witty short stories to magazines from time to time. Thus was she able to send her son and daughter to the best private schools, even during the Great Depression. Her daughter became a Phi Beta Kappa at Swarthmore.

She died three years ago, and is buried in Crown Hill Cemetery in Indianapolis, somewhere between John Dillinger, the bank robber, and James Whitcomb Riley, the "Hoosier Poet." I liked her a lot. She was a good friend of mine. She was my first mother-in-law.

I mention her in this chapter on obscenity because she imagined that I used certain impolite words in my books in order to cause a sensation, in order to make the books more popular. She told me as a friend that the words were having the opposite effect in her circle of friends, at least. Her friends could not bear to read me anymore.

Indianapolis Magazine said much the same thing in its article about me, from which I quoted in a previous chapter. It praised the themes of my early books, *Player Piano, The Sirens of Titan,* and *Mother Night:* ". . . anger at war and killing, at the void that technology is creating in contemporary life." But it went on to say: "From then on, though the themes remained constant, his style began to change. Small obscenities crept in, and four-letter words became frequent in *Breakfast of Champions* in a riot of indecorous line drawings and misbegotten words that were suggestive of a small boy sticking out his tongue at the teacher."

This small boy, sticking out his tongue, was fifty years old at the time. It has been many decades since I have wished to shock a teacher or anyone. I did want to make the Americans in my books talk as Americans really do talk. I wanted to make jokes about our bodies. Why not? Why not, I ask again, especially since Riah Fagan Cox, God rest her soul, assured me that she herself was not wobbled by dirty words.

If I had gone to Riah's friends, they would have told me, too, that they had heard all the dirty words I used many times before, that the words did not astonish them. They would have insisted that the words should not be published anyway. It was bad manners to use such words. Bad manners should be punished.

But even when I was in grammar school, I suspected that warnings about words that nice people never used were in fact lessons in how to keep our mouths shut not just about our bodies, but about many, many things—perhaps too many things.

When I was in the fourth grade or so, I had this hunch confirmed. My father hit me for my bad manners in front of guests. It was the only time either one of my parents ever hit me. I hadn't said "shit" or "piss" or "fart" or "fuck" or anything like that in front of the guests. I had asked them a question in the field of economics. But my father was so offended by my question that I might as well have called the guests "silly shitheads." They really were silly shitheads, by the way.

The Great Depression was going on. The year would have been 1932. I had been taken out of private school a couple of years before, so that my classmates were no longer the children of the rich and the powerful. They were the children of mechanics and clerks and mailmen and so on. I thought it was wonderful that their mothers could cook. That was more than my own mother could do. Also, their fathers could fart around with motors and so on. Peer pressure, which is the most powerful force in the universe, had actually made me a scorner of my parents' class.

But I was polite enough when these two silly upper-class shitheads came over to our house one night. They were husband and wife. I remember their names well enough, but I will call them "Bud and Mary Swan." This was at a time when securities had become nearly worthless, when many banks had closed forever. Factories and stores were dead. But the Swans had arrived in a new Marmon, and Mrs. Swan had a new fur coat and a new star sapphire ring.

We all had to look out through the front door at the car, and then at the coat and the ring. So Mother and Father, with their nice manners, said they were glad that things were going so well for the Swans. The whole thing looked fishy to me. Everybody else was broke. Where would the Swans get all that money? It was as though this one couple had been allowed to defy the law of gravity.

Mother and Father told me to take another look at the sapphire, so I could see the beautiful star in there. So I did. But then, to get a better understanding of what was going on, I asked Mr. Swan how much the ring had cost him. That was when Father hit me. He hit me with an underhand blow to the seat of my pants. It lofted me in the direction of the staircase, and I just kept on going upstairs to my bedroom. I was mad.

Now then: As my parents would eventually discover, to their grief, the Swans were cat's-paws for confidence men.

They had been bankrolled by crooks to put on a show for friends of theirs who might still have a little money squirreled away somewhere. My parents would want to know where the Swans got all their easy money. My parents needed some easy money, too. If they didn't find it somewhere, they would be bounced forever from the upper class. As I say, I myself had already sunk into the lower orders.

The Swans said that they had invested what little they had left after the crash of the securities market in a wonderful company which wanted to keep itself a secret. It was quietly putting together a coal monopoly which would be as rich and powerful as Standard Oil. It was buying mines and barge lines and controlling interest in coal-hauling railroads, was getting them for a minor fraction of their true value since it was paying cash. Almost nobody else had cash. The cash was coming from individuals like the Swans and my parents, who could keep a secret, and who could scrape up a little something from the bottoms of their barrels, if they really tried.

The value of the company would increase at least a hundred times, the instant prosperity returned to the world. Meanwhile, the company was already paying dividends because it was so efficient. It was the dividends which had bought the Marmon and the coat and the star sapphire ring.

My parents of course invested. They found buyers somewhere, I suppose, for some of their oil paintings or oriental rugs, or for some of Father's fine guns. During the boom years, Father had been a collector of guns.

My parents had been taught such nice manners in childhood that it was actually impossible for them to suspect that these old friends of theirs were in league with crooks. They had no simple and practical vocabularies for the parts and functions of their excretory and reproductive systems, and no such vocabularies for treachery and hypocrisy, either. Good manners had made them defenseless against predatory members of their own class.

There we have our old friend peer pressure again, of course.

And there was no coal monopoly, of course. Whoever got my parents' money spent most of it on racehorses and chorus girls, probably, except for maybe a quarter of it, which they sent to the Swans as dividends.

❦

I had a telephone conversation recently with a young Indianapolis cousin, a married woman, during which I said that I dreaded coming out there, since I did not consider it possible that my older relatives could love me but hate my books so. She replied that I had to understand that they were all Victorians and too old to change. They could not help themselves when it came to loathing dirty books.

So I thought about Victoria, Queen of the United Kingdom of Great Britain and Ireland, and the Empress of India, who lived from 1819, long before my first ancestor arrived in this country, until 1901, when my father was a junior in Shortridge High School. And I asked myself why any mention of bodily functions should have pained this queen so.

I cannot believe that Victoria herself would have suffered a moment's genuine dismay if I had shown her the picture of my asshole which I drew for my book *Breakfast of Champions.* My asshole looks like this:

I also feature my asshole in my signature, which looks like this:

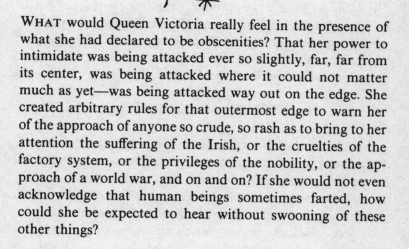

WHAT would Queen Victoria really feel in the presence of what she had declared to be obscenities? That her power to intimidate was being attacked ever so slightly, far, far from its center, was being attacked where it could not matter much as yet—was being attacked way out on the edge. She created arbitrary rules for that outermost edge to warn her of the approach of anyone so crude, so rash as to bring to her attention the suffering of the Irish, or the cruelties of the factory system, or the privileges of the nobility, or the approach of a world war, and on and on? If she would not even acknowledge that human beings sometimes farted, how could she be expected to hear without swooning of these other things?

WHAT a subtle scheme Queen Victoria evolved to make people hesitant about discussing their entitlement to more control over their lives. She persuaded them that they would deserve to be self-governing only after they had stopped thinking about all the things that human beings can't help thinking about all the time.

Genteel mothers of the era could do no less than to similarly discipline their children and their servants—and their husbands, if they could get away with it, and on and on.

✥

WHAT was the dirtiest story I ever wrote? Surely "The Big Space Fuck," the first story in the history of literature to have "fuck" in its title. It was probably the last short story I will ever write. I did it for my friend Harlan Ellison, who printed it in his anthology *Again, Dangerous Visions.* It was copyrighted by him in 1972, and appears here with his kind permission. It goes like this:

THE BIG SPACE FUCK

In 1987 it became possible in the United States of America for a young person to sue his parents for the way he had been raised. He could take them to court and make them pay money and even serve jail terms for serious mistakes they made when he was just a helpless little kid. This was not only an effort to achieve justice but to discourage reproduction, since there wasn't anything much to eat any more. Abortions were free. In fact, any woman who volunteered for one got her choice of a bathroom scale or a table lamp.

In 1989, America staged the Big Space Fuck, which was a serious effort to make sure that human life would continue to exist somewhere in the Universe, since it certainly couldn't continue much longer on Earth. Everything had turned to shit and beer cans and old automobiles and Clorox bottles. An interesting thing happened in the Hawaiian Islands, where they had been throwing trash down extinct volcanoes for years: a couple of the volcanoes all of a sudden spit it all back up. And so on.

This was a period of great permissiveness in matters of language, so even the President was saying shit and fuck and so on, without anybody's feeling threatened or taking offense. It was perfectly OK. He called the Space Fuck a Space Fuck and so did everybody else. It was a rocket ship with eight hundred pounds of freeze-dried jizzum in its nose. It was going to be fired at the Andromeda Galaxy, two-million light years away. The ship was named the *Arthur C. Clarke,* in honor of a famous space pioneer.

It was to be fired at midnight on the Fourth of July. At ten o'clock that night, Dwayne Hoobler and his wife Grace were watching the countdown on television in the living room of their modest home in Elk Harbor, Ohio, on the shore of what used to be Lake Erie. Lake Erie was almost solid sewage now. There were man-eating lampreys in there thirty-eight feet long. Dwayne was a guard in the Ohio Adult Correctional Institution, which was two miles away. His hobby was making birdhouses out of Clorox bottles. He went on making them and hanging them around his yard, even though there weren't any birds any more.

Dwayne and Grace marveled at a film demonstration of how jizzum had been freeze-dried for the trip. A small beaker of the stuff, which had been contributed by the head of the Mathematics Department at the University of Chicago, was flash-frozen. Then it was placed under a bell jar, and the air was exhausted from the jar. The air evanesced, leaving a fine white powder. The powder certainly didn't look like much, and Dwayne Hoobler said so—but there were several hundred million sperm cells in there, in suspended animation.

The original contribution, an average contribution, had been two cubic centimeters. There was enough powder, Dwayne estimated out loud, to clog the eye of a needle. And eight-hundred pounds of the stuff would soon be on its way to Andromeda.

"Fuck you, Andromeda," said Dwayne, and he wasn't being coarse. He was echoing billboards and stickers all over town. Other signs said, "Andromeda, We Love You," and "Earth Has the Hots for Andromeda," and so on.

There was a knock on the door, and an old friend of the family, the County Sheriff, simultaneously let himself in. "How are you, you old motherfucker?" said Dwayne.

"Can't complain, shitface," said the sheriff, and they joshed back and forth like that for a while. Grace chuckled, enjoying their wit. She wouldn't have chuckled so richly, however, if she had been a little more observant. She might have noticed that the sheriff's jocularity was very much on the surface. Underneath, he had something troubling on his mind. She might have noticed, too, that he had legal papers in his hand.

"Sit down, you silly old fart," said Dwayne, "and watch Andromeda get the surprise of her life."

"The way I understand it," the sheriff replied, "I'd have to sit there for more than two million years. My old lady might wonder what's become of me." He was a lot smarter than Dwayne. He had jizzum on the *Arthur C. Clarke,* and Dwayne didn't. You had to have an I.Q. of over 115 to have your jizzum accepted. There were certain exceptions to this: if you were a good athlete or could play a musical instrument or paint pictures, but Dwayne didn't qualify in any of those departments, either. He had hoped that birdhouse-makers might be entitled to special consideration, but this turned out not to be the case. The Director of the New York Philharmonic, on the other hand, was entitled to contribute a whole quart, if he wanted to. He was sixty-eight years old. Dwayne was forty-two.

There was an old astronaut on the television now. He was saying that he sure wished he could go where his jizzum was going. But he would sit at home instead, with his memories and a glass of Tang. Tang used to be the official drink of the astronauts. It was a freeze-dried orangeade.

"Maybe you haven't got two million years," said Dwayne, "but you've got at least five minutes. Sit thee doon."

"What I'm here for—" said the sheriff, and he let his unhappiness show, "is something I customarily do standing up."

Dwayne and Grace were sincerely puzzled. They didn't have the least idea what was coming next. Here is what it was: the sheriff handed each one of them a subpoena, and he said, "It's my sad duty to inform you that your daughter, Wanda June, has accused you of ruining her when she was a child."

Dwayne and Grace were thunderstruck. They knew that Wanda June was twenty-one now, and entitled to sue, but they certainly hadn't expected her to do so. She was in New York City, and when they congratulated her about her birthday on the telephone, in fact, one of the things Grace said was, "Well, you can sue us now, honeybunch, if you want to." Grace was so sure she and Dwayne had been good parents that she could laugh when she went on, "If you want to, you can send your rotten old parents off to jail."

Wanda June was an only child, incidentally. She had come close to having some siblings, but Grace had aborted them.

Grace had taken three table lamps and a bathroom scale instead.

"What does she say we did wrong?" Grace asked the sheriff.

"There's a separate list of charges inside each of your subpoenas," he said. And he couldn't look his wretched old friends in the eye, so he looked at the television instead. A scientist there was explaining why Andromeda had been selected as a target. There were at least eighty-seven chrono-synclastic infundibulae, time warps, between Earth and the Andromeda Galaxy. If the *Arthur C. Clarke* passed through any one of them, the ship and its load would be multiplied a trillion times, and would appear everywhere throughout space and time.

"If there's any fecundity anywhere in the Universe," the scientist promised, "our seed will find it and bloom."

One of the most depressing things about the space program so far, of course, was that it had demonstrated that fecundity was one hell of a long way off, if anywhere. Dumb people like Dwayne and Grace, and even fairly smart people like the sheriff, had been encouraged to believe that there was hospitality out there, and that Earth was just a piece of shit to use as a launching platform.

Now Earth really was a piece of shit, and it was beginning to dawn on even dumb people that it might be the only inhabitable planet human beings would ever find.

Grace was in tears over being sued by her daughter, and the list of charges she was reading was broken into multiple images by the tears. "Oh God, oh God, oh God—" she said, "she's talking about things I forgot all about, but she never forgot a thing. She's talking about something that happened when she was only four years old."

Dwayne was reading charges against himself, so he didn't ask Grace what awful thing she was supposed to have done when Wanda June was only four, but here it was: Poor little Wanda June drew pretty pictures with a crayon all over the new living-room wallpaper to make her mother happy. Her mother blew up and spanked her instead. Since that day, Wanda June claimed, she had not been able to look at any sort of art materials without trembling like a leaf and breaking out into cold sweats. "Thus was I deprived," Wanda June's lawyer had her say, "of a brilliant and lucrative career in the arts."

Dwayne meanwhile was learning that he had ruined his daughter's opportunities for what her lawyer called an "advantageous marriage and the comfort and love therefrom." Dwayne had done this, supposedly, by being half in the bag whenever a suitor came to call. Also, he was often stripped to the waist when he answered the door, but still had on his cartridge belt and his revolver. She was even able to name a lover her father had lost for her: John L. Newcomb, who had finally married somebody else. He had a very good job now. He was in command of the security force at an arsenal out in South Dakota, where they stockpiled cholera and bubonic plague.

The sheriff had still more bad news to deliver, and he knew he would have an opportunity to deliver it soon enough. Poor Dwayne and Grace were bound to ask him, "What made her *do* this to us?" The answer to that question would be more bad news, which was that Wanda June was in jail, charged with being the head of a shoplifting ring. The only way she could avoid prison was to prove that everything she was and did was her parents' fault.

Meanwhile, Senator Flem Snopes of Mississippi, Chairman of the Senate Space Committee, had appeared on the television screen. He was very happy about the Big Space Fuck, and he said it had been what the American space program had been aiming toward all along. He was proud, he said, that the United States had seen fit to locate the biggest jizzum-freezing plant in his "l'il ol' home town," which was Mayhew.

The word "jizzum" had an interesting history, by the way. It was as old as "fuck" and "shit" and so on, but it continued to be excluded from dictionaries, long after the others were let in. This was because so many people wanted it to remain a truly magic word—the only one left.

And when the United States announced that it was going to do a truly magical thing, was going to fire sperm at the Andromeda Galaxy, the populace corrected its government. Their collective unconscious announced that it was time for the last magic word to come into the open. They insisted that *sperm* was nothing to fire at another galaxy. Only *jizzum* would do. So the Government began using that word, and it did something that had never been done before, either: it standardized the way the word was spelled.

The man who was interviewing Senator Snopes asked him to stand up so everybody could get a good look at his codpiece, which the Senator did. Codpieces were very much in fashion, and many men were wearing codpieces in the shape of rocket ships, in honor of the Big Space Fuck. These customarily had the letters "U.S.A." embroidered on the shaft. Senator Snopes' shaft, however, bore the Stars and Bars of the Confederacy.

This led the conversation into the area of heraldry in

general, and the interviewer reminded the Senator of his campaign to eliminate the bald eagle as the national bird. The Senator explained that he didn't like to have his country represented by a creature that obviously hadn't been able to cut the mustard in modern times.

Asked to name a creature that *had* been able to cut the mustard, the Senator did better than that: he named two—the lamprey and the bloodworm. And, unbeknownst to him or to anybody, lampreys were finding the Great Lakes too vile and noxious even for *them*. While all the human beings were in their houses, watching the Big Space Fuck, lampreys were squirming out of the ooze and onto land. Some of them were nearly as long and thick as the *Arthur C. Clarke*.

And Grace Hoobler tore her wet eyes from what she had been reading, and she asked the sheriff the question he had been dreading to hear: "What made her *do* this to us?"

The sheriff told her, and then he cried out against cruel Fate, too. "This is the most horrible duty I ever had to carry out—" he said brokenly, "to deliver news this heartbreaking to friends as close as you two are—on a night that's supposed to be the most joyful night in the history of mankind."

He left sobbing, and stumbled right into the mouth of a lamprey. The lamprey ate him immediately, but not before he screamed. Dwayne and Grace Hoobler rushed outside to see what the screaming was about, and the lamprey ate them, too.

It was ironical that their television set continued to report the countdown, even though they weren't around any more to see or hear or care.

"Nine!" said a voice. And then, "Eight!" And then, "Seven!" And so on.

❧

THAT is a made-up story. Here is another true story:

When I was little, there was a female friend of my parents who was particularly admired for her vivacity and good taste and impeccable manners and so on. She married a German businessman.

When she came back to Indianapolis after the Second World War, she was as attractive as ever. She said vivaciously that Hitler had been right about most things, and that Germany should be admired for fighting so many powerful enemies all at once. "We almost won," she reminded us.

I had just come back from Germany, too. I had been a prisoner of war there. So I took my father aside, and I said to him, "Father, I can't help having mixed feelings about this old family friend."

He told me that I should pay no attention to her when she spoke of political matters, that she understood nothing about them, that she was just a charming, silly, innocent little girl.

He was right. It was impossible for her to think coherently about assholes or Auschwitz or anything else that might be upsetting to a little girl.

That's class.

XIII

CHILDREN

My first wife and both my daughters are born-again Christians now—working white magic through rituals and prayers. That's all right. I would be a fool to say that the Free Thinker ideas of Clemens Vonnegut remain as enchanting and encouraging as ever—not after the mortal poisoning of the planet, not after two world wars, with more to come.

Can I say now, with all my heart, what he said in his little book in 1900: "We believe in virtue, in perfectibility, in progress, in stability of the laws of nature, in the necessity of improving the social conditions and relations, which should be in harmony with that benevolence which conditions the coherence of men"?

No.

"Truth," he says, "must always be recognized as the paramount requisite of human society." As I myself said in another place, I began to have my doubts about truth after it was dropped on Hiroshima.

❦

CLEMENS Vonnegut wrote of powerful and rich families founded by criminals. He despised them. He himself founded a dynasty based on hard work, prudence, and honest dealing.

At the end of his life, eight years before the First World War, his many descendents, my father and grandfather among them, must have looked like innocent, happy sailors in a flotilla of freshly painted little catboats, running before the wind in a safe harbor, always in sight of land.

The harbor was Indianapolis. The sailboats were jobs and shares in the Vonnegut Hardware Company.

Seventy-four years later, the Vonnegut Hardware Company exists no more. The "Mile Square" in the heart of Indianapolis, where it once had its bustling main store, is a desert of parking lots now. At night the Mile Square is as eerily desolate as East Berlin. The retail outlets of the Vonnegut Hardware Company were ruined by perfectly fair competition—by discount stores.

So I can bequeath no Vonnegut Hardware stock to my own descendents, nor can I offer them jobs with that firm, if life on the outside becomes too rough-and-tumble. I am the last of my grandfather's branch of the family to have worked there, to have been given a little sailboat for a while.

In lieu of stock, I can only leave my descendents a story about the legendary times, now lost in the mists, when the name Vonnegut was synonymous with hardware in Indianapolis. That story will be lost forever, if I do not now take it out of my perishable head and write it down.

There was this Japanese jeweler in Indianapolis, you see, who, among other things, made class rings by hand for the graduates of Tudor Hall, the small and exclusive girls' school to which rich girls from all over Indiana were sent before going East to college. My sister, although her family was broke, went there. My first wife, although her family was broke, went there.

The name of the jeweler was Iku Matsu Moto. He had many secrets, probably because his customers asked him very little about himself. It turned out that he used to be a strong man with Ringling Brothers and Barnum & Bailey Circus.

So he appeared at the main store of Vonnegut Hardware Company on East Washington Street one day, and he wanted an anvil. His shop was on Monument Circle, three blocks away. In Indianapolis, which was laid out by Pierre Charles L'Enfant, the same Frenchman who laid out Washington, D.C., each block is one tenth of a mile on a side.

So Iku Matsu Moto found an anvil he liked, and he asked the salesman how much it cost. The salesman told him jocularly that he could have it for nothing if Iku Matsu Moto could carry it home. So Iku Matsu Moto carried it home.

I scarcely know any of the few Vonneguts still living in Indianapolis, and my own children will know and care about them as much as I know or care about my German relatives. Things fall apart.

There is a Bernard Vonnegut in Albany. That's my brother, I believe. And there is a Peter Vonnegut there, who is Bernard's son, and who is a librarian, and who married a woman named Michi Minatoya, who, like Iku Matsu Moto, is of Japanese ancestry. They have two children, Carl Hiroaki Vonnegut and Emiko Alice Vonnegut, my brother's only grandchildren. They, too, are, among other things, de St. Andrés. Strange and nice.

❀

THERE is a Dr. Mark Vonnegut in Brookline, Massachusetts. That's my son, I believe.

I am proud of Mark, and I praised him and drew on his experience in this manner at a meeting of the Mental Health Association in New Jersey in Morristown on June 4, 1980:

"The title of this speech in your programs is 'Must We Do without References?' Please cross that out, in case you want to remember later on what really happened here. The new title is 'Fear and Loathing in Morristown, New Jersey,' and I want you all to know how safe I feel up here. If I go crazy, you will know all the latest things to do about it. I will be out of the nuthouse and back on the streets in no time, coked to the gills on Thorazine.

"The title in your programs is a typographical error anyway. It should have been 'Must We Do without Reference *Points?*' You might want to add that word 'Points' to the original title before you cross the whole thing out, which reminds me of a very funny story. There was a man in a restaurant, and he called the waiter over, and he said, 'Waiter —there is a needle in my soup.' And the waiter said to him, 'Oh sir, I am so sorry. That is a typographical error. It should have been a noodle.'

"When I thought I was going to talk about reference points, I had in mind the fixtures in a simpler and more stable civilization than what we have today. Examples: Shakespeare's *Hamlet,* Beethoven's Fifth Symphony, Leonardo's *Mona Lisa,* Lincoln's Gettysburg Address, Mark Twain's *Huckleberry Finn*—the Great Wall of China, the Leaning Tower of Pisa, the Sphinx. These few works of art used to be enormous monuments in the minds of public school graduates in every corner of this country. They have now been drowned in our minds, like Atlantis, if you will, by the latest sensations on television and radio, and in our motion picture palaces and *People* magazine.

"Time was when a worker in the mental health field in America would have a few reference points in common with a native-born maniac, could begin a therapeutic conversation with comments on the smile of the Mona Lisa, say. It was a beginning. But nowadays, I would think, a therapist has to be prepared to discuss in depth *Beach Blanket Bingo* or *The Texas Chainsaw Murders* or *Howdy Doody* or *Romper Room* or Walter Cronkite—and just on and on and on. Farrah Fawcett-Majors. No subject of conversation lives much longer than a lightning bug these days. I have a son who is a gag writer on the West Coast, and he wrote what he thought was a very funny skit about Howdy Doody. I had to explain to him that there were millions of Americans older and younger than he was, who did not know or care who

Howdy Doody was. He was shattered. When he was seven years old, Howdy Doody was God to him.

"But I have scrapped that particular speech, as I say. I didn't have the brains to pull it off. It was too ambitious—not only for me but for lunch at a New Jersey motel. So I have decided to talk instead about how honored I am to be here. If some of you are taking notes, you should write that down: 'Honored to be asked to speak on mental health'—something like that.

"I don't know why you invited me. Perhaps it is because my son Mark went insane. He is not the gag writer. That is another son. The one who went insane is well now. He graduated from Harvard Medical School a year ago, and is an intern in Boston now. He, too, is a magnificent speaker. He loves to ask an audience of workers in the mental health field, 'How many of you have ever taken Thorazine?' Almost no hands go up, and my son the doctor gives a little smile, and he says: 'It won't hurt you. You really ought to try it sometime, just to get an inkling, anyway, of what your patients are going through.'

"Your organizers asked me what degrees I held. Even if I were a trapeze artist, they would have to ask me that, I guess. So I ransacked the drawers of my bedside table for documents. I found a long-lost pair of cuff links, unfortunately only gold-plated. I found a snapshot of my sister Alice when she was only sixteen. She died here in New Jersey at the age of forty-one, and not in the best of mental health. I found a diploma from the University of Chicago, which is west of here. It declared that I had earned a master's degree in anthropology. I looked up the word in a dictionary. It turned out to be the study of man.

"At the University of Chicago so long ago, I had to select

a specialty from these five fields in anthropology: archaeology, cultural anthropology, ethnology, linguistics, and physical anthropology. I chose cultural anthropology, since it offered the greatest opportunity to write high-minded balderdash. Culture, of course, is every object and idea which has been shaped by men and women and children, and not by God. Cultural anthropology is a broad specialty, you might say. I never heard of a cultural anthropologist who came down with claustrophobia.

"It was that damn fool diploma which made me believe for a moment that I could speak to you as an expert on culture, about that bed of Procrustes which maladjusted persons find so uncomfortable. My own son Mark found it so uncomfortable that he tried to beat his brains out on it, and had to be put in a padded cell. Really. That is how crazy he was. He would have tried to kill himself with a Stradivarius violin, if there had been one around—or the Leaning Tower of Pisa, or Walter Cronkite's mustache.

"But I am a storyteller, not a cultural anthropologist, no matter what the diploma says. And I am not even the best storyteller in my own family when it comes to the relationship of culture to mental health. My son Mark is the best storyteller in that area. He wrote an excellent book about going crazy and recovering. It is called *The Eden Express*. Mark remembers everything. His wish is to tell people who are going insane something about the shape of the roller coaster they are on. It helps sometimes to know the shape of a roller coaster. How many of you here have taken Thorazine?

"Mark has taught me never to romanticize mental illness, never to imagine a brilliant and beguiling schizophrenic who makes more sense about life than his or her doctor or even

241

the president of Harvard University. Mark says that schizophrenia is as ghastly and debilitating as smallpox or rabies or any other unspeakable disease you care to name. Society cannot be blamed, and neither, thank God, can the friends and relatives of the patient. Schizophrenia is an internal chemical catastrophe. It is a case of monstrously bad genetic luck, bad luck of a sort encountered in absolutely every sort of society—including the Australian aborigines and the middle class of Vienna, Austria, before the Second World War.

"Plenty of other writers at this very moment are writing a story about an admirable, perhaps even a divine schizophrenic. Why? Because the story is wildly applauded every time it is told. It blames the culture and the economy and the society and everything but the disease itself for making the patient unwell. Mark says that is wrong.

"As his father, though, I am still free to say this, I think: I believe that a culture, a combination of ideas and artifacts, can sometimes make a healthy person behave against his or her best interests, and against the best interests of the society and the planet, too.

"I have made up a story about that for this moment, and for this audience in this motel. It goes like this:

"There is this psychiatrist, you see. He is a colonel in the German SS in Poland during World War Two. His name is Vonnegut. That is a good German name. Colonel Vonnegut is supposed to look after the mental health of SS people in his area, which includes the uniformed staff at Auschwitz.

"Colonel Vonnegut has a skull and crossbones on his hat. Ordinarily, when an SS man wants to express his love for a woman, he gives her a skull and crossbones to wear. But Colonel Vonnegut is in love with an SS woman, and she

242

already has skulls and crossbones of her own. So he sends her candy instead.

"But that is not the major crisis in the story. The most moving part is when a young, idealistic SS lieutenant comes to Vonnegut for help. His name is Dampfwalze. *Dampfwalze* means 'steamroller.' *Vonnegut* means nothing. Ask any critic on *The New York Review of Books.*

"Lieutenant Dampfwalze, who could be played by Peter O'Toole, feels that he can't cut the mustard anymore on the railroad platform at Auschwitz, where boxcars of people are unloaded day after day. He is sick and tired of it, but he has the wisdom to seek professional help. Dr. Vonnegut is an eclectic worker in the field of mental health, incidentally, a pragmatic man. He is a little bit Jungian, a little bit Freudian, a little bit Rankian—and so on. He has an open and inquiring mind.

"Actually, he cures Dampfwalze with megavitamins, the same things that cured my son. The Nazis haven't received nearly the credit they deserve for pioneering megavitamin therapy.

"So Dampfwalze is ready to return to duty. His eyes are shining again. His appetite is good. He sleeps like a baby every night. And he asks Dr. Vonnegut how serious his illness had been.

"Dr. Vonnegut tells him that, if Dampfwalze hadn't recognized nature's little danger signals early and put himself into the hands of modern medicine, he might have tried to shoot Adolf Hitler by and by. That is how sick he was.

"And the moral of that story, I think, is that a society, on occasion, can be the worst possible describer of mental health.

"I thank you for your attention."

✢

THREE of my six children are adopted nephews. They have retained their original name, the most original of all names, which is Adams. My first wife and I adopted them after, within a period of only twenty-four hours, their father drowned when his commuter train went off an open draw-bridge in New Jersey and then their mother died of cancer in a hospital. Their mother was my only sister, and her death had been expected for quite a while.

There was a fourth Adams brother, an infant, who was adopted by a first cousin of his father in Birmingham, Alabama.

They were orphaned in September of 1958, nearly twenty-two years ago as I write. I came down from Cape Cod at once to run their house in Rumson, New Jersey. They held a meeting at which I was not present. They came downstairs together with a single demand: that they be kept together along with their dogs. One of the dogs, a sheep dog named Sandy, would become the closest friend I have ever had.

✢

JAMES Adams, the oldest of the orphans, as we continue to call them, was then fourteen. He is now thirty-six, the age I was when Jane and I adopted him. He attended college briefly, then became a Peace Corps volunteer in Peru, and then a goat farmer in Jamaica, and is now a cabinetmaker in Leverett, Massachusetts.

He is married to Barbara D'Arthanay, a former New England schoolteacher who lived and worked with him for several years on his goat farm on a mountaintop in Jamaica. They are as uninterested in social rank and property as was Henry David Thoreau.

They have given me a grandchild. The area in which they are raising that child consists largely of farmlands being recaptured by the wilderness. The name of the child resonates with the innocent imperialism of earlier white colonists. Her name is India Adams.

God watch over India Adams in the untamed American wilderness.

❦

A tale from Jim's bachelor days:

Jim went down the Amazon with two friends on a raft after he left the Peace Corps. One night, while the raft was tied up near Manaus, the old rubber boom town in Brazil, a speedboat came alongside. At the wheel was Yevgeny Yevtushenko, the Soviet poet. He had Brazilian friends along. He asked in English if he and his party could come aboard the raft for drinks. In exchange, he said, he would give his hosts a perfect name for their raft.

So there was some drinking on the raft, and fighting for some reason broke out between Yevtushenko and Jim.

So the party was over, and the visitors got back in their speedboat. Just before they cast off, Yevtushenko said: "I have not forgotten my promise. You should call your raft *The Huckleberry Finn.*"

Years later I myself would meet Yevtushenko, and I would ask him if the story was true.

"Ah!" he said. "Ah! That was your son? He is a very bad boy!"

Small world.

§

STEVEN Adams was eleven when we adopted him, the same age as my natural son Mark. He was the least dependent of the lot, being a superb athlete and having joined an alternative family long before his parents died, the worldwide family of coaches and teammates and competitors everywhere. Coaches on Cape Cod, just like the coaches in New Jersey, greeted him like a long-lost son.

Steve arrived on Cape Cod wearing a jacket with this emblazoned on the back: "New Jersey Little League All-Stars." Further introductions were unnecessary.

He went to Dartmouth, where he studied English literature and played end. He is in Los Angeles now, a professional writer of comedy for television shows. He is thirty-three and has never married, and he runs a lot.

I know Steve least well of all my children, since, to his credit, he has had the least need of me. At the same time, he is the only one who has chosen to become what I am, which is a full-time writer. His work now is entirely comical. As far as I know, he will not begin a piece unless it promises to lead him at once to a joke of some kind. He is well paid for unseriousness. If he ever became serious, he would lose his job.

His job also requires him to ignore all he learned at Dartmouth of history and literature and philosophy and what have you, and to joke only about matters with which his audience is familiar, recent television commercials, celebrities of the moment, big-grossing motion pictures of the past year, extraordinarily popular records, political figures in the news incessantly, and on and on. This must become tiresome.

He is the most rootless of my children, and the one most likely to drift away. If he reproduces, his children, in California, perhaps, will never find out, probably, unless they read this book, that they are de St. Andrés and have second cousins named Carl Hiroaki Vonnegut and Emiko Alice Vonnegut and on and on.

❦

STEVE'S younger brother Kurt Adams, nine years old when we adopted him, also lives in Leverett, near his brother Jim. Kurt was the first of the brothers to settle there. He is thirty-two now, and a pilot for Air New England, and a builder on speculation of beautiful post-and-beam houses which are entirely heated by wood stoves. He lives in such a house himself. He is married to an excellent artist named Lindsay Palermo. So far, they have not had a child.

Kurt is the only canny business person of the lot. He is of modest means, but he makes satisfying gains on small investments. He has a little victory garden of dollars that he tends.

The rest do not care for money games. They cannot pay attention—any more than my father or mother or sister could, than my brother can.

This is a matter of genetics, I think. People are born caring or not caring about managing money well.

We are all experiments in enthusiasms, narrow and preordained. I write.

❧

My brother is an enthusiast for the scientific study of thunderstorms. My late sister was born to be an enthusiast for painting and sculpture, but resisted. She said, very wisely, in my opinion, "Just because you have talent, it doesn't mean that you have to *do* something with it."

❧

There is a fourth Adams brother. He was an infant when his mother died. He was adopted by a first cousin of his father in Birmingham, Alabama, a judge. His mother died before she could have any influence over his character, and yet his attitudes toward life are identical with hers—and his jokes. His name is Peter Nice.

He talks of settling in Leverett—to be near his brothers, who are more like him than anyone else in the world.

❧

When we adopted the Adamses, two of our natural children got artificial twins. Steve Adams was the same age as Mark Vonnegut. Kurt Adams was the same age as Edith Vonnegut. This was purely delightful for Edith, who took her new twin to "Show and Tell" at the Barnstable Elementary School. She got two more strong older brothers, as well. For Mark, the benefits of a family merger weren't so apparent at once. He was no longer the oldest child and the only male child—and so on.

❦

ALL the children remain close these days, and think of themselves as genuine brothers and sisters. They are lucky to have so many interested and responsive relatives. There are many affectionate reunions a year in the big old house on Cape Cod where they were raised together. They were such a formidable gang when they were young that one policeman became a specialist in their habits and haunts. He had a lovely name, and always left his blue flasher on when he parked in our yard. His name was Sergeant Nightingale.

Whenever Sergeant Nightingale came to interrogate this child or that one, the flasher on his cruiser splashed our house with blue as it went around and around.

Nobody ever went to prison, though.

Nobody ever dealt dope.

❦

THERE was only one really fancy auto smashup. Mark rolled and totaled a Volkswagen Microbus with about eight people in it. It scattered people out along the shoulder of the road the way a saltshaker will scatter salt. People flew out through the sun roof, out through the side doors, out through the tailgate. Mark was the last one to fly out. He landed on his feet, and found himself facing oncoming traffic like a football lineman.

Nobody was killed or seriously hurt, thank God.

Jim Adams was not the only one of my children to come close to actual combat with a major literary figure. About the time Jim and Yevtushenko were menacing each other on the

Amazon, Mark Vonnegut was considering a fight with Jack
Kerouac in our kitchen on Cape Cod. These confrontations
even took place in the same time zone, but in different hemis-
pheres.

I knew Kerouac only at the end of his life, which is to say
there was no way for me to know him at all, since he had
become a pinwheel. He had settled briefly on Cape Cod, and
a mutual friend, the writer Robert Boles, brought him over
to my house one night. I doubt that Kerouac knew anything
about me or my work, or even where he was. He was crazy.
He called Boles, who is black, "a blue-gummed nigger." He
said that Jews were the real Nazis, and that Allen Ginsberg
had been told by the Communists to befriend Kerouac, in
order that they might gain control of American young people, whose leader he was.

This was pathetic. There were clearly thunderstorms in
the head of this once charming and just and intelligent man.
He wished to play poker, so I dealt some cards. There were
four hands, I think—one for Boles, one for Kerouac, one for
Jane, one for me. Kerouac picked up the remainder of the
deck, and he threw it across the kitchen.

It was then that Mark came in, unexpectedly home for a
weekend from Swarthmore College, where he was a religion
major. He was also a middleweight wrestler in very good
shape. He wore a full beard and a work shirt and blue jeans,
and carried a duffel bag. Everything about his costume and
even his posture might have been inspired by Kerouac's
books.

The moment Kerouac saw him, Kerouac stood and looked
him over smolderingly from head to toe. The calm before a
fight settled dankly over the room.

"You think you understand me," said Kerouac to Mark.

"You don't understand me at all. You want to fight about it?" Mark said nothing, not knowing who Kerouac was or what he was so mad about.

Kerouac praised himself as a fighter, asked Mark if he really thought he was man enough to take him on.

Mark understood this much, anyway: that he might really have to fight this person. He didn't want to, but then again, he wouldn't have minded fighting him all that much.

But then Kerouac sat back down in his chair heavily, shaking his head and saying over and over again, "Doesn't understand me at all."

Later on that night, after Kerouac and Boles left, Mark and I talked some about Kerouac, who was then completing his seventeenth and last book. He would die very soon.

It turned out that Mark had never read Kerouac.

❦

AND Mark is a physician now, married to Pat O'Shea, a schoolteacher, and they have one son, Zachary Vonnegut, the firstborn of my grandchildren, now three years old, and the only one so far to carry on my own curious last name. Mark is the first Vonnegut in America to be a healer, and only the second one to earn a doctor's degree of any sort. My brother Bernard, of course, has a doctor's degree in chemistry.

And Conrad Aiken, the poet, the one time I met him, told me that a child will compete with its father in an area where the father is weak, in an area where the father mistakenly believes himself to be quite accomplished. Aiken himself did this, by his own account. His father was a Renaissance man, a surgeon, an athlete, something of a musician, something of a poet, and on and on. Aiken said that he himself became a poet because he realized that his father's poetry really wasn't very good.

So what am I, if I believe that, to make of myself as mirrored in my own children, who cheerfully compete in every area, including writing, in which I have ever dabbled while they were watching? I played chess a little, and now all of them can beat me at chess. I painted and drew some, and now Jim Adams and Mark Vonnegut and Edith Vonnegut and Nanette Vonnegut can all paint and draw circles around me. Desperately, this old man is going to have a one-man show of his drawings this fall, but they're no damn good.

Yes, and I carpentered some, so now Jim Adams and Kurt Adams and Steve Adams and Mark Vonnegut can all do cabinet work. And on and on.

Mark has written a first-rate book. Edith has not only written but illustrated a first-rate book.

I noodled around some on the piano and the clarinet, so Steve Adams now composes his own music and performs with his guitar in cabarets, and Mark plays saxophone and a little piano in a jazz band composed entirely of physicians, and on and on.

This is terrible.

❦

I find that I want to protect the privacy of my two daughters, and so will talk about them very little. Nanette and Edith are both gifted artists. Both have found the life of an artist a lonely one. Edith has determined that loneliness is not too high a price to pay. Nanette is becoming a nurse who will make pictures for fun.

❦

AND meanwhile the man-made weather of politics and economics and technology will blow them this way and that.

❦

WHAT is my favorite among all the works of art my children have so far produced? It is perhaps a letter written by my youngest daughter Nanette. It is so *organic!* She wrote it to "Mr. X," an irascible customer at a Cape Cod restaurant where she worked as a waitress in the summer of 1978. The customer was so mad about the service he had received one evening, you see, that he had complained in writing to the management. The management posted the letter on the kitchen bulletin board.

Nanette's reply went like this:

Dear Mr. X,

As a newly trained waitress I feel that I must respond to the letter of complaint which you recently wrote to the ABC Inn. Your letter has caused more suffering to an innocent young woman this summer than the inconvenience you experienced in not receiving your soup on time and having your bread taken away prematurely and so on.

I believe that you did in fact receive poor service from this new waitress. I recall her as being very flustered and upset that evening, but she hoped that her errors, clumsy as they were, would be understood sympathetically as inexperience. I myself have made mistakes in serving. Fortunately, the customers were humorous and compassionate. I have learned so much from these mistakes, and through the support and understanding of other waitresses and customers in the span of only one week, that I feel confident now about what I am doing, and seldom make mistakes.

There is no doubt in my mind that Katharine is on her way to becoming a competent waitress. You must understand that learning how to waitress is very much the same as learning how to juggle. It is difficult to find the correct balance and timing. Once these are found, though, waitressing becomes a solid and unshakable skill.

There must be room for error even in such a finely tuned establishment as the ABC Inn. There must be allowance for waitresses being human. Maybe you did not realize that in naming this young woman you made it necessary for the management to fire her. Katharine is now without a summer job on Cape Cod, and school is ahead.

Can you imagine how difficult it is to find jobs here now? Do you know how hard it is for many young students to make ends meet these days? I feel it is my duty as a human being to ask you to think twice about what is of importance in life. I hope that in all fairness you will think about what I have said, and that in the future you will be more thoughtful and humane in your actions.

Sincerely,
Nanette Vonnegut.

xlv

JONATHAN SWIFT
MISPERCEIVED

Is it possible for a man of my eminence to write so badly that he is rejected? Yes, indeed. It takes some doing, though. As my own vanity publisher, I intend to thrust one such fizzle into our culture anyway. It is an essay on Jonathan Swift, which I submitted as a preface for a new edition of *Gulliver's Travels.*

The publisher's objection was that I had sentimentalized Swift, having failed, apparently, to have read any detailed accounts of his life and character. Here is how I did it:

"Go, traveler," says his epitaph in Latin, "and imitate, if you can, one who strove with all his strength to champion liberty." Jonathan Swift (1667–1745), an Anglican priest, wrote this about his own long life. He is buried beside his wife in Dublin's St. Patrick's Cathedral, where he was dean for his final thirty-two years. It was in Dublin that he wrote *Gulliver's Travels,* a book as enduring as any cathedral. The appointment to St. Patrick's had disappointed him. He had hoped for a bishopric in England. Be that as it may, he became, according to Swift scholar Ricardo B. Quintana, "Dublin's foremost citizen and Ireland's great patriotic dean." In our own thin-skinned and solemn society, it would be impossible for such a ferocious satirist to become the head of a cathedral and a treasured public man.

He began to write *Gulliver's Travels* when he was about my age, which is fifty-four. He finished it when he was sixty. He was already recognized as one of the most bitterly funny writers of his or any time. His motives were invariably serious, however, and I now suggest that *Gulliver's Travels* can be read as a series of highly responsible sermons, delivered during a crisis in Christian attitudes, one that is far from over yet. The crisis is this, in my opinion: It simply will not do for adult Christians to think of themselves as God's little lambs anymore.

Swift died before the invention of the steam engine or the iron plow—or of the Constitution of the United States, for that matter. But he was aware of microscopes and telescopes and the calculus, and Harvey's theories about the circulation of human blood, and Newton's laws of motion, and all that. There were certainly strong hints around that the natural orders of things, so long so stubborn and mysterious, might in fact be wonderful clocks which could be tinkered with, which might even be taken apart and reassembled. Human reason was in the process of assuming powers to change life such as only armies and disasters had possessed before. So Dublin's first citizen found it urgent that we take an unsentimental look, for the good of the universe, at the great apes that were suddenly doing such puissant thinking. Lambs, indeed!

In *Gulliver's Travels,* Swift sets such high standards for unsentimentality about human beings that most of us can meet those standards only in wartime, and only briefly even then. He shrinks us, urinates on us, expands us and peers into all our nauseating apertures, encourages us to demonstrate our stupidity and mendaciousness, makes us hideously old. On paper he subjects us to every humiliating test that imaginative fiction can invent. And what is learned about us in the course of these Auschwitzian experiments? Only this, according to Swift's hero, Captain Gulliver: that we are disgusting in the extreme. We can be sure that this is not Swift's own opinion of us, thank God—for, before he allows Gulliver to declare us no better than vomit, he makes Gulliver insane. That *has* to be the deepest meaning of Gulliver's adoration of horses, since Swift himself had no more than average respect for those dazed and skittish animals. Gulliver is no longer the reliable witness he was in Chapter I.

I had a teacher in high school who assured me that a person has to be at least a little insane to harp on human disgustingness as much as Swift does. And Swift harps on it long before Gulliver has gone insane. I would tell that teacher now, if she were still alive, that his harping is so relentless that it becomes ridiculous, and is meant to be ridiculous, and that Swift is teaching us a lesson almost as important as the one about our not being lambs: that our readiness to feel disgust for ourselves and others is not, perhaps, the guardian of civilization so many of us imagine it to be. Disgust, in fact, may be the chief damager of our reason, of our common sense—may make us act against our own best interests, may make us insane.

Swift does not develop this theme, but the history of the past hundred years or so has surely done it for him. What is it that has allowed civilized human beings to build and operate death camps? Disgust. What has encouraged them to bomb undefended cities, to torture prisoners, to beat up their own spouses and children, to blow out their own brains? Disgust. Yes. In my opinion, *Gulliver's Travels* is a remarkable effort to inject us with an overdose of disgustedness, and thus to immunize us from that most dangerous disease.

This Book-of-the-Month Club edition of *Gulliver's Travels* is based on the Oxford University Press edition of 1971, which was edited by Paul Turner, Lecturer in English Literature at Oxford. That edition has what this one lacks: an introduction and hundreds of fascinating notes by him. I recommend that edition to all who want the pleasure of relating the tale to Swift's own adventures and times, and who would like help in speculating as to the plausibleness of Captain Gulliver's endless lies. Mr. Turner tells us, for example: "The scale of Lilliput is one inch to a foot of the ordinary world. Mogg mentions [F. Mogg, *Scientific American,* Vol. CLXXIX, 1948] some biological difficulties: a Lilliputian would have room for far fewer cortical cells (so far less intelligence) than a chimpanzee; his head would be too small to carry useful eyes; and he would need eight times as many calories per ounce of body-weight as a full-scale man needs —twenty-four meals a day instead of three." As for the giants of Brobdingnag, he refers to Mogg again, who "calls a sixty-foot man 'an engineering impossibility.' The skeleton would need considerable modification to support the weight (about ninety tons): shorter legs, smaller head, thicker neck, and larger trunk (to accommodate adequate internal organs to power such a huge machine)." And so on.

The justification for publishing an edition as naked of notes as this one is, of course, is that the author, like all authors, wished his book to be loved for itself alone. If the ghost of Jonathan Swift is among us, it must resent terrifically my own Yahoolike intrusion here. I apologize. Next to my being in this volume at all, my most serious offense is failing to convey how much rage and joy and irrationality must have gone into the creation of this masterpiece. In praising the sanity of *Gulliver's Travels,* I have made it sound altogether *too* sane.

XV

JEKYLL AND HYDE
UPDATED

L EE Guber, the Broadway producer, became a friend
of mine when we served on the New York State
Council for the Arts. During the summer of 1978 he asked
me to write a modern version of Robert Louis Stevenson's
Dr. Jekyll and Mr. Hyde for the musical stage. The original,
by the way, is a tiny thing, no more than sixty pages. There
is very little characterization in the original, which is surpris-
ingly sketchy and sparsely populated. It was the first piece
of writing for which Stevenson was paid.

I never got paid for my version. I consider it excellent, if
a little slapdash and short. It is called *The Chemistry Professor,* and it goes like this:

PALM SUNDAY

THE TIME: THE PRESENT, SPRINGTIME. THE PLACE:
SWEETBREAD COLLEGE, A SMALL, LIBERAL-ARTS
INSTITUTION OUTSIDE PHILADELPHIA.

SCENE 1: THE COLLEGE GATE, NOON.

[*At the rise: A chorus of male and female students is
discovered, desperately unhappy, making extravagant
demonstrations of grief. A particularly pretty and
scatterbrained coed is named KIMBERLY. Her
studious boyfriend is named SAM. Each person has a
fresh copy of the student newspaper, which has told
them that the college is bankrupt, and will probably
close forever.*]

KIMBERLY: I can't stand it!
SAM: What kind of a world is this, where a thing like this can
    happen?
STUDENT 1: What a rotten, stinking society this is!

[*And so on. The cries become more musical and the
milling more formal, so that a song and dance about
outrageous fortune materializes. No mention has yet
been made, however, as to what the misery is all
about. The number ends with the students strewn
about in poses of dejection.*]

STUDENT 1: I feel like getting drunk.
SAM: What good would that do?
STUDENT 1: At least I could throw up.
KIMBERLY: You always do.

261

[*SALLY CATHCART, a Judy Garland look-alike,
enters boisterously in cheerleading garb, carrying
pom-poms high. She has not heard the news.*]

SALLY: Hey, gang—what's there to be so blue about? It's
springtime!
KIMBERLY: Where have you been, Sally?
SALLY: Cheerleading practice. [*A sample cheer*] With an S,
with a W, with an E, E, T! With a B, with an R, with an
E, A, D! Sweetbread! Sweetbread! Sweetbread!
SAM: The college is bankrupt, Sally.
SALLY: Oh, no!
SAM: [*Handing her a paper*] It's in the *Daily Pancreas.*
KIMBERLY: They wouldn't dare print it, if it weren't true.
SALLY: [*Reading*] "Bankrupt! Closing its doors forever in
two weeks' time." The most innocent college in the world.
SAM: Drop your pom-poms, Sally. Nothing to cheer for here
anymore.
SALLY: I won't drop them yet, Sam—but I'll carry them low.
CHORUS: [*Singing   as   one,   a   rich   chord*]
Lowwwwwwwwwwwwwwwwww.

[*JERRY RIVERS, a Mickey Rooney look-alike and
president of the student body, enters with his
stepfather, FRED LEGHORN, shrewd hayseed king
of the mechanized chicken industry.*]

SAM: Hey—it's Jerry Rivers, the president of the student
body.
JERRY: Gang—this is my mother's fifth and possibly final
husband, Fred Leghorn, the largest producer of chickens
in the world.

SALLY: Do you ever get tired of chickens, Mr. Leghorn?

LEGHORN: Anybody who is tired of chickens is tired of life.

SAM: You hear about the bankruptcy, Jerry?

JERRY: Yeah. I keep wondering what an ordinary bunch of kids like us can do.

[*JERRY puts his hands behind his back, does a tap dance as he ponders the problem. He stops, speaks to the chorus.*]

JERRY: You kids got any ideas?

[*Members of the chorus put their hands behind their backs and duplicate his steps in unison. They stop and sing the next line with a gorgeous choral effect.*]

CHORUS: [*Singing*]   What can ordinary kids like us do about anything?

LEGHORN: Maybe you could have a cake sale.

SALLY: Mr. Leghorn—couldn't you give us a few million buckaroonies or so?

LEGHORN: I came down here to see what this stepson of mine was getting for ten thousand dollars a year, and I must say I'm not overwhelmed with respect. It looks like Disneyland without the rides to me.

KIMBERLY: But we're your nation's future!

LEGHORN: That's what I mean.

JERRY: Wait a minute! I've got it! We'll put together a Broadway musical with all the talent we've got right here!

CHORUS: [*Thunderstruck, as one*]   Wow! Do you think we really could?

JERRY: Why not? We could take a piece of meretricious kid

263

crap up there and make enough in a season to keep this academic bucket shop running for years!

CHORUS: [*As one*] Holy smokes!

SALLY: Jerry—just one question: Are we still in love?

JERRY: You mean in spite of the bankruptcy? It's too early to tell.

SALLY: I'll wait.

[*ELBERT WHITEFEET, the beloved old college president and philosopher, enters wild with grief over the bankruptcy. He is comforted by DR. HENRY JEKYLL, the venerable head of the chemistry department, and by POPS, the doddering campus cop. WHITEFEET and JEKYLL wear academic caps and gowns. POPS is uniformed like a Keystone Cop. It is a wild scene. Students look on in horror and pity as WHITEFEET tears out handfuls of his own hair, rends his garments, dumps a trash container over himself, and so on.*]

WHITEFEET: I don't want to live anymore!

POPS: Please, sir—the student body is watching.

WHITEFEET: I don't care!

POPS: They shouldn't see the president of their college in this condition. They might write home.

WHITEFEET: They should hang me from the Senior Elm for what I've done.

JEKYLL: Elbert—you haven't done anything a million other nincompoops might not have done.

WHITEFEET: [*Embracing Jekyll*] Ah—Dr. Henry Jekyll— the head of the chemistry department and my closest friend. Faithful old Henry, the only faculty member with a statewide reputation.

264

JERRY: President Whitefeet—Dr. Jekyll—what happened to the endowment, which was supposed to be so big and well invested—the Xerox, the Polaroid, the IBM.

WHITEFEET: [*Echoing tragically*] The Xerox, the Polaroid, the IBM.

CHORUS: The Xerox, the Polaroid, the IBM.

> [*This sets off a terrific rhythm number that builds and builds, and consists of the chanting of the names of common stocks. Everybody is caught up in a mad, slobbering war dance about wealth. It ends in panting exhaustion.*]

LEGHORN: What did happen to all those stocks?

KIMBERLY: [*Sexually aroused by wealth*] All those woo-zum, coozum, squoozum blue chip stocks. Yum, yum! Yum, yum!

WHITEFEET: A clean-cut young investment counselor with a silver tongue came into my office two months ago. I was reading Plato at the time.

SAM: What part of Plato, sir?

WHITEFEET: [*Indignantly*] I don't have to answer pip-squeak questions like that anymore. I was reading Plato. Period.

SAM: Yes, sir.

WHITEFEET: It's all kind of one big mixed up thing anyway. Can't tell where one thing stops and the next thing begins. This investment counselor said to me, "Lift your blood-shot eyes from the yellowed page, old philosopher. Look at the world as it has come to be! There's money to be made! In two months' time, Sweetbread College could be twice as rich as Harvard!"

265

SALLY: But Harvard's too big!

KIMBERLY: Harvard's too hard!

SAM: They're really serious up there.

WHITEFEET: "Put everything you've got into cocoa futures," he said.

LEGHORN: Oh Lord.

WHITEFEET: Please, for the love of God, don't anybody ever mention cocoa in my presence again.

SALLY: What are cocoa futures?

WHITEFEET: I still don't know.

KIMBERLY: I'll go to the library and look it up.

WHITEFEET: That's what you're here for—to learn how to look things up.

LEGHORN: [*To Kimberly*] Look under "C."

KIMBERLY: [*Sincerely*] Thanks for the tip.

[*KIMBERLY exits.*]

WHITEFEET: If my doctor's thesis had not been about philosophical arguments against suicide, I would be a dead man now.

JERRY: Dr. Whitefeet—?

WHITEFEET: [*Indicating that he is non compos mentis with self-loathing*] Bluh, bluh, bluh.

JERRY: Sir—I've been talking to the rest of the kids, and we thought maybe we could put on a Broadway musical.

WHITEFEET: Uck.

LEGHORN: The smartest thing you ever said.

JERRY: I haven't figured out what it should be about.

SALLY: You're a show business genius, Jerry. You can do anything.

SAM: We could do the story of Jesus Christ.

JERRY: Maybe.

SALLY: [*Singing to tune of "Ach Du Lieber Augustine"*]
Oh, I am Mary Magdalene,
Magdalene, Magdalene—
I am Mary Magdalene.
How do you do?

POPS: [*To same tune*]   I have got the leprosy,
Leprosy, leprosy.
I have got the leprosy.
Who will cure me?

JERRY: No, no. Kids have done Jesus Christ to death on-stage. (A double take) Say, Pops, I didn't know you could sing.

POPS: I was on my way to being a star of stage, screen, and radio. But then my dog was run over, and I entered a period of deep depression from which I never recovered. Nobody starts out to be a campus cop.

JEKYLL: Cripes—you know, I ought to be able to do something to help. Come up with a chemical discovery of some kind.

WHITEFEET: You've already given the world the recipe for Betty Crocker banana cake.

JEKYLL: I'm thinking of something really dangerous, Nobel prize stuff. You can't scare the pants off people with a banana cake.

JERRY: Come on, kids! Let's get cracking! Let's go over to the Mildred Peasely Bangtree Memorial Theater, and see what we can put together. We'll stay up all night!

JEKYLL: I'll stay up all night, too! This is exciting! This is just the kind of a kick in the butt I've needed for years.

[*All students exit.*]

LEGHORN: Who was Mildred Peasely Bangtree?
WHITEFEET: Beats me.

[*KIMBERLY enters.*]

KIMBERLY: Excuse me—

[*LEGHORN, JEKYLL, WHITEFEET, and POPS gather together as a barbershop quartet, and sing a heart-rending ballad, "How Can We Help You, Little Girl?"*]
KIMBERLY: You all through?
LEGHORN, JEKYLL, WHITEFEET, POPS: [*Still singing in harmony*] All through.
KIMBERLY: Which building is the library?

CURTAIN

❦

SCENE 2: DR. JEKYLL'S LABORATORY. TEN O'CLOCK AT NIGHT. A PAINTED BACKDROP WITH AN OPERATING WINDOW AND DOOR IN IT.

[*At the rise: Library clock strikes ten. Dog howls. DR. JEKYLL is alone and going through hell, trying to think of something really good to discover. The theater is within hailing distance.*]
JEKYLL: Gosh darn it to heck. Let's put on the old thinking cap, and cogitate. Jesus, this is really a doozy, trying to

think up something nobody ever thought up before. Everything I think of has been thought of.

[*JERRY appears in the window. He is dejected.*]

JERRY: Dr. Jekyll—looks like you're going to have to save the college singlehanded. We can't think up a story.

JEKYLL: Things are none too brisk in the lab, my boy. Why is it that every time you need a Nobel prize-type idea, you never can think of one?

JERRY: I'm sending over some inspiration for you. Hope it helps.

JEKYLL: Inspiration?

JERRY: You'll see.

[*JERRY exits. LEGHORN knocks on the door.*]

JEKYLL: *Entrez.*

[*LEGHORN enters with a bottle containing a green chemical.*]

LEGHORN: I wonder if you'd run an analysis on this for me. It's some kind of dope one of my competitors is feeding his chickens. I'd like to know what's in it. I'll pay you well.

JEKYLL: That's like asking Albert Einstein to balance your checkbook.

LEGHORN: He couldn't tie his own shoelaces. Everybody knows that. [*Spotting a row of bottles*] A half gallon of LSD! Amphetamines! Barbiturates! Quaaludes! Vitamin E! What are you doing with this stuff?

JEKYLL: Taken from students at different times.

LEGHORN: No wonder they think they're so talented. I'll give you five hundred bucks if you can give me an analysis of this stuff before I get out of here—tomorrow at noon. That's only in the event, of course, that your Nobel prize project falls through. Good night.

[*LEGHORN exits. JEKYLL sniffs the sample.*]

JEKYLL: Whoooeee! That'll put hair on your chest! Smells like a mixture of crème de menthe and athlete's foot to me.

[*SALLY knocks on the door, calls through it seductively.*]

SALLY: Dr. Jekyll, Dr. Jekyll.
JEKYLL: *Entrez.*

[*SALLY enters at the head of a line of coeds in diaphanous nightgowns. They have come to inspire him. KIMBERLY is among them.*]

JEKYLL: [*Petrified, retreating*]   What kind of a frame-up is this? I've never had anything to do with sex in my life!
SALLY: This isn't sex.
JEKYLL: It isn't?
SALLY: We're Muses. Jerry had us dress up like Muses, and told us to come over and inspire you.
JEKYLL: I'd hate to have to explain that to the state police.
SALLY: You just relax and enjoy it.

[*The music starts up, and the girls do a sort of here-we-go-gathering-nuts-in-May dance with and around JEKYLL, tickling him, blowing in his ears, decking him with flowers, and so on. The dance ends*] *with JEKYLL in a sensationally compromising position.*

WHITEFEET enters without knocking, and is scandalized.]

WHITEFEET: I am revolted! I am disillusioned! I am scandalized!

JEKYLL: It isn't what it looked like.

WHITEFEET: It looked like a full professor playing here-we-go-gathering-nuts-in-May.

SALLY: It was our fault, Dr. Whitefeet.

WHITEFEET: What do you foolish virgins know? You couldn't find your own behinds with both hands.

KIMBERLY: [*Proudly, innocently*]   I just found mine.

WHITEFEET: [*Pointing to JEKYLL*]   There is the man I hold responsible. He is not only a Dr. Jekyll—he is a Dr. Jekyll and Mr. Hyde.

SALLY: [*Echoing wonderingly*]   Dr. Jekyll and Mr. Hyde. [*More firmly*] Dr. Jekyll and Mr. Hyde! That's it!

JEKYLL: Who's Mr. Hyde?

SALLY: That's the story for our musical! Dr. Jekyll and Mr. Hyde—it's never been done. Wait till I tell Jerry!

WHITEFEET: Just a minute! What about this moral outrage I saw here?

SALLY: [*On her way out, leading the other coeds*]   Buster—when you peed away the endowment on cocoa futures, you ceased to exist as a moral leader for me. You don't have the brains God gave a clay pigeon.

[*SALLY and the coeds exit.*]

WHITEFEET: I suppose I had that coming. It's probably good for me that people speak to me like that from time to time.

JEKYLL: Who's Mr. Hyde?

WHITEFEET: From the famous story, "Dr. Jekyll and Mr. Hyde," by Clare Boothe Luce.

JEKYLL: I never heard of it.

WHITEFEET: Your name is Jekyll, and you never heard of one of the most famous stories in all of our literature—a story with your own name in it?

JEKYLL: I don't make you feel like something the cat drug in because you don't know any chemistry. Don't you make me feel like something the cat drug in because I don't know any literature.

WHITEFEET: It's about a man who discovers a substance that changes his whole personality and appearance when he drinks it. He changes from nice Dr. Jekyll to terrible Mr. Hyde.

JEKYLL: He drinks it himself?

WHITEFEET: And becomes a monster.

JEKYLL: Doesn't give it to somebody else. He drinks it himself.

WHITEFEET: That's right.

JEKYLL: [*Inspired*]   Boy—that's what I call balls.

[*Cheers come from the theater as SALLY delivers the good news.*]

JERRY: [*Off, far away*]   That's it, kids! Jekyll and Hyde!

CURTAIN

❧

SCENE 3: THE BARE STAGE OF THE MILDRED PEASELY
BANGTREE MEMORIAL THEATER—A FEW MINUTES
LATER.

> [*At the rise: All the students, except for JERRY,
> SALLY, KIMBERLY, and SAM, are onstage. They
> are excited about doing* Dr. Jekyll and Mr. Hyde.
> POPS *is looking on. The girls are still in nightgowns.*
>
> *Accompanied by scary music, they experiment with
> turning into monsters, uttering maniacal laughs, and
> generally trying to scare the hell out of each other.*
>
> JERRY, SALLY, KIMBERLY, *and* SAM *enter,
> loaded down with Victorian costumes and props.*]

JERRY: Okay, kids—we found all this stuff in the costume
loft. Come and get it.

> [*They throw down the costumes, and people set about
> clothing themselves, including SALLY, KIMBERLY,
> and SAM.*]

POPS: Can I pick a costume, too?

JERRY: No. You're perfect as you are. We need a comedy cop.

POPS: [*Offended*]   There's real bullets in my gun.

JERRY: You're kidding! They shouldn't trust you with a
squirt gun loaded with lemonade!

POPS: Thanks a lot.

JERRY: Any time.

> [*LEGHORN enters from the wings, impressed by a
> machine he has seen back there.*]

LEGHORN: Mind if I watch you geniuses work?

JERRY: Glad to have you, Dad.

[*Everybody but JERRY and LEGHORN and POPS turns his or her back to the audience, and applies monster makeup, becoming Dracula or Frankenstein or Wolfman or whatever.*]

LEGHORN: You can stop calling me that. Your mother and I have filed for divorce.

JERRY: Well, whoever you are, take a seat somewhere.

LEGHORN: There's a hell of a machine back here. Looks like one of my old industrial chicken roasters—from the early days.

[*JERRY has a look, is thrilled.*]

JERRY: Oh, boy! A fog machine—left over from our rock and roll version of *Macbeth*.

LEGHORN: Some boat whistles, too.

JERRY: Left over from our rock and roll version of *The Old Man and the Sea.* [*He takes his place stage center.*] Okay, gang—face this way, please.

[*Everybody faces him—with horrifying effect.*]

JERRY: Oh, no—everybody can't be the monster!

SALLY: But everybody loves monsters so.

[*This starts off a production number about how everybody loves monsters, but that not everybody is lucky enough to be a monster, that some people have to be good-looking and therefore hated by everyone, and so on.*]

JERRY: Gee—I wonder how the real-life Jekyll is doing over in the lab?

LEGHORN: He can't even light a Bunsen burner, if you ask me.

CURTAIN

❁

SCENE 4: DR. JEKYLL'S LABORATORY—A FEW MINUTES
LATER.

[*At the rise: Idiotic rock music can be heard coming
from the theater through the open window. It consists
of a repetition of "Jekyll and Hyde! whoe whoe, baby,
good old Jekyll and Hyde!" JEKYLL is alone,
happily adding LSD and the unknown diet
supplement for chickens and so forth to a large
beaker, which is giving off unwholesome fumes.*

*JEKYLL closes the window, shutting out the music.
He continues about his business, singing to himself, to
the tune of "Humoresque."*]

JEKYLL: [*Singing*]   We were walking through the park,
A-goosing statues in the dark.
If Sherman's horse can take it,
So can you—oo!

[*There is a knock on the door.*]

JEKYLL: [*Aside*] Hmmmm. A possible guinea pig. [*To
knocker*] *Entrez, s'il vous plait.*

[*Jekyll's wife, a gorgeous, tragically neglected older
woman, enters. He does not recognize her. She
immediately sings to him in a rich contralto a
show-stopping song about her total devotion to him.*]

275

JEKYLL: May I ask who you are?

MRS. JEKYLL: I'm your wife, Henry.

JEKYLL: Right, right, right. Got it now.

MRS. JEKYLL: When you failed to come home for supper, I called around to find out what had become of you.

JEKYLL: [*Genuinely concerned*] Am I all right?

MRS. JEKYLL: Here you are.

JEKYLL: Thank God. I could be lying in a ditch somewhere.

MRS. JEKYLL: They said you were going all out for the Nobel prize.

JEKYLL: [*Intensely*] It's the new me, Mildred.

MRS. JEKYLL: [*Correcting him*] Hortense.

JEKYLL: It's the new me, Hortense. Say—you look thirsty to me.

MRS. JEKYLL: Thirsty?

JEKYLL: [*Offering the beaker*] This'll put hair on your chest.

MRS. JEKYLL: Why would I want hair on my chest?

JEKYLL: Just a friendly expression. You have to pick me up on every last little thing? I don't know how our marriage has lasted as long as it has.

MRS. JEKYLL: That stuff smells vile!

JEKYLL: But you love me so much. That was you, wasn't it?

MRS. JEKYLL: Yes—it was I.

JEKYLL: Okay—so drink, chug-a-lug, chug-a-lug; so drink, chug-a-lug, chug-a-lug!

MRS. JEKYLL: This is the first thing I have ever refused you.

[*MRS. JEKYLL exits with dignity.*]

JEKYLL: [*Aside*] If it's anything that burns me up, it's women's lib. [*To himself*] Okay, big boy—if you're ever going to get to Stockholm, you'd better drink this stuff yourself. Here goes nothing.

[*He holds his nose and drinks. Nothing happens for a moment, then a horrible transformation starts to take place. He claws at his throat, makes subhuman sounds, drops to the floor, rolls out of sight under a desk. When he emerges, he has become an enormous, homicidal chicken. He flings open the window, and, flapping his wings, jumps out into the night.*]

CURTAIN

❦

INTERMISSION

❦

SCENE 5: THE STAGE AT MIDNIGHT THE SAME NIGHT. THE STUDENTS HAVE BUILT A SET TO REPRESENT A NINETEENTH-CENTURY LONDON STREET. THERE ARE THREE FACADES FROM LEFT TO RIGHT: A LOW-LIFE PUB, A SINISTER STOREHOUSE WHERE JEKYLL DOES HIS EXPERIMENTS, AND JEKYLL'S RESPECTABLE HOME. ALL HAVE OPERATING DOORS. THERE ARE STREETLAMPS. THERE IS A PROMINENT SIGN ON THE SECRET LAB SAYING, "SECRET LAB."

[*Before the rise: College library clock strikes twelve.*

At the rise: Full cast, except for WHITEFEET, DR. JEKYLL, and MRS. JEKYLL, is onstage. All except LEGHORN, who is a mere observer in his regular business suit, are dressed in Victorian costumes from every level of society. POPS is a bobby, already on duty. SALLY is a whore with a heart of gold, already waiting for customers under a lamppost. JERRY, who is going to be Dr. Jekyll, wears a top hat and evening cape, and directs many students who are still working on the set, painting, driving nails. Among them is SAM, wearing a tweed suit and derby, who is to be Utterson, Jekyll's best friend, and KIMBERLY, who is dressed as a nursery maid. Her elaborate perambulator is parked on the street. LEGHORN has been interesting himself in the fog machine, which is now putting out wisps of fog.]

JERRY: Okay, kids—that's close enough. We just want to give the general idea. No point in getting it absolutely perfect tonight.

[*Students put down their tools, assemble on the street, awaiting instructions. LEGHORN goes to JERRY.*]

LEGHORN: I got your fog machine going.

JERRY: I see.

LEGHORN: It really is one of my old industrial chicken roasters. Didn't realize they were being sold now as fog machines.

JERRY: It wasn't cheap.

LEGHORN: Nothing ever is. If you ever wanted to roast a half a ton of chicken in five minutes, you still could—feathers and all.

JERRY: That's nice to know.

SALLY: I love you, Jerry. I'd die for you, if you wanted me to.

JERRY: That's nice to know. Places, everybody!

> [*JERRY goes into Jekyll's house. LEGHORN withdraws to one side of apron. SALLY stays under lamppost. POPS continues to patrol. Lower-class types go into pub. KIMBERLY, with her pram, and SAM exit into wings. The rest compose a London street scene in the late afternoon.*
>
> *A rock band in the pit strikes up appropriate music to be written by somebody else, and a nonstop rock ballet about Jekyll and Hyde begins.*
>
> *The story, to be choreographed by somebody else, goes roughly like this, with some information being sung:*
>
> *Everybody on the street is happy, but worried about nightfall and fog. There has been, only a few days before, the murder of a whore under the lamppost where SALLY stands.*
>
> *Dr. Jekyll, played by JERRY, comes out of his house, the image of civic decency, and is recognized and adored by all. He is trying to get into his secret lab without being observed. While biding his time, he performs acts of civic virtue which are noted and admired by one and all. He picks up a piece of trash dropped by somebody else, puts it in a waste barrel, gives money to a beggar, politely declines an invitation*

from SALLY the whore, giving her a gentle lecture, and so on. KIMBERLY enters with her perambulator, and he admires the baby, chucks it under its chin. KIMBERLY exits into wings, to return, going in the opposite direction, a few minutes later.

A fight breaks out in the pub, spills into the street. POPS rushes in to break it up. Everybody but Jekyll goes to watch. Jekyll takes the opportunity to duck into his lab. Lights go on in there.

The fight is broken up, and one of the fighters invites everyone into the pub for a drink on him.

Many accept, go into pub. Some refuse, exit into the wings instead. SALLY resumes her post by the lamppost. The street is otherwise deserted.

Utterson, the lawyer, played by SAM, enters in a state of agitation. He carries a huge briefcase on which is written, "Lawyer." He is on his way to Jekyll's house, is propositioned by SALLY. They dicker. Her price is too high and her services too limited, and he is too busy anyway. He goes and bangs on Jekyll's door. Nobody is home. He sings to the audience that his client and closest friend, Dr. Jekyll, has just written a will leaving everything to a man named Hyde, about whom Utterson has never heard before. He fears that Jekyll has gone insane or is being blackmailed. He gives up, dickers briefly with the whore again, goes into pub for a needed drink.

JERRY, now as the monstrous Mr. Hyde, peers furtively out the secret lab door, sees nobody around but the whore. He whistles to her, crooks his finger at her. She is appalled, but needs the work. She goes into the lab with him, and the door is closed.

A drunk comes out of the pub, sings a song about the beauty of love, staggers off into the wings.

The lab door opens. The whore reels out, her clothes in frightful disarray. Hyde throws money after her, heaps scorn on her as she picks it up. She exits in disorder and shame. Hyde remains in the doorway, looking up and down the street for other opportunities to do evil.

KIMBERLY enters with her perambulator, on her way home from the park. She seems an ideal target of opportunity. She pauses, giving him a chance to duck into the lab to get a black spherical bomb with a fuse sticking out of it, which he shows to the audience. She starts coming again, and he stops her, pretending to be solicitous, hiding the bomb behind his back. He tells her that she should be careful, that he thinks someone may be following her. She looks back, and he tucks the bomb in with the baby and lights the fuse. She moves on, looking back over her shoulder, exits. Hyde ducks into lab, closes door.

There is a terrific explosion offstage, people come pouring out of the pub, exit in direction of explosion.

They return, filled with horror. Some carry pieces of the perambulator. Utterson carries a wheel. Last of all come POPS and KIMBERLY. Pops has his pad and pencil out, trying to get Kimberly's story. Most of Kimberly's clothing has been blown away. Her face is black. She still holds the handle of the perambulator.

Utterson draws aside, muses over the clue of the wheel. He sings that he knows his friend Jekyll has been performing secret experiments of great importance and behaving queerly. He wonders if he could be making bombs.

Somebody suggests that everybody go into the pub to have a drink. KIMBERLY says that she certainly needs one. All exit into the pub, except for Utterson, who goes to Jekyll's house and knocks again. JERRY, now a respectable Jekyll again, comes out of the lab unobserved, again picks up a piece of trash, puts it into a barrel.

Jekyll comes up behind Utterson, scares the daylights out of him. Utterson asks him if his research involves bombs. Jekyll says he has discovered a means of controlling human character with chemicals. Utterson says this is more dangerous than bombs. Jekyll says it is perfectly safe, with no harmful side effects. He confesses that he turned himself into Hyde many times, and that he isn't going to do it anymore, that Hyde is dead. "No harmful side effects?" says Utterson. Jekyll echoes this, but with qualifications— blurred vision sometimes, constipation, swollen ankles, nothing serious. Utterson asks how he feels now. Jekyll says he never felt better, but then has an attack. He turns into Hyde.

He chokes Utterson to death. There are Grand Guignol effects, with Utterson spitting out catsup, sticking out an impossibly long tongue, and so on.

Still clinging to Utterson's throat, Hyde, played by JERRY, sings a tragic song about how the most idealistic experiments can sometimes go wrong.

KIMBERLY, POPS, and a few others come out of the pub, all half in the bag. KIMBERLY is still holding the handle of the perambulator. They see Hyde choking the dead Utterson. KIMBERLY identifies him as the man who probably blew up the baby, tells POPS to shoot him like a mad dog.

POPS draws his real pistol, which is loaded, and is so carried away by the drama that he actually takes a shot at JERRY, shattering a streetlamp.

Everything stops.]

JERRY: [*As JERRY, dropping Utterson*] That was a real bullet.

POPS: I told you I had real bullets in my gun. Nobody kills babies while I'm around.

JERRY: Imbecile!

LEGHORN: [*Striding onstage to disarm Pops*] I'll take that thing. [*He sticks the pistol under his belt.*]

POPS: I lost my head.

JERRY: I almost lost my life. Get out of here!

POPS: What can I say after I've said I'm sorry?

JERRY: Try "Good-bye."

POPS: This thing is never going to make it to Broadway anyway. [*He exits.*]

LEGHORN: Well—if this show has accomplished nothing else, at least it's disarmed a campus cop.

JERRY: The whole thing stunk. I really let you down this time, gang. I resign as head of the student body.

[*SALLY enters, still a mess, deeply concerned about Jerry.*]

SALLY: Jerry—

JERRY: You don't have to tell me: You don't love me anymore. I don't even love myself anymore.

SALLY: It wasn't your fault, Jerry. I mean—it was a story we found in the public domain. Everybody knows there's nothing but picked-over garbage in the public domain.

LEGHORN: A little chicken would cheer us all up about now —but I don't know where we could find a chicken this time of night.

[*POPS screams in terror outside the theater. The screams go on and on. Nobody is much concerned.*]

SALLY: What's that?

JERRY: It sounds like Pops got himself caught in his zipper again.

SAM: Happens all the time.

KIMBERLY: I don't know—that doesn't quite sound like his zipper scream.

[*POPS enters, mad with terror, breathless.*]

POPS: [*Pointing, gasping*] I just saw—I just saw—I just saw—

LEGHORN: You're not making any sense.

POPS: I just saw the biggest chicken in history.

LEGHORN: Uh huh. The biggest chicken in history weighed fifty-six pounds and four ounces, and was found on Bikini Atoll after a hydrogen bomb test there.

POPS: Bigger than that.

LEGHORN: And what was this chicken doing?

POPS: As God is my witness—it was eating a Doberman pinscher alive.

JERRY: He just wants his gun back.

LEGHORN: I don't know. Strange things happen in the chicken world. [Aside] Often profitable. [To Pops] How much would you say this chicken weighed?

POPS: With or without the Doberman inside?

LEGHORN: Without the dog.

POPS: A hundred and eighty pounds, medium build, white—yellow feet, yellow beak—believed to be dangerous. Somebody better get out an APB.

LEGHORN: A hundred-and-eighty-pound chicken would feed about two hundred people. A few birds like that would go a long way toward ending the protein shortages in India, in Africa, in Moscow—in Bangladesh. [He considers going out to have a look.]

POPS: Oh, sir—I hate your guts, but I beg of you, please don't go out there alone.

LEGHORN: I never met the chicken I could not dominate. Besides, gumshoe, I have a gun with five shots left in it. Remember?

[LEGHORN draws the pistol, blows down the barrel, and exits.]

JERRY: Well—that's all very interesting, but it doesn't have a heck of a lot to do with saving the college, does it?

POPS: You'd think it had to do with everything there ever was, if you saw a chicken that size.

SALLY: Maybe somebody should call the Humane Society.

POPS: The National Guard!

JERRY: Maybe we *should* put on a cake sale.

[*A pistol is fired outside.*]

POPS: Four shots left.

SALLY: Is it legal to shoot a chicken that size?

POPS: A chicken, no matter how big, has no rights in the state of Pennsylvania.

[*Two more pistol shots*]

POPS: Two shots left.

[*LEGHORN rushes back in, holding the smoking gun.*]

LEGHORN: Everybody out! Grab a hammer, a broom—anything! I'm gonna need help with this one. This one must have been fed pure plutonium on Mars. I think I winged it, but I can't be sure.

[*All but KIMBERLY grab makeshift weapons and rush out. SAM is the last one out.*]

SAM: You coming, Kimberly?

KIMBERLY: No. I am a follower of Albert Schweitzer. I have reverence for life. Besides, I'm very sleepy.

SAM: Okay, you take a nap.

[*SAM exits. Sounds of a chase come from outside, fading off into the distance, as KIMBERLY makes a pillow of a discarded garment and goes to sleep on Dr. Jekyll's doorstep. She snores softly, sweetly.*

There are clumsy, subhuman sounds in the wings. The great chicken which the head of the chemistry department has turned himself into enters, desperately hoping to elude its hunters. It is wounded and enraged. It does not see Kimberly at first, and KIMBERLY goes on sleeping. It tears off the door of the pub, uproots a lamppost and bends it double, and so on.

It sees Kimberly at last, approaches her sleeping form with a mixture of dim-witted awe and lust, after the fashion of King Kong. It decides to do something with her—whether to rape her or abduct her or consume her, it is not clear.

We never find out, for just in the nick of time, LEGHORN enters with his pistol cocked and aimed. He is followed by SAM, SALLY, and JERRY.]

LEGHORN: Reach for the sky.

[*The chicken raises its wings, turns around slowly.*]

LEGHORN: Don't try anything fancy. One false move, and you're fricassee.

JERRY: Some bird!

LEGHORN: I had a hunch this one would double back to the Mildred Peasely Bangtree Memorial Theater and try to hide in here. Do I know chickens, or do I know chickens?

SALLY: Who was Mildred Peasely Bangtree?

JERRY: No time to wonder that now.

LEGHORN: Quiet now. I'm going to interrogate this roaster.

SALLY: Rooster?

LEGHORN: Roaster.

> [*LEGHORN now conducts a conversation in chicken language with the chicken. It takes quite a while. It is expressive, with moments of excitement and sadness and so on.*]

JERRY: What did it say?

LEGHORN: I thought I had heard every chicken story possible, but this is a new one on me. This is the head of your chemistry department here. He drank a mixture of LSD and chicken tonic and Drano and God only knows what else, in the hopes of winning a Nobel prize. There's more of the stuff back in his laboratory.

SALLY, JERRY, AND SAM: Dr. Jekyll.

> [*LEGHORN says something rueful in chicken language, and the chicken agrees.*]

SAM: What did you just say to him?

LEGHORN: Said he couldn't go to Stockholm looking like that.

> [*Chicken says more, resignedly.*]

LEGHORN: Says he's got three bullets in him, and is dying anyway.

[*The chicken begins a tragic dying scene, which takes a minute or two.*

WHITEFEET and MRS. JEKYLL enter while it is going on. MRS. JEKYLL is carrying the beaker. Everybody is profoundly moved but WHITEFEET, who is overwhelmed with mirth.]

WHITEFEET: That's the funniest costume I ever saw!

MRS. JEKYLL: Shut up you lightweight—you intolerable sparrowfart! That is my husband there. I watched it all through the laboratory window. I have the fatal mixture here. [*She shows the beaker.*]

[*The chicken struggles upright one last time, and sings a farewell aria in chicken language, with orchestral accompaniment. It dies, its feet straight up in the air.*]

SAM: Kimberly, are you all right?

KIMBERLY: I think so. But I'll never be the same. I don't think I can be a follower of Albert Schweitzer anymore.

[*The remainder of the cast enters quietly to gawk.*]

MRS. JEKYLL: What was its last song about?

LEGHORN: I'm liable to bust out crying when I tell you. I never thought a chicken could get to me like that. There's precious little sentimentality in the modern chicken business, believe you me. It sang about the disposal of its remains. It asked to be roasted and wrapped in Reynolds Wrap and given to an orphanage.

MRS. JEKYLL: The first unselfish act of his life.

LEGHORN: Well, we're all in this together now—and the reputation of the college, not that it ever amounted to a hill of beans, depends on what we decide to do. All in favor of roasting it?

ALL: Aye.

LEGHORN: All in favor of wrapping it in Reynolds Wrap?

ALL: Aye.

LEGHORN: All in favor of giving it to an orphanage?

ALL BUT MRS. JEKYLL: No.

MRS. JEKYLL: Abstain.

LEGHORN: Abstention noted. I think you have voted wisely. Allowing even orphans to eat a chicken produced by this method is morally repugnant in a Christian society at this time. Future generations may feel differently. It is the sense of the meeting, then, that the roasted chicken be buried in an unmarked grave as soon as possible, and that nothing more be said about it, since the story, if it ever got out, would interfere with recruiting and fund raising activities of the college, and only confuse the county prosecutor.

CHORUS: [*Singing, directed by JERRY*] Aaaaaaaaaaaaa-men! Aaaaaaaaaaaa-men! Aaaaaaaaaaaaaaa-men!

[*Sobbing, MRS. JEKYLL throws herself on the remains.*]

CURTAIN

XVI

A NAZI SYMPATHIZER DEFENDED AT SOME COST

I have spoken in another chapter of the thunderstorms in the head of Jack Kerouac when I knew him, or to be more truthful, when he was unknowable—near the end of his life. He was to be pitied and forgiven, of course, for all he said while the thunder and lightning was going on.

We arrive now, though, at the case of a writer who not only thought loathsomely on occasion, but who sometimes acted on those loathsome thoughts, and who, as many people have told me very pointedly, can never be forgiven. It is common for people to find his work impossible to read, not because of what he happens to be saying on a given page but because of unforgivable things he has said or written elsewhere.

291

He said often enough himself, one way or another and as a universally despised old man and war criminal, that he had nothing to apologize for, and that forgiveness would be yet another insult from nincompoops.

He would not like me. The evidence is that he was not strikingly fond of any human beings. He loved his cat, which he was forever carrying from here to there like a baby.

He considered himself at least the equal of any living writer. I am told that he once said of the Nobel prize: "Every Vaseline-ass in Europe has one. Where's mine?"

And yet, compulsively, with no financial gain in prospect, and understanding that many people will believe that I share many of his authentically vile opinions, I continue to say that there were good things about this man. And my name is most snugly tied to his in the Penguin paperback editions of his last three books, *Castle to Castle, North,* and *Rigadoon.* My name is on each cover: "With a new introduction," it says, "by Kurt Vonnegut, Jr."

That introduction to all three paperbacks goes like this:

He was in the worst possible taste, by which I mean that he had many educational advantages, becoming a physician, and he was widely traveled in Europe and Africa and North America—and yet he wrote not a single phrase that hinted to similarly advantaged persons that he was something of a gentleman.

He did not seem to understand that aristocratic restraints and sensibilities, whether inherited or learned, accounted for much of the splendor of literature. In my opinion, he discovered a higher and more awful order of literary truth by ignoring the crippled vocabularies of ladies and gentlemen and by using, instead, the more comprehensive language of shrewd and tormented guttersnipes.

Every writer is in his debt, and so is anyone else interested in discussing lives in their entirety. By being so impolite, he demonstrated that perhaps half of all experience, the animal half, had been concealed by good manners. No honest writer or speaker will ever want to be polite again.

Céline has been praised as a stylist. He himself mocked the endlessly repeated typographical trick that made every page he wrote easily recognizable as being his: 'Me and my three dots . . . my supposedly original style! . . . all the real writers will tell you what to think of it! . . .'

The only writers who admire that style enough to imitate it, as far as I know, are gossip columnists. They like its looks. They like the sense of urgency it imparts, willy-nilly, to any piece of information at all.

With no especial help from his eccentric typography, in my opinion, Céline gave us in his novels the finest history we have of the total collapse of Western civilization in two world wars, as witnessed by hideously vulnerable common women and men. That history should be read in the order in which it was written, for each volume speaks knowingly to the ones that came before it.

And the resonating chamber for this intricate system of echoes through time is Céline's first novel, *Journey to the End of the Night,* published in 1932, when the author was thirty-eight. It is important that a reader of any Céline book know in his heart what Céline knew so well, that his writing career began with a masterpiece.

Readers may find their experience softened and deepened, too, if they reflect that the author was a physician who chose to serve patients who were mainly poor. It was common for him not to be paid at all. His real name, by the way, was Louis-Ferdinand Auguste Destouches.

His sympathy may not have lain with the poor and powerless, but he surely gave them the bulk of his time and astonishment. And he did not insult them with the idea that death was somehow ennobling to anybody—or killing, either.

He and Ernest Hemingway died on the same day, incidentally, on July 1, 1961. Both were heroes from World War I. Both deserved Nobel prizes—Céline for his first book alone. Céline didn't get one, and Hemingway did. Hemingway killed himself, and Céline died of natural causes.

All that remains is their books.

And Céline's slowly fading infamy.

After years of unselfish and often brilliant service to mankind in literature and medicine, he revealed himself as a fierce anti-Semite and a Nazi sympathizer. This was in the late 1930s. I have heard no explanation for this, other than that he was partly insane. He never claimed to have been insane, and no physician ever declared him so.

He was sane enough, at any rate, to virtually exclude his racism and cracked politics from his novels. The anti-Semitism appears only flickeringly here and there, and usually in a context of his being absolutely gaga about all the varieties of treacherous and foolish human beings.

For what it may be worth, he wrote these words only a few days before he died: "I say that Israel is a real fatherland that welcomes its children home and my country is a shit-house . . ."

His words are contemptible to anyone who has suffered from anti-Semitism. And so, surely, were the amnesty and exoneration he received from the French government in 1951. He was punished with heavy fines and imprisonment and exile before that.

As for the words I quoted: They don't, after all, imply an apology or a wish to be forgiven. They are envious, and little more.

Since he is punished and dead, and since the Nazi nightmare is so long ago now, it may at last be possible to perceive a twisted sort of honor in his declining to speak of remorse or to offer excuses of any kind. Other collaborators with the Nazis, of whom there were tens of thousands in France and millions in all of Europe, had stories to tell of how they were forced to behave as badly as they did, and of daring acts of resistance and sabotage they committed, at the risk of their lives.

Céline found that sort of lying ludicrous in a very ugly way.

I get a splitting headache every time I try to write about Céline. I have one now. I never have headaches at any other time.

As the war was ending, he headed for the center of the holocaust—Berlin.

I know when he began to influence me. I was well into my

forties before I read him. A friend was startled that I didn't know anything about Céline, and he initiated me with *Journey to the End of the Night,* which flabbergasted me. I assigned it for a course in the novel which I was giving at the University of Iowa. When it was time for me to lecture for two hours about it, I found I had nothing to say.

The book penetrated my bones, anyway, if not my mind. And I only now understand what I took from Céline and put into the novel I was writing at the time, which was called *Slaughterhouse-Five.* In that book, I felt the need to say this every time a character died: 'So it goes.' This exasperated many critics, and it seemed fancy and tiresome to me, too. But it somehow had to be said.

It was a clumsy way of saying what Céline managed to imply so much more naturally in everything he wrote, in effect: "Death and suffering can't matter nearly as much as I think they do. Since they are so common, my taking them so seriously must mean that I am insane. I must try to be saner."

Which has brought us back to our old friend insanity again. Céline claimed from time to time to have been trepanned in the First World War, as the result of a head wound. Actually, according to his fascinating biographer Erika Ostrovsky (*Voyeur Voyant,* Random House, 1971), he was wounded in his right shoulder. And, in his final novel, *Rigadoon,* he tells of being hit in the head by a brick during an air raid in Hannover. So it might be said that he found it necessary sometimes to explain a head that so many people found unusual.

He himself must have become thoroughly sick of his head occasionally, and I will guess as to its chief defect. I think it lacked the damping apparatus which most of us have, which keeps us from being swamped by the unbelievability of life as it really is.

So perhaps Céline's style isn't as arbitrary as I've thought it was. It may have been inevitable, if his mind was so undefended. There may have been nothing for him to do, as though he were caught in an artillery barrage, but to exclaim and exclaim and exclaim.

And his works cannot be called a triumph of the human imagination. Almost everything he exclaimed about was really going on.

He was wonderful about inventors and machines.

The inscription on his tombstone is the one with which I began this essay. Erika Ostrovsky calls it a "terse summary of a double life."

Good for her.

He expected his writings to live on and on. He described himself when he was about to die like this: ". . . by your leave, a writer, a terrific stylist, the living proof: they put me in the 'Pleiade' with La Fontaine, Clement Marot, du Bellay . . . not to mention Rabelais! and Ronsard! . . . just to show you that I'm not worried . . . in two or three centuries I'll be helping the kids through high school . . ."

At the time I write, which is the autumn of 1974, it has become apparent even to ordinary people, with their mental dampers operating perfectly, that life is in fact as dangerous and unforgiving and irrational as Céline said it was. There is some question as to whether we have two or three centuries remaining to us in which to prepare civilization for the teaching of Céline in high school.

Until that day, if it comes, I suspect that fellow writers will keep his reputation alive. We are especially shocked and enlightened by what he says. We are filled with a giddy sort of gratitude.

I have heard it suggested that Céline may live on far longer in English than in French—for technical rather than political reasons. The argument goes that Céline's gutter French was so specialized as to time and place that gobs of it are incomprehensible to Frenchmen.

Those who have translated it into English, however, have used more durable crudities, which will be clear enough still, God willing, in one hundred years.

As I say, this is not my idea. I heard it somewhere. I pass it on. If it turns out to be true, it seems that simple literary justice would eventually require that his translators be acknowledged as coauthors of Céline. Translation is that important.

There is at least one significant document by Céline that is out of print in English. And it would be punctilious of me to say that it was written not by Céline but by Dr. Destouches. It is the doctoral thesis of Destouches, "The Life and Work of Ignaz Philipp Semmelweis," for which he received a bronze medal in 1924. It was written at a time when theses in medicine could still be beautifully literary, since ignorance about diseases and the human body still required that medicine be an art.

And young Destouches, in a spirit of hero-worship, told of the futile and scientifically sound battle fought by a Hungarian physician named Semmelweis (1818–1865) to prevent the spread of childbed fever in Viennese hospital maternity wards. The victims were poor people, since persons with decent sorts of dwellings much preferred to give birth at home.

The mortality rate in some wards was sensational—25 percent or more. Semmelweis reasoned that the mothers were being killed by medical students, who often came into the wards immediately after having dissected corpses riddled with disease. He was able to prove this by having the students wash their hands in soap and water before touching a woman in labor. The mortality rate dropped.

The jealousy and ignorance of Semmelweis's colleagues, however, caused him to be fired, and the mortality rate went up again.

The lesson Destouches learned from this true story, in my opinion, if he hadn't already learned it from an impoverished childhood and a stretch in the army, is that vanity rather than wisdom determines how the world is run.

XVII

A NAZI CITY
MOURNED AT
SOME PROFIT

I have not only praised a Nazi sympathizer, I have expressed my sorrow at the death of a Nazi city as well. I am speaking of Dresden, of course. And I have to say again that I was an American soldier, a prisoner of war there, when the city was simultaneously burned up and down. I was not on the German side.

I mourned the destruction of Dresden because it was only temporarily a Nazi city, and had for centuries been an art treasure belonging to earthlings everywhere. It could have been that again. The same was true of Angkor Wat, which military scientists have demolished more recently for some imagined gain.

Being present at the destruction of Dresden has affected my character far less than the death of my mother, the adopting of my sister's children, the sudden realization that those children and my own were no longer dependent on me, the breakup of my marriage, and on and on. And I have not been encouraged to go on mourning Dresden—even by Germans. Even Germans seem to think it is not worth mentioning anymore.

So I myself thought no more about Dresden until I was asked by Franklin Library in 1976 to write a special introduction to a deluxe edition they were bringing out of my novel, *Slaughterhouse-Five*.

I said this:

This is a book about something that happened to me a long time ago (1944)—and the book itself is now something else that happened to me a long time ago (1969).

Time marches on—and the key event in this book, which is the fire-bombing of Dresden, is now a fossilized memory, sinking ever deeper into the tar pit of history. If American school children have heard of it at all, they are surely in doubt as to whether it happened in World War One or Two. Nor do I think they should care much.

I, for one, am not avid to keep the memory of the fire-bombing fresh. I would of course be charmed if people continued to read this book for years to come, but not because I think there are important lessons to be learned from the Dresden catastrophe. I myself was in the midst of it, and learned only that people can become so enraged in war that they will burn great cities to the ground, and slay the inhabitants thereof.

That was nothing new.

I write this in October of 1976, and it so happens that only two nights ago I saw a screening of Marcel Ophul's new documentary on war crimes, "The Memory of Justice," which included movies, taken from the air, of the Dresden raid—at night. The city appeared to boil, and I was down there somewhere.

I was supposed to appear onstage afterwards, with some other people who had had intimate experiences with Nazi death camps and so on, and to contribute my notions as to the meaning of it all.

Atrocities celebrate meaninglessness, surely. I was mute. I did not mount the stage. I went home.

The Dresden atrocity, tremendously expensive and meticulously planned, was so meaningless, finally, that only one person on the entire planet got any benefit from it. I am that person. I wrote this book, which earned a lot of money for me and made my reputation, such as it is.

One way or another, I got two or three dollars for every person killed. Some business I'm in.

THE
SEXUAL
REVOLUTION

So I left my first wife and Cape Cod home forever in 1971. All our children save for the youngest, Nanette, had lit out for the Territory, so to speak. I became a soldier in what many were calling a sexual revolution. My departure itself was so sexual that a French name for orgasm describes it to a tee. It was a "little death."

There were similar little deaths going on all around me, of course, and that continues to be the situation today. In the case of long marriages, such departures really are make-believe dying, a salute to a marriage in its good old days, sheepish acknowledgment that the marriage could have been perfect right up to the end, if only one partner or the other one had managed to die peacefully just a little ahead of time. Can I say this without seeming to praise death? I hope so. I am praising literature, I think—praising stories that satisfy because they end where they should, before they stop being stories.

I left the house and all its furnishings and the car and the bank accounts behind, and taking only my clothing with me, I departed for New York City, the capital of the World, on a heavier-than-air flying machine. I started all over again.

As for real death—it has always been a temptation to me, since my mother solved so many problems with it. The child of a suicide will naturally think of death, the big one, as a logical solution to any problem, even one in simple algebra. Question: If Farmer A can plant 300 potatoes an hour, and Farmer B can plant potatoes fifty percent faster, and Farmer C can plant potatoes one third as fast as Farmer B, and 10,000 potatoes are to be planted to an acre, how many nine-hour days will it take Farmers A, B, and C, working simultaneously, to plant 25 acres? Answer: I think I'll blow my brains out.

❦

IF the story of an American father's departure from his hearth is allowed to tell itself, if it is allowed to wag tongues when he isn't around, it will tell the same story it would have told a hundred years ago, of booze and wicked women.

Such a story is told in my case, I'm sure.

Closer to the truth these days, in my opinion, is a tale of a man's cold sober flight into unpopulated nothingness. The booze and the women, good and bad, are likely to come along in time, but nothingness is the first seductress—again, the little death.

To the middle-class wives and children across this land whose male head of household has recently departed, learn the truth of his present condition from yet another great contemporary poem by the Statler Brothers, "Flowers on the Wall":

> I keep hearing you're concerned
> About my happiness.
> But all the thought you've given me
> Is conscience, I guess.
> If I were walkin' in your shoes
> I wouldn't worry none.
> While you 'n' your friends are worryin'
> 'Bout me
> I'm havin' lots of fun:
> Countin' flowers on the wall,
> That don't bother me at all,
> Playin' solitaire till dawn
> With a deck of fifty-one,
> Smokin' cigarettes and watchin'
> Captain Kangaroo.
> Now don't tell me
> I've nothin' to do.
>
> Tonight I dressed in tails
> Pretending I was on the town;
> Long as I can dream it's hard to
> Slow this swinger down.
> So please don't give
> A thought to me,

305

KURT VONNEGUT

I'm really doin' fine,
And you can always find me here,
I'm havin' quite a time:
Countin' flowers on the wall,
That don't bother me at all,
Playin' solitaire till dawn
with a deck of fifty-one,
Smokin' cigarettes and watchin'
Captain Kangaroo.
Now don't tell me
I've nothin' to do.

It's good to see you,
I must go,
I know I look a fright;
Anyway my eyes are not
Accustomed to this light.
And my shoes are not
Accustomed to this hard concrete,
So I must go back to my room
And make my day complete:
Countin' flowers on the wall,
That don't bother me at all,
Playin' solitaire till dawn
With a deck of fifty-one,
Smokin' cigarettes and watchin'
Captain Kangaroo.
Now don't tell me
I've nothin' to do.

❧

THIS was written by Lew DeWitt, the only one of the four Statler Brothers to have been divorced. It is not a poem of escape or rebirth. It is a poem about the end of a man's usefulness.

The man understands that his wife deserves the tragic dignity of being a widow now.

❧

OR so he feels.

And much of what any human being feels is oceanic. The wife of a man counting the flowers on the wall may not yearn so much to be a widow, and yet the culture in which the man is floating may be telling him that it is right for her to yearn for that.

He is no longer needed as a father, and no longer useful as a soldier who could stop a bullet winging toward his loved ones, and he has no hope for being honored for his wisdom, for it is well understood that people only become more tiresome as they grow old.

The man is experimenting with the Christian idea of heaven without actually dying, and more and more women, of course, are doing it, too. In heaven, you see, or so the childish dream goes, people are liked and honored simply for having been alive. They don't have to have any utility up there.

The man counting flowers on the wall has no appreciable utility anymore. He probably wasn't all that good in earning money even when he was in his prime. What is he waiting for?

For an angel to knock on his door. Angels love anybody who has simply been alive.

❧

IT seems to me that the most universal revolutionary wish now or ever is a wish for heaven, a wish by a human being to be honored by angels for something other than beauty or usefulness.

The women's liberation movement of today in America, in its most oceanic sense, is a wish by women to be liked for something other than their reproductive abilities, especially since the planet is harrowingly overpopulated. And the rejection of the Equal Rights Amendment by male state legislators is this clear statement by men, in my opinion: "We're sorry, girls, but your reproductive abilities are about all we can really like you for."

The truth.

❧

THERE are other hard truths about the old and those without friends and those without skills or capital, and on and on.

❧

NO angel knocked on my door while I was counting flowers on the wall, but an old friend with the gambling sickness was quick to find me. He had never borrowed anything from me, but now my turn had come. He told me of a family emergency, and asked for a sum that was just about the size of the little grubstake I had built. I ran into him about five years later, and he told me that he scarcely thought of anything but the day when he could pay me back with interest.

And people reached me by mail, most often asking me to read this or that new novel and write some words of praise for the jacket.

No book had been published in the past ten years for which I had not written a blurb.

But then an old friend wrote a book so bad that even I, crossing my eyes and ransacking it from end to end, could find nothing in it which could be mistaken for even a winsome sort of imbecility. So I declined to write a blurb. This may have been a major turning point in my life.

It was a crisis in the life of another writer, too, it turned out. He had written a blurb for the book I had spurned. He called me up in the middle of the night, long distance and sounding as though he had just swallowed Drano. "My God," he said, "you just can't leave me on that book jacket all alone."

❧

AND so on. Somewhere in there my son Mark went crazy and recovered. I went out to Vancouver and saw how sick he was, and I put him in a nut house. I had to suppose that he might never get well again.

He never blamed me or his mother, as I have said before. His generous wish not to blame us was so stubborn that he became almost a crank on the subject of chemical and genetic causes of mental illness. Talk therapy made sense as poetry but not as a means to a cure, he thought.

But now, as a physician, as an open-minded scientist, he has delivered himself into the hands of a talk therapist, blabbing his head off about Jane and me and his sisters and his cousins and all that, I hope, and finding it hilariously beneficial.

Hooray.

There will be talk about how people wronged him. It's about time. It's about time.

❦

EVERYTHING is about time.

Yes, and somewhere in there I looked in on George Roy Hill while he made a motion picture based on a novel of mine, *Slaughterhouse-Five*.

There are only two American novelists who should be grateful for the movies which were made from their books. I am one of them. The other one? Margaret Mitchell, of course.

❦

THE Eastern Seaboard's intellectual ranks will probably always require one woman to be so brilliant, supposedly, that everybody else is scared to death of her. Mary McCarthy used to hold that job. Susan Sontag has it now.

Susan Sontag approached me at a party one time. I was petrified. What brilliant question would she ask me, and what would be my pip-squeak reply?

"How did you like the movie they made of *Slaughterhouse-Five*?" she said.

"I liked it a lot," I confessed.

"So did I," she said.

How sweet and easy that was, and what a great motion picture *Slaughterhouse-Five* must really be!

❦

THERE was a depression going on in the movie industry in Hollywood back then. Only two pictures were being made, both based on works of mine. The other one was *Happy Birthday, Wanda June.*

This movie, starring Rod Steiger and Susannah York, turned out so abominably that I asked that my name be taken off it. I had heard of other writers doing that. What could be more dignified?

This proved to be impossible, however. I alone had done the thing the credits said I had done. I had really written the thing.

❦

YES, and it wasn't the only bad job I ever did. I have graded my separate works from A to D. The grades I hand out to myself do not place me in literary history. I am comparing myself with myself. Thus can I give myself an A-plus for *Cat's Cradle,* while knowing that there was a writer named William Shakespeare. The report card is chronological, so you can plot my rise and fall on graph paper, if you like:

Player Piano	B
The Sirens of Titan	A
Mother Night	A
Cat's Cradle,	A-plus
God Bless You, Mr. Rosewater	A

Slaughterhouse-Five	A-plus
Welcome to the Monkey House	B-minus
Happy Birthday, Wanda June	D
Breakfast of Champions	C
Wampeters, Foma & Granfalloons	C
Slapstick	D
Jailbird	A
Palm Sunday	C

❦

WHAT has been my prettiest contribution to my culture? I would say it was a master's thesis in anthropology which was rejected by the University of Chicago a long time ago. It was rejected because it was so simple and looked like too much fun. One must not be too playful.

The thesis has vanished, but I carry an abstract in my head, which I will here set down. The fundamental idea is that stories have shapes which can be drawn on graph paper, and that the shape of a given society's stories is at least as interesting as the shape of its pots or spearheads.

In the thesis, I collected popular stories from fantastically various societies, not excluding the one which used to read *Collier's* and *The Saturday Evening Post.* I graphed each one.

Anyone can graph a simple story if he or she will crucify it, so to speak, on the intersecting axes I here depict:

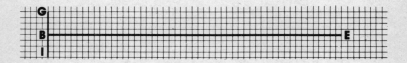

"G" stands for good fortune. "I" stands for ill fortune. "B" stands for the beginning of a story. "E" stands for its end.

The late Nelson Rockefeller, for example, would be very close to the top of the G-I scale on his wedding day. A shopping-bag lady waking up on a doorstep this morning would be somewhere nearer the middle, but not at the bottom, since the day is balmy and clear.

A much beloved story in our society is about a person who is leading a bearable life, who experiences misfortune, who overcomes misfortune, and who is happier afterward for having demonstrated resourcefulness and strength. As a graph, that story looks like this:

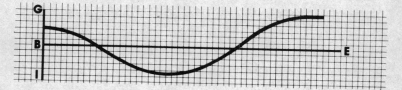

Another story of which Americans never seem to tire is about a person who becomes happier upon finding something he or she likes a lot. The person loses whatever it is, and then gets it back forever. As a graph, it looks like this:

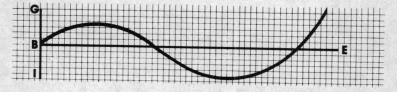

An American Indian creation myth, in which a god of some sort gives the people the sun and then the moon and then the bow and arrow and then the corn and so on, is essentially a staircase, a tale of accumulation:

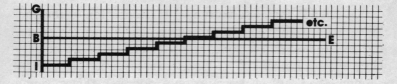

Almost all creation myths are staircases like that. Our own creation myth, taken from the Old Testament, is unique, so far as I could discover, in looking like this:

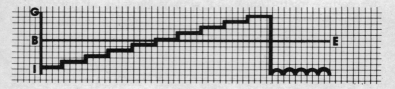

The sudden drop in fortune, of course, is the ejection of Adam and Eve from the Garden of Eden.

Franz Kafka's "The Metamorphosis," in which an already hopelessly unhappy man turns into a cockroach, looks like this:

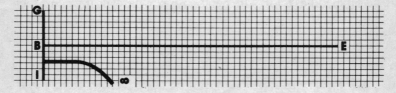

But could my graphs, when all was said and done, be useful as anything more than little visual comedies, cartoons of a sort? The University of Chicago asked me that, and I had to ask myself that, and I say again what I said at the beginning: that the graphs were at least as suggestive as pots or spearheads.

314

But then I had another look at a graph I had drawn of Western civilization's most enthusiastically received story, which is "Cinderella." At this very moment, a thousand writers must be telling that story again in one form or another. This very book is a Cinderella story of a kind.

I confessed that I was daunted by the graph of "Cinderella," and was tempted to leave it out of my thesis, since it seemed to prove that I was full of shit. It seemed too complicated and arbitrary to be a representative artifact—lacked the simple grace of a pot or a spearhead. Have a look:

The steps, you see, are all the presents the fairy godmother gave to Cinderella, the ball gown, the slippers, the carriage, and so on. The sudden drop is the stroke of midnight at the ball. Cinderella is in rags again. All the presents have been repossessed. But then the prince finds her and marries her, and she is infinitely happy ever after. She gets all the stuff back, and *then* some. A lot of people think the story is trash, and, on graph paper, it certainly looks like trash.

But then I said to myself, Wait a minute—those steps at the beginning look like the creation myth of virtually every society on earth. And then I saw that the stroke of midnight looked exactly like the unique creation myth in the Old Testament. And then I saw that the rise to bliss at the end was identical with the expectation of redemption as expressed in primitive Christianity.

The tales were identical.

315

I was thrilled to discover that years ago, and I am just as thrilled today. The apathy of the University of Chicago is repulsive to me.

They can take a flying fuck at the mooooooooooooooooon.

❧

AND, my goodness, haven't we come far afield from the stated subject of this chapter, which is the sexual revolution? I have spoken elsewhere of how neophyte writers, and even some old poops in the field, will veer away from subjects which alarm them. Just look how far I myself have veered away from the subject of sex. There is little that is genuinely sexual in telling a great university to take a flying fuck at the mooooooooooooooooon.

Am I too much of a sissy to discuss anal intercourse, aphrodisiacs, armpits, bidets, birth control, bisexuality, bondage, buttocks, chastity belts, circumcision, clitorises, condoms, dildoes, discipline, ejaculation, feathers, femoral intercourse, fetishes, foursomes, frigidity, genitals, hair, hair-trigger trouble, impotence, karezza, kisses, and so on? I have lifted this list from the index of *The Joy of Sex: A Gourmet Guide to Love Making* (illustrated), edited by Alex Comfort, M.B., Ph.D. (Crown, 1972). Actually, I feel quite free to discuss any and all of those matters, and even to laugh some while doing so.

What isn't congenial is an admission that I have been forced to be celibate for long periods of time. I search the index of *The Joy of Sex* in vain for "celibacy," which happens to be the most common human sexual adventure, and which could be illustrated nicely by a page as white as a snowdrift.

To take an example: I was a private in the United States Army (actually the Army of the United States, since I was a volunteer) for three years. I was one warrior ant in an enormous colony of identical ants, imprisoned in rural areas, and sent finally to an all-male battlefield in a foreign country. How many women eager to fuck me do you suppose I encountered in three long years? I could ask the same question about months and months in my civilian life, and get the same answer: to all practical purposes, none.

I was talking one time to my friend Robert Penn Warren, a lusty old gentleman and a great poet and novelist, and I asked him about another majestic literary figure, dead, who had been an acquaintance of his. Mr. Warren is seventeen years older than I am. He was born in Guthrie, Kentucky, in 1905. He drew in words an enchantingly Edwardian caricature of the man I had asked about, and he concluded it with a statement which was in no wise a joke. It was meant to have clinical significance. A person versed in psychology and medicine, he seemed to say, would be able to extrapolate an entire syndrome from this one small clue. This was the clue: "He was a masturbator, of course."

This ended the conversation. I did not protest. I was grateful, though, to remember something far more casual about masturbation which had been said to me with all possible cheerfulness by my friend Milos Forman, the motion picture director.

"You know what I like about masturbation?" he asked me.

"What is it you like about it, Milos?" I said.

"You don't have to talk afterward," he replied.

I peruse what is at this moment the number one nonfiction best seller in America, written by Gay Talese, *Thy Neighbor's Wife*. It is meant to be a quite universal analysis of the current sexual revolution. According to Talese, women are becoming more hospitable and casual, less discriminating with respect to sexual contacts. I oversimplify but do not entirely misrepresent that supposed revolution if I describe it this way: Whereas an ideal woman in olden times might have given a dusty male wayfarer on the road of life a piece of pie—a modern woman may now give him a hand job or a blow job as well.

I am sorry, but that is how I read it.

I do not wish to mock the book, even having said that, for it is to me a secretly deep history of a generation of middle-class American males, my own, which was taught by parents and athletic coaches and scoutmasters and military chaplains and quack doctors and so on to be deeply ashamed of masturbation and wet dreams.

And the hidden plea in the book is one which first appeared in my eyes when I was fourteen, say, and which has not vanished entirely to this day. It is part of the mystery of me. The plea is addressed by old-fashioned males forever full of jism to any pretty human female, on the street, in a magazine, in a movie—anywhere. The plea is this: "Please, pretty lady, don't make me play with my private parts again."

XIX

IN THE CAPITAL OF THE WORLD

S
o here I sit on the fourth floor of a town house on the East Side of New York City, the Capital of the World, with a report card on the past thirty years of my life —signed by myself and tacked to the wall. I look at all those grades, some high, some low, and I think that I am like the compulsive gambler who borrowed so much money from me and who could not pay me back: I could not help myself.

I have spoken elsewhere of the mentor I had at the University of Chicago, who was so brilliant, who could not find anyone to publish his most audacious work, and who committed suicide. I have not proved how brilliant he was. As I set out to do so now with an example, I am hesitant, not only because I have his reputation in my hands for a moment, but because all the good things he said which I remember were so simple and clear. It has been my experience with literary critics and academics in this country that clarity looks a lot like laziness and ignorance and childishness and cheapness to them. Any idea which can be grasped immediately is for them, by definition, something they knew all the time.

So it is with literary experimentation, too. If a literary experiment works like a dream, is easy to read and enjoy, the experimenter is a hack. The only way to get full credit as a fearless experimenter is to fail and fail.

❦

A music critic once regaled a party I attended with a list of composers of serious music in the past. Nobody had heard of any of them, and the critic told us that they were all regarded in their own time as being the greatest composers alive. These were contemporaries of Beethoven and Brahms and Wagner and so on, composers for full orchestras in the Romantic mode.

We asked him why they weren't admired today. He had made it his business to hear as much of their work as he could, and he had this to say: "It was all gesture." By this he meant that musical promise after musical promise of great themes to come were made, and were not kept. The composers were honored in their own time for the gorgeousness of the promises they made but could not keep. They perhaps made promises which not even an archangel could keep.

Some of the most imposing literary reputations of my own time, it seems to me, are based on just that sort of promising.

❦

THE example of my mentor's brilliance:

Using the Socratic method, he asked his little class this: "What is it an artist does—a painter, a writer, a sculptor—?"

He already had an answer, which he had put down in the book he was writing, a book which would never be published. But he would not tell us what it was until the end of the hour, and he might discard it entirely if our answers to his question made more sense than his. This was a class composed entirely of veterans of the Second World War in the summertime. The class had been put together in order that we might continue to receive our living expenses from our government when most of the rest of the university was on vacation.

If any of us came up with good answers, I now have no idea what they might have been. His answer was this: "The artist says, 'I can do very little about the chaos around me, but at least I can reduce to perfect order this square of canvas, this piece of paper, this chunk of stone.' "

Everybody knows that.

❦

MOST of my adult life has been spent in bringing to some kind of order sheets of paper eight and a half inches wide and eleven inches long. This severely limited activity has allowed me to ignore many a storm. It has also caused many of the worst storms I ignored. My mates have often been angered by how much attention I pay to paper and how little attention I pay to them.

I can only reply that the secret to success in every human endeavor is total concentration. Ask any great athlete.

To put it another way: Sometimes I don't consider myself very good at life, so I hide in my profession.

❦

I know what Delilah really did to Samson to make him as weak as a baby. She didn't have to cut his hair off. All she had to do was break his concentration.

❦

ABOUT nine years ago I was asked to deliver an address to the American Institute and Academy of Arts and Letters here. I was not then a member, and was terrified. I had left home, and was spending most of my time counting flowers on the wall and watching Captain Kangaroo in a tiny apartment on East Fifty-fourth Street. My friend with the gambling sickness had just cleaned out my bank account and my son had gone insane in British Columbia.

I asked my wife please not to come, since I was rattled enough as it was. I asked a woman with whom I had been keeping company some not to come, either—for the same reason. So they both came, all dressed up for a fancy execution.

What saved my life? Pieces of paper eight and a half inches wide and eleven inches long.

❦

I am sorry for people who have no knack for reducing to seeming order some little thing. More and more people are doing it with film and video tape these days. My chief objection to motion pictures as art is their expensiveness. A filmmaker is like Benvenuto Cellini, who worked with raw materials which were priceless to begin with—with silver and platinum and gold.

❦

I was born into a house which was designed and built by my father in 1922, the year of my birth. It was so full of treasures that it was like a museum, and it was meant to be inherited by my brother, my sister, or me. I would not like to live there. Edwardian lives of a sort were conducted there for seven years. That isn't a long period of time, you know. To my parents, who were great lovers of music, it must have been as though a full orchestra had played the first seven bars of a symphony, and then gone home.

The house I now inhabit was built in this busy seaport by a speculator named L. S. Brooks in 1860–61, at the outbreak of the Civil War. Spiritually, it is as much my house as anyone's, since Brooks built it, along with a lot of other ones just like it in this neighborhood, with no inhabitant in particular in mind.

The first person who liked it enough to move into it, the way a hermit crab might move into an empty snail shell, was another German, Ferdinand Traud. He was president of the German Free School down at 142 East Fourth Street.

The Trauds moved out in 1875, and Julius Bruno, a broker, moved in. Julius Bruno moved out in 1887, and Peter Goetz moved in. Peter Goetz moved out in 1891, and Louisa Gerlach moved in. And on and on.

I myself bought the house eight years ago from Robert

Gottlieb, the editor in chief of Alfred A. Knopf, who moved to a house across the street—and Jill Krementz, who is now my wife, and I moved in.

Jill runs her photographic business out of the bottom floor. I run my writing business out of the top floor. We share the two floors in between.

❦

THE people in this city have been very friendly to me, although I was born far away. They have uses for strangers who do good work in the arts here, and I have done reasonably good work as a novelist from time to time.

The most satisfying kindness which has been done me here was an invitation from St. Clement's Episcopal Church, whose congregation includes many actors, to preach on Palm Sunday in 1980. It is the custom of that church, which is also a theater, to have a stranger preach just once a year.

The altar there is portable, since the front of the church is also a stage. Very few plays would work well with an altar as a fixed centerpiece. So, on the morning I preached, the altar had been trundled temporarily onto a set which was the kitchen of a Manhattan tenement of perhaps sixty years ago or more—before I was born.

I do not know what play the set was for. I have not asked. I want to imagine that it was for a play about European immigrants to New York City and their children. I was happy to speak from that set as a descendent of immigrants who settled much farther inland, immigrants about whom native New Yorkers often know nothing and imagine the worst.

I had this to say:

"I am enchanted by the Sermon on the Mount. Being merciful, it seems to me, is the only good idea we have received so far. Perhaps we will get another idea that good by and by—and then we will have two good ideas. What might that second good idea be? I don't know. How could I know? I will make a wild guess that it will come from music somehow. I have often wondered what music is and why we love it so. It may be that music is that second good idea's being born.

"I choose as my text the first eight verses of John twelve, which deal not with Palm Sunday but with the night before —with Palm Sunday Eve, with what we might call 'Spikenard Saturday.' I hope that will be close enough to Palm Sunday to leave you more or less satisfied. I asked an Episcopalian priest the other day what I should say to you about Palm Sunday itself. She told me to say that it was a brilliant satire on pomp and circumstance and high honors in this world. So I tell you that.

"The priest was Carol Anderson, who sold her physical church in order that her spiritual parish might survive. Her parish is All Angels—on West Eightieth, just off Broadway. She sold the church but hung on to the parish house. I assume that most, if not all, of the angels are still around.

"Now, as to the verses about Palm Sunday Eve: I choose them because Jesus says something in the eighth verse which many people I have known have taken as proof that Jesus himself occasionally got sick and tired of people who needed mercy all the time. I read from the Revised Standard Bible rather than the King James, because it is easier for me to understand. Also, I will argue afterward that Jesus was only joking, and it is impossible to joke in King James English. The funniest joke in the world, if told in King James English, is doomed to sound like Charlton Heston.

"I read:

" 'Six days before the Passover, Jesus came to Bethany, where Lazarus was, whom Jesus had raised from the dead. There they made him a supper; Martha served, but Lazarus was one of those at table with him.

" 'Mary took a pound of costly ointment of pure nard and anointed the feet of Jesus and wiped his feet with her hair; and the house was filled with the fragrance of the ointment.

" 'But Judas Iscariot, one of his disciples (he who was to betray him), said, "Why was this ointment not sold for three hundred denarii and given to the poor?" This he said, not that he cared for the poor but because he was a thief, and as he had the money box he used to take what was put into it. Jesus said, "Let her alone, let her keep it for the day of my burial. The poor you always have with you, but you do not always have me." '

"Thus ends the reading, and although I have promised a joke, there is not much of a chuckle in there anywhere. The reading, in fact, ends with at least two quite depressing implications: That Jesus could be a touch self-pitying, and that he was, with his mission to earth about to end, at least momentarily sick and tired of hearing about the poor.

"The King James version of the last verse, by the way, is almost identical: ' "For the poor always ye have with you; but you do not always have me." '

"Whatever it was that Jesus really said to Judas was said in Aramaic, of course—and has come to us through Hebrew and Greek and Latin and archaic English. Maybe he only said something a lot like, 'The poor you always have with you, but you do not always have me.' Perhaps a little something has been lost in translation. And let us remember, too, that in translations jokes are commonly the first things to go.

"I would like to recapture what has been lost. Why? Because I, as a Christ-worshiping agnostic, have seen so much un-Christian impatience with the poor encouraged by the quotation, 'For the poor always ye have with you.'

"I am speaking mainly of my youth in Indianapolis, Indiana. No matter where I am and how old I become, I still speak of almost nothing but my youth in Indianapolis, Indiana. Whenever anybody out that way began to worry a lot about the poor people when I was young, some eminently respectable Hoosier, possibly an uncle or an aunt, would say that Jesus himself had given up on doing much about the poor. He or she would paraphrase John twelve, Verse eight: 'The poor people are hopeless. We'll always be stuck with them.'

"The general company was then free to say that the poor were hopeless because they were so lazy or dumb, that they drank too much and had too many children and kept coal in the bathtub, and so on. Somebody was likely to quote Kin Hubbard, the Hoosier humorist, who said that he knew a man who was so poor that he owned twenty-two dogs. And so on.

"If those Hoosiers were still alive, which they are not, I would tell them now that Jesus was only joking, and that he was not even thinking much about the poor.

"I would tell them, too, what I don't have to tell this particular congregation, that jokes can be noble. Laughs are exactly as honorable as tears. Laughter and tears are both

327

responses to frustration and exhaustion, to the futility of thinking and striving anymore. I myself prefer to laugh, since there is less cleaning up to do afterward—and since I can start thinking and striving again that much sooner.

"All right:

"It is the evening before Palm Sunday. Jesus is frustrated and exhausted. He knows that one of his closest associates will soon betray him for money—and that he is going to be mocked and tortured and killed. He is going to feel all that a mortal feels when he dies in convulsions on the cross. His visit among us is almost over—but life must still go on for just a little while.

"It is again suppertime.

"How many suppertimes does Jesus have left? Five, I believe.

"His male companions for this supper are themselves a mockery. One is Judas, who will betray him. The other is Lazarus, who has recently been dead for four days. Lazarus was so dead that he stunk, the Bible says. Lazarus is surely dazed, and not much of a conversationalist—and not necessarily grateful, either, to be alive again. It is a very mixed blessing to be brought back from the dead.

"If I had read a little farther, we would have learned that there is a crowd outside, crazy to see Lazarus, not Jesus. Lazarus is the man of the hour as far as the crowd is concerned.

"Trust a crowd to look at the wrong end of a miracle every time.

"There are two sisters of Lazarus there—Martha and Mary. They, at least, are sympathetic and imaginatively helpful. Mary begins to massage and perfume the feet of

Jesus Christ with an ointment made from the spikenard plant. Jesus has the bones of a man and is clothed in the flesh of a man—so it must feel awfully nice, what Mary is doing to his feet. Would it be heretical of us to suppose that Jesus closes his eyes?

"This is too much for that envious hypocrite Judas, who says, trying to be more Catholic than the Pope: 'Hey—this is very un-Christian. Instead of wasting that stuff on your feet, we should have sold it and given the money to the poor people.'

"To which Jesus replies in Aramaic: 'Judas, don't worry about it. There will still be plenty of poor people left long after I'm gone.'

"This is about what Mark Twain or Abraham Lincoln would have said under similar circumstances.

"If Jesus did in fact say that, it is a divine black joke, well suited to the occasion. It says everything about hypocrisy and nothing about the poor. It is a Christian joke, which allows Jesus to remain civil to Judas, but to chide him about his hypocrisy all the same.

" 'Judas, don't worry about it. There will still be plenty of poor people left long after I'm gone.'

"Shall I regarble it for you? 'The poor you always have with you, but you do not always have me.'

"My own translation does no violence to the words in the Bible. I have changed their order some, not merely to make them into the joke the situation calls for, but to harmonize them, too, with the Sermon on the Mount. The Sermon on the Mount suggests a mercifulness that can never waver or fade.

"This has no doubt been a silly sermon. I am sure you do

not mind. People don't come to church for preachments, of course, but to daydream about God.

"I thank you for your sweetly faked attention."

END